A Matter of Style?

Organizational Agency in Global Public Policy

International public administrations (IPAs) have become an essential feature of global governance, contributing to what some have described as the 'bureaucratization of world politics'. While we do know that IPAs matter for international politics, we neither know exactly to what extent nor how exactly they matter for international organizations' policy making processes and subsequent outputs. This book provides an innovative perspective on IPAs and their agency in introducing the concept of administrative styles to the study of international organizations and global public policy. It argues that the administrative bodies of international organizations can develop informal working routines that allow them to exert influence beyond their formal autonomy and mandate. The theoretical argument is tested by an encompassing comparative assessment of administrative styles and their determinants across eight IPAs, providing rich empirical insight gathered in more than 100 expert interviews.

LOUISA BAYERLEIN is a research fellow at LMU and a doctoral researcher at the EUI in Florence. She works on the intersection of organizational theory, public administration, and comparative policy analysis. Her research focus lies on comparing bureaucracies, their agency, and their ways of influencing policy-making processes.

CHRISTOPH KNILL is Chair of Political Science and Public Administration at LMU Munich. He is director of the Research Unit 'International Public Administration' and won two ERC Advanced Grants (2010 and 2018). In 2018, he received two best paper prizes for publications in *Policy Sciences* and the *Journal of European Public Policy*.

YVES STEINEBACH is an Assistant Professor at LMU Munich. His main research interests are analyses of the effectiveness of public policies and governing institutions. In 2018, Steinebach won the best paper awards of the internationally renowned peer-reviewed journals *Journal of European Public Policy* and *Policy Sciences*.

T0384524

Cambridge Studies in Comparative Public Policy

The **Cambridge Studies in Comparative Public Policy** series was established to promote and disseminate comparative research in public policy. The objective of the series is to advance the understanding of public policies through the publication of the results of comparative research into the nature, dynamics, and contexts of major policy challenges and responses to them. Works in the series will draw critical insights that enhance policy learning and are generalizable beyond specific policy contexts, sectors, and time periods. Such works will also compare the development and application of public policy theory across institutional and cultural settings and examine how policy ideas, institutions, and practices shape policies and their outcomes. Manuscripts comparing public policies in two or more cases as well as theoretically informed critical case studies which test more general theories are encouraged. Studies comparing policy development over time are also welcomed.

General Editors: M. Ramesh, National University of Singapore; Xun Wu, Hong Kong University of Science and Technology; Michael Howlett, Simon Fraser University, British Columbia and National University of Singapore

A Matter of Style?

Organizational Agency in Global Public Policy

LOUISA BAYERLEIN
European University Institute
CHRISTOPH KNILL
Ludwig-Maximilians-Universität Munich
YVES STEINEBACH
Ludwig-Maximilians-Universität Munich

Shaftesbury Road, Cambridge CB2 8EA, United Kingdom

One Liberty Plaza, 20th Floor, New York, NY 10006, USA

477 Williamstown Road, Port Melbourne, VIC 3207, Australia

314–321, 3rd Floor, Plot 3, Splendor Forum, Jasola District Centre, New Delhi – 110025, India

103 Penang Road, #05–06/07, Visioncrest Commercial, Singapore 238467

Cambridge University Press is part of Cambridge University Press & Assessment, a department of the University of Cambridge.

We share the University's mission to contribute to society through the pursuit of education, learning and research at the highest international levels of excellence.

www.cambridge.org
Information on this title: www.cambridge.org/9781108818964

DOI: 10.1017/9781108864671

First published 2020
First paperback edition 2023

A catalogue record for this publication is available from the British Library

Library of Congress Cataloging-in-Publication data
Names: Bayerlein, Louisa, 1991– author. | Knill, Christoph, author. |
Steinebach, Yves, 1987– author.
Title: A matter of style? : organizational agency in global public policy / Louisa Bayerlein, Christoph Knill, Yves Steinebach.
Description: Cambridge ; New York, NY : Cambridge University Press, 2020. |
Includes bibliographical references and index.
Identifiers: LCCN 2019058108 (print) | LCCN 2019058109 (ebook) |
ISBN 9781108836371 (hardback) | ISBN 9781108864671 (ebook)
Subjects: LCSH: International agencies – Administration. | International organization. | Political planning. | Management.
Classification: LCC JZ4850 .B39 2020 (print) | LCC JZ4850 (ebook) |
DDC 352.3/4211–dc23
LC record available at https://lccn.loc.gov/2019058108
LC ebook record available at https://lccn.loc.gov/2019058109

ISBN   978-1-108-83637-1   Hardback
ISBN   978-1-108-81896-4   Paperback

This book is dedicated to Klaus Bayerlein,
who would have been so proud of his daughter.

Contents

Tables and Figures

Preface

This book was inspired by the idea that in order to better understand international organizations' agency, we need to redirect our attention from their formal characteristics and exceptional achievements or failures to the ordinary, informal workings of their staff. Much ink has been spilled on international public administrations' role in shaping various extraordinary events and policy outputs. Yet, we can learn a lot about (international) organizations by examining their staffers' actions not in critical moments but in their daily work. Likewise, formal characteristics alone fail to capture the deeper running, less easily quantifiable intricacies of international organizations. There is simply more to international public administrations than single indicators can tell us.

Consider the very simple example of wanting to learn more about a person. When we observe someone dressed up quite extravagantly one day, we would not immediately consider them a flamboyant dresser based on this snapshot. Only at the point where the person regularly, often intuitively, chooses attire of that kind would we speak of a personal style. This style is an expression of the person, his or her spirit, ambitions, and the like. When interested in what really 'makes somebody tick', these distinctive patterns of behaviour are at least as informative as considering single, exceptional acts. In this book, we are of course less interested in appearances or individual attire, but in 'how things are done' in international public administrations as a whole. There is a certain way of going about quotidian tasks which is distinct to a given organization. Similar to the quite mundane example above, these administrative styles only emerge in regularity, as a routine. They are so deeply embedded in the respective organizational culture that they can be considered an organization's default way of working. These defaults teach us about an organization's underlying orientations just as a clothing style clues us in on someone's personality.

Similarly, knowing exactly how tall or short, young or old, rich or poor said person is only reveals a small part of the story of who they are. These readily quantifiable bits of information could hint at certain character traits, but no one would seriously claim to really know somebody based on these statistics alone. Just as demographic characteristics are thus only loosely coupled with who a person truly is, administrative styles are not entirely determined by formal organizational characteristics, such as size, membership, budget, or mandate. Although shifting attention away from these characteristics obviously comes with the risk of introducing complications, what drives international public administrations, their underlying orientations in policy making, is more elusive than numbers can tell. Hence we believe this effort, which we undertake in this book, to be worthwhile.

After more than three years in the making, this book really came together in the summer of 2018. The effort of eventually putting everything in place was made bearable – fun even – by a good portion of team spirit, long walks, and Munich beer gardens. We would like to thank our colleagues of the Research Unit 1745 on 'International Public Administrations (IPAs)' funded by the German Science Foundation (DFG) for continuously providing valuable input and stimulating discussions. In supporting this research group, the DFG also provided generous funding for the specific research carried out for this book (grant no. KN 891/7–1). Especially in the earlier stages of this research project, Jan Enkler, Stephan Grohs, Steffen Eckhard, Christina Kern, Lucia de Grandi, and Sylvia Schmidt gave very valuable input on the overall concept and manuscript. We are also greatly indebted to them for their efforts and assistance in gathering the data for this book. Throughout the years, Dionys Zink has been a tremendous help in preparing and finalizing the manuscript for this book. Kim Greenwell has provided excellent language editing assistance. We are especially grateful to our editor at Cambridge University Press, Joe Ng, and the series editors Michael Howlett, M. Ramesh, and Xun Wu for their time and encouragement, as well as to the three anonymous reviewers for their willingness to truly and thoroughly engage with our work. Above all, we would like to thank the over 100 staffers who took the time to provide us with insights into their work routines. Despite all this invaluable help in making this book possible, all errors of course remain ours.

Abbreviations

AusAid	Australian Agency for International Development
BIS	Bank for International Settlement
BRICS	Brazil, Russia, India, China, South Africa
CDG	Center for Global Development
CFC	Chlorofluorocarbon
COFO	Committee on Forestry
CPF	Country Programming Framework
CPR	Committee of Permanent Representatives
DEWA	Division of Early Warning and Assessment
DFID	Department for International Development
DTIE	Division of Technology, Industry, and Economics
ExCom	Executive Committee of the High Commissioner's Programme
FAO	Food and Agriculture Organization
G20	Group of 20
GEF	Global Environment Facility
GEO	Global Environment Outlook
GMG	Global Migration Group
ICAO	International Civil Aviation Organization
IEO	Independent Evaluation Office
IHR	International Health Regulations
ILC	International Labour Conference
ILO	International Labour Organization
IMF	International Monetary Fund
IMS	International Military Staff
IO	International Organization
IOM	International Organization for Migration
IPA	International Public Administration
IPPC	International Plant Protection Convention
IR	International Relations

IS	International Staff
ITC-ILO	International Training Centre of the International Labour Organization
ITPGRFA	International Treaty on Plant Genetic Resources for Food and Agriculture
LFA	Logical Framework Approach
MTS	Mid-term Strategy
MOPAN	Multilateral Organization Performance Assessment Network
NAC	North Atlantic Council
NATO	North Atlantic Treaty Organization
NGO	Non-governmental Organization
OECD	Organization for Economic Co-operation and Development
OSCE	Organization for Security and Co-operation in Europe
PHEIC	Public Health Emergency of International Concern
PoW	Programme of Work
QUART	NATO's four biggest budget holders, US, UK, France, and Germany
QUINT	NATO's five biggest budget holders, US, UK, France, Germany, and Italy
RTS	Regional Thematic Specialists
SRI	Socially Responsible Investment
TC	Technical Cooperation
TSR	Triennial Surveillance Reviews
UN	United Nations
UNCSD	United Nations Conference on Sustainable Development
UNDP	United Nations Development Programme
UNEA	United Nations Environmental Assembly
UNEO	United Nations Environment Organization
UNEP	United Nations Environment Programme
UNESCO	United Nations Educational, Scientific and Cultural Organization
UNFCCC	United Nations Framework Convention on Climate Change
UNHCR	United Nations High Commissioner for Refugees
WEA	World Environment Organization

WFP	World Food Programme
WHA	World Health Assembly
WHO	World Health Organization
WMO	World Meteorological Organization
WTO	World Trade Organization

1 | *Introduction*

Of Illusory Giants and Dwarfs:
Do International Public Administrations
Matter for Policy Making Beyond the
Nation-State?

Among the many memorable characters created by Michael Ende, the author of *The Neverending Story*, Mr Tur Tur, who appears in Ende's lesser-known children's book *Jim Button and Luke the Engine Driver* (1963), quite literally stands out. In the book, protagonists Jim and Luke, travelling across a vast desert, spot a giant figure far on the horizon. Although initially frightened, the two decide to approach the colossus, who miraculously becomes smaller and smaller the closer they get to him. When they finally face the creature up close, they learn that far from being scary or even a giant, Mr Tur Tur is a perfectly ordinary-sized and, moreover, very kind man, who later proves to be a valuable ally in finding a way out of the dangerous desert. Mr Tur Tur, it turns out, is an illusory giant. Only when seen from a distance does he appear to be gigantic; the closer one approaches him, the more clearly one sees his true shape and colour.

This little tale has much to tell us about real-life problems of governance beyond the nation-state and, more specifically, about the role of international public administrations (IPAs) therein. IPAs – the administrative corpus of international organizations (IOs) – have led a shadowy existence as 'analytical wallflowers'. In the realm of international relations (IR), IPAs were perceived, at best, as distant points on the horizon, the examination of which was deemed unnecessary to the understanding of international policy making. Yet over the last few years, the analytical perception of IPAs as 'dwarfs' in the international arena has turned out to be as illusory as Mr Tur Tur's gigantism; the closer we approach them, the more clearly we see their agency in policy making beyond the nation-state. IPAs, in short, are only illusory dwarfs.

The story of Mr Tur Tur draws attention to the importance of per-spective, of distance in particular. The assessment of how big a player an IPA is often depends on the perspective that defines the level of analysis from which a certain phenomenon is assessed. While those who view IPAs from a great distance run the risk of being taken in by the illusion and of thus misjudging an IPA's actual (informal) agency, those who see IPAs from too close a perspective might overestimate the magnitude of their administrative influence. For the purposes of comparison, one needs a perspective that is both remote enough to see the bigger picture beyond the formal, initially visible and close enough to take account of as much informal detail as possible. In this book, we advocate for a meso-perspective on IPA agency and influence that is sufficiently close to capture what really happens beyond formal rules and distant enough to make comparisons. Once we know how 'big' or 'small' a given set of IPAs are in terms of agency and potential influence, we need theories that can coherently account for differences across the board.

This book is guided by two main questions. First, being interested in IPA agency in policy making beyond the nation-state, we ask, *To what extent do international administrations have the potential to influence the initiation, formulation, and implementation of their IOs' policies?* In terms of analytical levels, or 'distance from our subject', we aim to strike a balance between comparability and close attention to the day-to-day workings of IPAs in proposing the concept of administrative styles. By focusing on these informal, quotidian procedures, we present a novel way to systematically assess IPA agency across different orga-nizations and different issue areas. We are also able to discern specific kinds of potential IPA influence by making the distinction between policy advocacy and institutional consolidation. Taking the middle ground between near and far, we are able to see the gestalt of the phenomenon in comparatively assessing IPA's actual form and size.

Second, once we know about the IPAs' administrative styles, we ask, *How do we explain variation? What makes an IPA a dwarf or a giant? Why are some giants leaning towards institutional consolidation while others are strong in policy advocacy, and still others do both?* We argue that the formation of different administrative styles comes along with different influence potential and orientations. Administrative style is affected by two dimensions: the internal challenges and the external challenges that a bureaucracy faces and perceives. This approach allows for systematic, generalized statements about the factors that determine the potential policy influence of IPAs against the backdrop of the structural and institutional context in which they operate. A focus on administrative styles may thus enhance our theoretical understanding of the determinants of IPA agency and enable the conceptually guided comparison and measurement of IPAs over time and across the IO landscape.

In this introductory chapter, we show how the analytical view of IOs as actors in their own right has fuelled a growing interest in IPA influence in international policy making. While we do know that IPAs matter, we lack systematic knowledge and a comparative perspective on their informal agency. In the following pages, we argue that the study of IPA agency and its determinants has brought about important insights yet still lacks a meso-perspective on the phenomenon. We then go on to introduce our main argument and elaborate on the contributions we hope to make, before sketching out the structure and plan of the book.

1.1 Research Perspectives on International Public Administrations

Research on IPAs has gained strong momentum over the last two decades. This development is especially remarkable in view of the analytical neglect that has long characterized this field of inquiry. Although the growing interest in IPAs has brought about highly valuable findings on IPA agency and influence in international policy making, we are caught between analytical perspectives that take on either too remote or too proximate a view, implying that assessments of IPAs are either confined to their formal features or are rather idiosyncratic. We contend that there is a need for a meso-level perspective on IPAs that goes beyond merely formal assessments but that is sufficiently abstract to allow for systematic comparisons across different IPAs.

1.1.1 Seeing through the Dwarf Illusion: The Changing View on International Public Administrations

Globalization and the end of the Cold War fuelled the establishment and growing relevance of IOs in nearly all areas of global governance. IOs have been delegated a wide variety of tasks and are part of the global attempt to define effective means against climate change; they command armed troops deployed to protect civilians in fragile states; they assist nation-states in solving humanitarian and refugee crises and they administrate the world financial system. While IOs are increasingly significant to both our understanding and the actual making of global governance, until the new millennium, they have played the role of 'ugly duckling' in IR theory (Verbeek, 1998). In a sense, IPAs were not even seen as illusory dwarfs; they were not seen at all. 'The question of what IOs actually do, a conception of IOs as actors as well as an understanding and explanation of their actions, had ... been largely overshadowed by the more fundamental theoretical entanglement of whether they matter at all' (Venzke, 2010, p. 68). Due to the discursive prevalence of realism and functionalism in the realm of IR, IOs (and hence IPAs even more so) had long been discarded as actors and research subjects in their own right (Reinalda & Verbeek, 2003). Even the emergence of a less statist perspective as a side product of regime theory left the general perception of passive IOs almost unchanged (Verbeek, 1998). To this day, IOs are often viewed as mere instruments of their member states or as forums for intergovernmental bargaining (Archer, 2015; Hurd, 2013; Rittberger & Zangl, 2006).[1]

It was not until the approaching new millennium that a major theoretical and analytical shift took place with regard to IOs. Theoretical advances in (sociological) institutionalism (Barnett & Finnemore, 1999, 2004) and principal–agent theory (Abbott & Snidal, 1998; Hawkins, Lake, Nielson, & Tierney, 2006; Stone, 2011) led scholars in global governance and IR to reopen the organizational black box and to look at IOs more seriously. Increasingly, IOs were theorized to matter,[2] since their broad spectrum of delegated authority and policy functions constitutes them as actors that influence their member states and the larger environment. By treating IOs as players in their own right, their conceptualization as actors goes far beyond their possessing a legal personality, since 'part of the point of creating international

---

[1] For a more detailed account of how different theoretical traditions in IR view IOs and their secretariats, see Biermann et al. (2009).

[2] Note here that constructivists and organizational theorists were certainly pivotal in pushing this research agenda at the time, but naturally not the first to ever claim that IOs matter more generally. Liberal-idealists going back to Woodrow Wilson have made the same claim almost a century ago in emphasizing their role as a means to foster and uphold peace between states (Wilson, 1919; Woolf, 1916).

organizations is to have a body that is distinct from any of the states within it, and so agency on the part of the IO is an essential part of its function, purpose, and indeed existence' (Hurd, 2013, p. 17). This agency – the ontological potential and capacity to act according to their own will – enables IOs to influence their own output and processes, to thus 'act' and even to 'behave'. As actors, IOs can creatively work the rule structure in which they are embedded (Martin, 2006, p. 141).

When implying that an IO 'behaves', however, one is actually talking about the collective decisions of either member states or – more interestingly for the purpose of this book – their bureaucracies. The realization that 'if IOs matter, their staff must be significant too' (Xu & Weller, 2004, p. 11) profoundly challenged the dwarf illusion, which became less and less tenable the closer scholars zoomed in on IOs. Zooming in on IOs entails viewing the secretariat as a distinct part of the organization, as a political system that interacts with the IO's other parts and with the broader environment.

We refer to these bureaucratic bodies as 'international public administrations' (IPAs), which can more specifically be defined as 'hierarchically organised groups of international civil servants with a given mandate, resources, identifiable boundaries, and a set of formal rules of procedures within the context of a policy area' (Biermann et al., 2009, p. 37). IOs as actors, thus, are far from being monolithic, since they typically comprise several different, interacting bodies. Major formal decisions are normally made in the political arm of an IO, that is, the plenary organ and the executive body. These two elements are political in the sense that they usually consist of member states' representatives acting in the interest of their respective home countries. The bureaucratic[3] part of the IO – that is, the IPA – provides the

---

[3] We generally conceive of IPAs as more-or-less bureaucratic organizations. Similar to their national counterparts, IPAs carry out administrative tasks on the basis of clearly specified competencies within a fixed hierarchical structure. Although the extent to which IPAs (and, of course, any other public or private administration) resemble patterns of Max Weber's ideal-typical conceptualization of bureaucracies varies, all of these organizations share the basic ingredients typically associated with bureaucratic structures, namely the principles of rule-bound behaviour, in particular neutrality, hierarchy, and action on the basis of recorded and written rules (Weber, 1978). Note that in order to avoid too many repetitions and enhance readability, we will henceforth use the terms 'bureaucratic' and 'administrative' interchangeably.

organizational infrastructure. Similar to nation-states, IOs thus possess an administrative apparatus designed to carry out the actual day-to-day business of the IO, such as researching and formulating documents, or planning and preparing conferences and assemblies. Typically, IPAs are headed by a secretary general,[4] and personnel are usually accountable not to the member states but to the organization, which – at least in principle – defies direct member-state control.

These bureaucratic bodies, as the 'institutional backbones of governance', indeed do 'behave'. Since at least the time of Barnett and Finnemore's (2004) seminal publication on the authority and pathologies of IOs' secretariats, a growing number of studies that have been inspired by sociological institutionalism, organizational sociology, and principal-agent approaches have adopted the view that IPAs are far from being dwarfs in analytical terms (see inter alia Bauer & Ege, 2016; Biermann & Pattberg, 2012; Biermann & Siebenhüner, 2009c; Dingwerth, Kerwer, & Nölke, 2009; Liese & Weinlich, 2006; Nay, 2011; Nielson & Tierney, 2003). These undertakings have been paralleled by recent efforts of public administration, scholars to systematically investigate IPAs as a genuine type of public administration (Bauer, Knill, & Eckhard, 2016; Knill & Bauer, 2016; Knill, Bayerlein, Grohs, & Enkler, 2019). Research combining IR and organization theories fuelled a renewed interest in studying IOs as political systems and their IPAs 'as organizations' (Brechin & Ness, 2013; Dingwerth et al., 2009; Ness & Brechin, 1988), recognizing that the internal structure and political personnel of IOs can be sources of policy change (Biermann & Siebenhüner, 2009c) or organizational dysfunctions (Barnett & Finnemore, 2004). Building on the now classical contributions of Cox and Jacobsen (1973), Haas (1964), and Weiss (1982), the main contribution of these efforts was to highlight that IOs' secretariats, just like IOs, are not just epiphenomenal and instrumental (Mearsheimer, 1994) but wield a certain level of influence. This research thus highlights the agency of both IOs and their IPAs (Ellis, 2010; Rochester, 1986). Increasingly, IOs are disentangled from their bureaucratic bodies, which are now almost univocally conceived to be *actors* in various settings, such as the secretariats of the International Monetary Fund (IMF) and the World Bank (Martin, 2006; Vetterlein, 2012) or the

---

[4] We use the term secretary general uniformly for all IOs; note that this also includes functional equivalents, since the particular denomination varies from IO to IO.

administrative apparatus of United Nations bodies involved in peace-building (Eckhard, 2016; Weinlich, 2014). With many scholars now taking IPAs seriously, it is safe to say that the long-standing dwarf illusion of IPAs has been debunked.

1.1.2 Actual Dwarfs or Giants? IPA Influence in Policy Making

Once the literature has moved past the analytical problem of whether IOs matter or not, scholars began closing in on the subject. '[A]n international organization is most clearly an actor when it is most distinctly an "it", an entity distinguishable from its member states' (Claude, 1984, p. 13). The extent to which an IO is an 'it' – that is, IPA agency as a potential – becomes visible in its actions. Given the complex setup of IPAs' being embedded in the broader structure, action comes to mean 'independent action'. By definition, to be attributable to the IPA, agency must materialize in those actions taken by the IPA that would not have happened if an IO were simply the sum of its member states. In other words, IPA agency becomes visible in the influence IPAs exert on IOs' policies and processes. As a logical consequence of this and with the realization that IPAs are not dwarfs after all, the question arises as to if and how bureaucracies employ their agency, that is, how they actually influence IO policies and processes. We know from research on domestic administrations that bureaucrats may exert considerable influence on the contents and methods of policy making, which reach far beyond the street level. Bureaucracies can be highly active in initiating the development of new policies and typically play a pronounced role in the drafting of policy proposals to be adopted by the legislature. In short, it is established in the national context that public administrations are far from merely constituting instruments or means for policy makers and governments but pursue their own interests and objectives in policy making (inter alia Rourke, 1969; Heclo, 1977; Knill, 2001; Peters & Pierre, 2004).

Indeed, IPAs have similarly been found to exert considerable influence on IOs' policy outputs. Although different disciplines apply a variety of conceptual perspectives when addressing IPAs, the literature is surprisingly united in finding that IPAs matter as significant actors in international politics (see reviews by Busch, 2014; Eckhard & Ege, 2016; Liese & Weinlich, 2006). IPAs can influence IOs' substantive policies, such as economic programmes by the IMF and the World Bank (Martin, 2006; Sharma, 2013; Vetterlein, 2012), for example, or the emergence and change of the World Health Organization's (WHO's) global AIDS initiative (Harman, 2010; Nay, 2011), the implementation of IOs' policies (e.g. Eckhard, 2016; Stone, 2008; Yi-Chong & Weller, 2004), and institutional policies that affect the design and change of IOs (Barnett & Coleman, 2005; Hanrieder, 2014; Hawkins & Jacoby, 2006; Johnson & Urpelainen, 2014; Weaver & Leiteritz, 2005). Although political control and responsibility over the decisions taken on all these questions remains well in the hands of member states, international policy making is clearly more than merely the sum of IO interests.

While the literature seems to have agreed that IPAs possess a certain degree of agency of their own, the actual extent of their influence in policy making continues to be debated (see Bauer et al., 2016; Reinalda, 2013). Despite the fact that the bureaucratic bodies form the major share of an IO, and notwithstanding a growing academic interest in IPAs, we lack systematic comparative knowledge of IPA agency in policy making beyond the nation-state. As we have seen, a variety of studies empirically assessed IPAs' influence in single or small-N case studies and concluded that IPAs can indeed be influential. This research highlights the agency of IOs and their IPAs (Ellis, 2010; Rochester, 1986) and has provided valuable insights into the various ways IPAs might matter for concrete IO policy outputs (Biermann & Siebenhüner, 2009a). These pronounced efforts of a large number of scholars examining IPAs' involvement in and influence on IO policy making notwithstanding, from what we know so far, they could be real or illusory dwarfs or giants.

1.1.3 *Dwarf or Giant Is a Matter of Perspective: IPAs from Near and Far*

While we know that IOs do matter when trying to understand international policy and that IPAs can be relevant actors in this regard, we know little about whether – and if so, which – IPAs can really be considered active players in the field. We contend that one reason for this lies in the analytical perspectives applied. Our assessment of how and how much IPAs matter in international policy making crucially depends on perspectives: in other words, how closely we delve into the workings of IPAs.

On the one hand, we find thick descriptions, which are analytically too close to allow for generalizable statements about IPA agency. While the above-mentioned qualitative single- or small-N case studies provide rich empirical information on the ways IPAs have exerted concrete influence in a given time period or case, the idiosyncratic assessment of IPA influence naturally renders comparisons across different bureaucracies highly difficult. While this is certainly a general drawback of the method and should not be held against the research itself, this case-specific research comes with a second problem. Usually, we find interpretations of instances in which bureaucratic influence was successful (i.e. actually visible). Yet this focus on visible cases of influence bears the danger of a biased case selection, since non-visibility does not necessarily imply that IPA influence was not present at all (Beach, 2004).

On the other hand, we see studies that approach IPAs (or IOs) from afar. Many scholars explicitly acknowledge these problems associated with the qualitative approach and systematically analyse a large number of IPAs on the basis of quantitative research designs. Focusing on the formal autonomy of IOs and IPAs, their independence, or the amount of authority delegated to them (Bauer & Ege, 2016; Ege, 2019; Haftel & Thompson, 2006; Hooghe & Marks, 2015), IPA influence has been mapped and measured in medium- and large-N studies. Although highly innovative and doubtlessly valuable, these approaches similarly come with a number of drawbacks associated with the analytical perspective. Because the informal is infamously hard to quantify, often these studies implicitly assume that formal discretion automatically implies that an IPA will actually make use of this room for manoeuvre. The basis of policy influence is located in the formal autonomy of IPAs as fixed in the founding treaties and other statues of the IO (Bauer & Ege, 2016). From an informal governance perspective (Stone, 2013), however, the presence of autonomy does not automatically mean that bureaucracies also seek to exert influence on policy making. Likewise, the absence of autonomy does not necessarily imply that bureaucracies dispense with the development of informal activities to overcome their formal autonomy limitations. Put simply: knowing about what IPAs can do in principle (knowing the boundaries of their discretion) does not tell us much about what they do de facto.

In sum, no analytical concepts have thus far been developed that would allow for systematic comparison of informal IPA influence and agency across different IOs. Existing research is either based on single case studies or fully quantitative approaches. While certainly fruitful, both approaches bear distinctive problems. While cases studies suffer from potential selection bias and idiosyncratic explanations, quantitative approaches have the problem of relying on formal assessments of IPA influence, that is, on data that are comparatively easy to collect for a larger number of organizations. What is missing, however, are comparative assessments that *combine* the strengths of in-depth studies on administrative influence with a broader comparative perspective.

1.1.4 Why Some IPAs Are Dwarfs While Others Are Giants: Explanations for IPAs' Potential for Policy Influence

In the young but rich literature on IPAs, their agency, and their influence, we are confronted with a plethora of loosely connected theoretical assessments of the conditions under which IPA influence might be more or less pronounced. Why are some IPAs considered giants while others are considered dwarfs? In the last ten years, several relevant factors have been suggested that might enable or constrain IPA action. The long list included bureaucratic expertise and expert authority (Barnett & Finnemore, 2004; Nay, 2012), politicization (Cox & Jacobsen, 1973; Hanrieder, 2014), member state control capacities (Best, 2012), and contextual factors such as policy uncertainty and organizational crises (Broome, 2012; Chorev, 2013). Scholars also pointed towards factors like the degree of administrative discretion, administrative resources, organizational structures (fragmentation versus concentration) (Graham, 2014), hierarchical structures (Eckhard, 2016), mandates (Hall, 2015, 2016), funding structures (Graham, 2017), and the nature of the political problem to be addressed, to name only some of the most prominent arguments in this regard (Snidal, 1990; Biermann et al., 2009; Lenz, Bezuijen, Hooghe, & Marks, 2015).

All these factors have been used convincingly to explain specific cases or important aspects of IPA agency. Informal institutions and behaviour, however, can rarely be explained against the backdrop of purely structural factors, let alone singular explanations. In sum, we have seen that while the literature has clearly moved past the dwarf illusion by seriously engaging with IOs as actors and the role of their IPAs, there are still a number of unresolved issues.

The story of Mr Tur Tur is an example of how the proximity to a given subject can change what one sees. We have argued that in the case of IPAs, we lack an intermediate perspective – in analytical terms, a meso-level analysis – of IPAs that is abstract enough for comparison yet that still allows us to capture the *informal* elements of IPAs' doings, which are of special relevance for those interested in agency and influence. Finally, once we arrive at conclusions as to how much of a giant or a dwarf an IPA is in reality, we need to account for the complex and multifaceted factors that give way to their behaviour. Here, we argue that we need to move beyond single, structural variables and instead focus on the sum of broader, perceived constraining and enabling factors.

1.2 Main Argument and Contributions: IPA Agency and Administrative Styles

These lacunae in the literature point to the central question of this book. Essentially, we are interested in the presence or absence of IPA agency in policy making beyond the nation-state. To what extent do international administrations have the potential to influence their IOs' policies, and why so? In answering this question, we hope to make a conceptual, theoretical, and empirical contribution to the literature.

First, we argue for a middle ground in the problem of perspective by relying on the concept of administrative styles, thus adding an analytical meso-perspective (Knill et al., 2019) to existing accounts of IPAs. In so doing, we avoid problems of biased case selection centred around 'visible' cases and conceive of administrative influence as independent from formal autonomy and thus not entirely determined by it. At the same time, the administrative styles concept allows us to compare behavioural routines across different IPAs. It is sufficiently abstract to enable meaningful comparisons across any kind of administration, regardless of the institutional level at which the administrative body is located. In short, it allows us to recognize and compare dwarfs and giants.

We start from the proposition that when an IPA regularly intends to influence the policy-making process (and policy outputs subsequently), we should be able to identify patterns of informal administrative behaviour directed at accomplishing this objective – even if, at times, the endeavour might fail. The previous considerations indicate that administrative influence along these lines can hardly be captured by merely considering an IPA's formal autonomy and rules. Rather, they require the study of informal practices and routines. Just like people, places, or epochs, each IPA has a certain individual style that becomes visible in an informal, routinized modus operandi that is part of an IO's culture more broadly. Administrative styles can hence be considered as behavioural routines and practices that have been internalized collectively over time.

The concept captures what makes public administrations 'tick' when it comes to their role in initiating, formulating, and implementing the policies of their respective IOs. We argue in this book that an IPA can be driven by very distinct orientations that are informative of the kind of influence they may exert. IPA behaviour can be shaped simply by the goal of fulfilling all their principals' wishes and needs; they can be guided predominantly by the desire to enhance the policy effectiveness and hence problem-solving capacity of their IO; or they can strive to preserve and enhance their institutional position and legitimacy. Each of these orientations should make a difference for the overall policy record of an IO.

The concept of style thus captures both the presence and direction of bureaucratic influence orientations. More specifically, we distinguish between two orientations – functional and positional – that can be more or less prevalent in shaping administrative routines. The functional orientation becomes apparent in administrative routines geared towards enhancing the effectiveness and quality of an IO's policies; the positional orientation, by contrast, refers to routines directed at institutional consolidation, that is, the bureaucracy's institutional standing and position. Depending on the extent to which these orientations can be observed in bureaucratic routine behaviour, we can distinguish between four ideal-typical IPA styles: (1) a servant style (neither functional nor positional orientation), (2) an entrepreneurial style (both orientations high), (3) an advocacy style (high functional but low positional orientation), and (4) a consolidator style (low functional but high institutional orientation). To assess an IPA's degree of functional or positional orientation, we rely on a range of indicators that capture different elements of administrative routines for different stages of the policy process (initiation, drafting, implementation). This way, we are able to classify and compare administrative styles across IOs.

Administrative styles as conceptually developed in this book provide an innovative basis for measuring administrative influence on policy making. First, we overcome long-standing problems of actually delineating which elements or components of a policy can be attributed to political or administrative aegis or other sources by conceiving of administrative influence as orientation, that is, as routinized intentions rather than concrete policy manifestations. Second, we perceive administrative influence as an informal potential that is not determined by an IPA's autonomy. Third, informality also means that we explicitly focus on influence that goes beyond mere formal rule orientation. Rather, formal rules constitute the benchmark for assessing the extent to which administrations seek to informally go beyond or remain behind these formal arrangements. And finally, it is inherent to the administrative styles concept that we assess influence orientations as stable organizational routines rather than strategic interactions that might vary from case to case within an organization.

The second contribution of this book refers to the theoretical interpretation of different administrative styles. Which factors account for variation of administrative styles across different organizations? Why are the routines and standard operating procedures in some IPAs more entrepreneurial, while others are more servant-like? Why are some dwarfs and others giants? To account for variation in administrative styles across different IOs, we propose two factors that are of special importance for the explanation of the respective styles: the extent to which an IPA perceives itself to be challenged externally, and the extent to which an IPA perceives itself to be challenged internally. The first captures perceived exogenous threats to the bureaucracy's institutional status and operation emerging from political intervention and competition from within an IPA's organizational domain. The second refers to constraints on the bureaucracy's cognitive resources and expertise. This analytical distinction enables us to identify distinctive configurations of internal and external challenges that render the emergence of certain administrative styles more or less likely. In conjunction, internal and external challenges hence go beyond singular structural features that have been identified as potential causes of IPA influence in previous research and instead combine configurations of different structural aspects. Moreover, we argue that the extent to which these configurations affect the formation of administrative styles is crucially affected by their perception through the IPA rather than through their factual characteristics.

Based on these theoretical considerations, we challenge classic assumptions inherent to principal–agent approaches on administrative agency, as the latter continue to be 'blind' to sources of IPA influence that might emerge outside of and not determined by formal autonomy and principal controls. Contrary to these accounts, we show that agents need not always make full use of the formal discretion granted to them by their principals. Our findings demonstrate that IPAs can develop informal routines that might go beyond their formal autonomy. Yet, different administrative styles might also entail that IPAs typically remain below their formally granted space for action. Discretion, therefore, does not equal agency (Cortell & Peterson, 2006). Moreover, we add to sociological institutionalist and constructivist theorizing in emphasizing that bureaucratization and autonomization, i.e., IPAs' alleged tendency to increasingly insulate themselves from political control, should not be considered an automatism. We argue that, rather than being a quasi-deterministic endogenous development, bureaucratic orientations emerge out of the interaction of internal and external factors.

Third, in empirical terms, we provide an encompassing *comparative* assessment of administrative styles across a broad range of structurally different IOs, some of which have not received much scholarly attention with regard to their IPAs. More specifically, we analyse administrative styles in the following eight IOs: the Food and Agriculture Organization of the United Nations (FAO), the International Labour Organization (ILO), the IMF, the International Organization for Migration (IOM), the United Nations Environment Programme (UNEP), the United Nations High Commissioner for Refugees (UNHCR), the North Atlantic Treaty Organization (NATO), and the WHO. Based on this assessment, we are able to demonstrate not only that administrative styles display pronounced variation across different IPAs, but also that this variation is affected by the configuration of internal and external challenges that an IPA faces. IPAs that perceive similar challenges display similar styles, although they might vary strongly in their formal autonomy and structural features, such as their size, budget, staff, functions, or organizational form. While the NATO and the ILO display styles that come very close to the servant ideal, the UNHCR and the IMF can be classified as entrepreneurial.

The FAO and the IOM, by contrast, predominantly display adminis- trative routines reflecting a consolidator style, and the WHO and UNEP come quite close to the advocate ideal.

In sum, this book provides a systematic analysis of IPA policy influ- ence in policy making beyond the nation-state. It does so based on the innovative concept of administrative styles reflecting different degrees and directions of administrative influence orientation. Moreover, it identifies configurations that affect the emergence of distinctive styles and demonstrates the plausibility of these arguments for a broader set of different IPAs. In other words, we are getting close enough to see the gestalt of IPAs in terms of different administrative styles while keeping enough distance to compare them across different bureaucratic bodies. Moving away from the theoretical question of whether IPA 'size' – its agency – is an illusion or not, we thus turn to empirical assessments of which IPAs are dwarfs, which are giants, and why.

1.3 Structure and Plan of the Book

In the chapters to come, we first develop in more detail our conceptua- lization of administrative styles. On this basis, we are able to system- atically analyse the degree and direction of IPA influence. We analytically distinguish between four ideal-typical patterns to identify differences in bureaucratic routines of exerting influence: servants, advocates, consolidators, and entrepreneurs. In addition to this con- ceptual innovation, we offer a theoretical framework accounting for the variation in administrative styles across different international bureaucracies (Chapter 2).

In Chapter 3, we outline how these conceptual and theoretical con- siderations can be studied empirically. This begins with the operatio- nalization of administrative styles and key explanatory factors for variation in administrative styles. Thereafter, we elaborate on our methodological approach to assess IPAs' informal bureaucratic rou- tines and the considerations guiding our case selection.

In Chapters 4 to 7, we provide in-depth empirical analyses of admin- istrative styles in the eight IOs under investigation. In each chapter, we compare two IPAs that exhibit the same administrative style despite differences in several key structural features of their respective IOs. For each of the four pairings, we show that this similarity in styles is due to shared perceptions of internal and external challenges.

In Chapter 4, we focus on the IMF and the UNHCR as two IPAs that display a highly entrepreneurial administrative style. Both IPAs share routines that combine strong policy advocacy with institutional consolidation. Taking into account the considerable differences in formal autonomy between both IPAs, these similarities in administrative styles are striking. In particular, one might intuitively expect that in view of its limited autonomy, the UNHCR should display a servant style. Yet what both IPAs have in common is the perception of similarly low internal and high external constraints that facilitate the emergence of similar entrepreneurial routines in both IPAs.

By contrast, in comparing the IOM and the FAO, Chapter 5 highlights how internal challenges in the absence of serious external threats favour the emergence of a similar consolidator style in both IPAs. Both IPAs combine pronounced routines directed towards institutional consolidation with only weak policy advocacy. We show that none of the prominent structural characteristics – size, budget, mandate, or organizational structure – can convincingly account for both the IPAs' pronounced positional orientation and their lack of functional orientation geared towards advocacy.

In Chapter 6, we are concerned with the WHO and UNEP as examples of advocate-style IPAs. The two IPAs share behavioural patterns that have allowed them to establish themselves as advocates in the area of environmental and global health matters. Despite their apparent common capability to solve problems of global scale, the two IPAs could hardly be more different when considering only their structural features. We show that this commonality in styles, despite structural dissimilarities, is due to the similarly strong perception of external threats and the comparatively low level of internal challenges.

In Chapter 7, we compare NATO and the ILO as servants, despite their having almost nothing formally in common. While NATO's servant style is not particularly astounding, given its policy area, mandate, and functional design, the ILO's case is puzzling. Despite its being an organization with rather broad autonomy, normative authority, and high legitimacy, the ILO's IPA regularly behaves very passively when it comes to leaving its own mark on the IO's outputs. We show that in conjunction, the constraints arising from high internal challenges and the sense of security stemming from low subjective external pressures render more entrepreneurial behaviour neither possible nor necessary.

Finally, in Chapter 8, we present an overview of our key results and critically reassess our conceptual and theoretical approach in light of our empirical findings. We discuss theoretical implications and some limitations to our study and conclude by pointing out future avenues for research, including the need to investigate the link between administrative styles and policy outputs, the interaction of formal autonomy and administrative styles, and issues of stability and change of administrative styles.

2 | Conceptualizing and Explaining Bureaucratic Influence: Administrative Styles

In this book, we focus *not* on what IPAs ought to do (as in their formal autonomy), not on what they can do (in exceptional cases), but on what they actually do beyond manifestations in outputs and their mandates. To what extent do international administrations have the potential to influence the initiation, drafting, and implementation of IOs' policies and why? We are interested in the presence or absence of IPA agency in policy making beyond the nation-state. In reality, should we consider a given IPA a dwarf or a giant?

Administrative agency in practice captures the extent to which an IO's policy outputs and policy outcomes can be shaped by its administrative body. Regardless of its formal mandate, an IPA can be active or reactive when it comes to identifying new problems and pushing new initiatives on an IO's agenda. Moreover, as we know from research on national ministerial bureaucracies and the European Commission (Knill, Enkler, Schmidt, Eckhard, & Grohs, 2017; Peters, 2010; Pollitt & Bouckaert, 2004), bureaucratic bodies can be highly active in shaping the political agenda or pursuing a more instrumental role refraining from strategic anticipation of their political masters' interests. The same scenario applies when it comes to the implementation stage. Again, bureaucracies can interpret their role rather formally, going strictly 'by the book', or they can pursue a more strategic role in sanctioning and monitoring compliance. In short, there is a range of potential ways through which IPAs might make a considerable difference to an IO's policies. Our previous considerations also indicate that administrative influence along these lines can hardly be captured by merely considering an IPA's formal autonomy and rules, but rather requires the study of informal practices and routines. It is exactly these patterns that we want to explore in this book.

To this end, we develop the concept of *administrative styles*. Not all public administrations work the same way. This fact does not come as a surprise to anyone who studies bureaucracies or has ever been in contact with one in everyday life. Administrative involvement, operations, and decision making may differ across policy sectors, countries (Peters & Pierre, 2004; Schnapp, 2004), and international organizations (Knill & Grohs, 2015). Beyond formal rules, administrations can develop lives of their own. This inner life of bureaucracies becomes visible in an informal, routinized modus operandi, which is part of administrative culture more broadly. There are distinct characteristics to the ways and procedures through which they typically accomplish their daily tasks. Administrative styles can generally be defined as informal routines that characterize the behaviour and activities of public administrations in the policy-making process (Knill, 2001). This concept, which we elaborate on in the following section, is sufficiently precise to capture informal routines and practices of IPAs in the policy-making process (Section 2.1) and at the same time allows us to describe the central orientations underlying administrative behaviour (Section 2.2).

What makes public administrations tick when it comes to their role in initiating, formulating, and implementing the policies of their respective IO? We argue that IPAs can be driven by very distinct orientations that are informative of the kind of influence they may exert on policy outputs. An IPA's behavioural routines can be shaped simply by the goal to fulfil all their principals' needs and wishes; they can be predominantly guided by the desire to enhance the policy effectiveness and hence problem-solving capacity of their IO, or they can strive to preserve and advance their institutional position and legitimacy. Each of these orientations might make a difference for the overall policy record of an IO. On this basis, we are able to identify four ideal-typical administrative styles that serve as analytical benchmarks for measuring and mapping real-world styles of IPAs (Section 2.3). This leaves us with the important question of which factors favour the emergence of different administrative styles that will be addressed in the final part of this chapter (Section 2.4).

2.1 The Concept of Administrative Styles

Any attempt to capture the influence of public administrations on policy outputs and policy outcomes is confronted with considerable analytical challenges. Policy making is usually highly complex and involves many actors with different interests. This is even more the case when we leave the realm of national politics and turn to the international level. Properly delineating the policy influence of ministerial bureaucracies in the national context has been identified as an extremely difficult task (Page, 1985, 2012; Peters, 2010), and there is no reason to believe that this task gets easier when focusing on IPAs. It has proven to be very challenging to dissect the concrete influences of different actors on a given output of policy making beyond the nation-state (Zürn, Binder, & Ecker-Ehrhardt, 2012).

The methodological difficulties of convincingly isolating and uncovering administrative policy influence prompted the reliance on indirect approaches to measure such effects. Rather than studying administrative behaviour directly, the focus of earlier studies is on political attempts to control administrative behaviour through different formal means. From this perspective, administrative influence is simply viewed as a reflection of the extent of political control of the IPA, that is, the administration's formal autonomy. Yet this approach of reducing IPA influence to formal autonomy hardly seems feasible in light of our interest in IPA agency and our subsequent focus on de facto administrative practices and routines. Moreover, even if we were to stick to a merely formal approach, we would learn nothing about the underlying orientations behind behavioural patterns. What exactly is it that IPAs seek to influence and what is their underlying rationale? Theories of formal control of the administration, such as principal–agent models, simply speak of agency drift, but they remain relatively silent about the ways in which agents actually make use of their discretion. In short, while highly valuable in assessing their relationship to their principals, these approaches usually contain little information about what administrative agents actually do (Hawkins, Lake, Nielson, & Tierney, 2006).

We posit that a concept for assessing the influence of IPAs in shaping public policies beyond the nation-state must fulfil two essential requirements: it must demonstrate the presence (or absence) of influence (beyond formal bureaucratic autonomy), and it must identify the orientations guiding bureaucratic influence. In addressing these challenges, we rely on the conception of administrative styles that departs from existing accounts in four ways: administrative influence is analysed (1) as intention rather than policy manifestation; (2) as an informal potential that is not fully conditioned by an IPA's autonomy; (3) as sticky organizational routines rather than purposeful action that might vary from case to case; and (4) as a distinctive dimension of organizational culture.

2.1.1 Administrative Styles as a Potential to Influence the Policy Process

First, we think of administrative influence as a potential rather than a policy manifestation. Hence, we analyse potentials of administrative influence rather than trying to attribute certain elements of IOs' policy outputs to the behaviour of their bureaucracy. Instead of trying to disentangle interdependent actions and trying to isolate the share of IPAs' influence on policy outputs, we depart from the proposition that if IPAs work *towards* influencing the policy-making process (and outputs, subsequently), we should be able to identify patterns of administrative behaviour directed towards accomplishing this objective.

An IPA's general inclination to exert policy influence renders it a potentially relevant actor in the policy-making process, even if these attempts are more or less successful and even if they fail from time to time. By conceptualizing IPA influence in this way, we avoid selection biases inherent in studies that restrict their focus to constellations in which IPA influence is easily visible: in other words, bureaucratic action was found to have made a difference for policy making beyond the nation-state (Eckhard & Ege, 2016). Our approach, by contrast, is not restricted to situations in which an IPA's influence actually materialized. The absence of clearly attributable policy influences should not lead us to neglect the systematic potential of informal agency if an IPA generally has a strong disposition to making a difference in the policy process.[1]

---

[1] This is because, naturally, successful policy influence is not determined by IPA characteristics alone, but depends on the coincidence of a multiplicity of favourable conditions. For instance, it might matter whether domestic developments allow for a member state to be convinced of the IPA's cause and whether a given policy issue is of low political salience or, rather, a critical topic that is subject to intergovernmental decision-making mechanisms. Thus, depending on all these contingencies, within the same IPA some efforts to influence the policy process will ultimately make a difference whilst others do not. On average, however, some IPAs will still routinely invest more efforts than others, depending on their administrative style.

This way, we avoid measurement and attribution problems that can hardly be overcome in light of the multitude of interdependent actors involved in international policy making (Bauer & Ege, 2017; Hooghe & Marks, 2015). Because we do not claim to measure the 'effect size' of IPA influence but rather the presence or absence of the potential to exert influence, we capture influence even where it is to be considered minor at first glance. This approach is especially useful when, in addition, it incorporates the possibility that IPA influence can be consciously concealed. An influential IPA can 'sell' its ideas as being those of their principals or deceive their principals by decoupling or buffering (DiMaggio & Powell, 1991; Hawkins et al., 2006). We therefore study the IPAs' own intentions – not their member states' – and what the IPAs are actually doing in their day-to-day practices.

2.1.2 Bureaucratic Agency as Informal Potential Relative to Formal Rules

Second, we argue that it is predominantly informal factors that shape administrative behaviour since those factors define the way in which administrations try to achieve their objectives given the opportunities and constraints provided by the structural and institutional context they operate in. These patterns of everyday routines will be equally visible if the administration fails to actually exert influence on policy processes and outputs. To assess IPA agency, it is crucial that we go beyond merely considering formal autonomy. We hence perceive bureaucratic agency as informal potential that is not determined by an IPA's formal autonomy. By focusing on IPAs' styles and intentions to influence policy making, we avoid the problems of approaches that consider their influence to be a direct function of formal autonomy. This view is especially pronounced in principal–agent models of administrative behaviour (Graham, 2014; Pollack, 2006). By contrast, we argue that the presence of autonomy does not automatically mean that bureaucracies seek to exert influence on policy making. In a similar vein, the absence of autonomy does not necessarily mean that bureaucracies dispense with the development of informal activities to overcome their formal autonomy limitations. Highly autonomous bureaucracies are not by definition more influence-orientated than those enjoying less discretion. Lisa Martin succinctly summarized the relationship between formal autonomy and informal agency as follows:

While formal autonomy is the amount of authority states have explicitly delegated to agents, informal autonomy defines a situation in which the agent is able to manoeuvre within the existing rule structure. I distinguish between formal agency, which is the amount of authority states have explicitly delegated to an IO, and informal agency, which is the autonomy an IO has in practice, holding the rules constant. (2006, p. 141)

It is the very nature of informal behaviour that it is not fully determined or programmed by the formal rules and regulations governing bureaucratic activities. Rather than restricting our analytical focus to these rules, we are interested in the extent to which an IPA develops informal routines that allow it to exert influence beyond formal rules or whether its informal activities remain in line with, or even behind, the behavioural options provided by existing rules and regulations. Formal rules are not an explanation for administrative influence but serve as a benchmark in assessing informal agency. Administrative styles describe behaviour that is precisely not the essential function of an IPA. They are hence not a direct result of the rational design of the organization but rather evolve within it. This conception of administrative influence is well in line with classic findings of organizational studies and the public administration literature that emphasize the limits of programming administrative behaviour through formal rules as well as the potentially dysfunctional consequences of exclusively rule-orientated behaviour (March & Simon, 1993; Merton, 1957; Blau, 1955; Selznick, 1949). Formal rules are not expected to automatically generate the desired organizational behaviour.

2.1.3 *Administrative Styles as a Stable Modus Operandi*

Third, we conceive of administrative styles as a relatively stable behavioural orientation characterizing an organizational body. They are an institutionalized informal modus operandi that ideationally materializes as a guiding principle over time by repetition and subsequent routinization. We assume that these informal routines shape organizational behaviour. This is not to neglect that the role understandings and values of individual administrators within an organization might vary to some extent. Yet the constant reproduction of informal modes of operation and processes of organizational socialization justifies aggregating individual behaviours at the meso-level of the organization

(Knill, 2001; Simon, 1997). This way, we depart not only from macro-level accounts focusing on general features determining an IPA's formal autonomy or cultural traditions, but also from micro-level accounts interested in the behaviour of individual bureaucrats (Downs, 1967; Dunleavy, 1991).

Under conditions of uncertainty and complexity, individual bureaucrats develop routines for coping with shortages of knowledge, information-processing capacities, and time (Simon, 1997). Similarly, and depending on their underlying rationale, administrators can develop and internalize behavioural patterns that can influence their organization's policies. At the level of the organization, administrative strategies of influence can consolidate into stable patterns of administrative behaviour. The repeated modus operandi of the organization becomes part of its specific organizational identity, manifesting itself as an informal or a formal institution over the long run (Wilson, 1989). Such routines are 'most likely to be treated as fixed' because they 'give stability to the organization and direction to activities that are constantly recurring' (Cyert & March, 1963, p. 103). In line with early conceptions of organizational routines (Simon, 1997; Stene, 1940), administrative styles have hence been assumed to constitute 'unitary and unchanging' (Feldman & Pentland, 2003, p. 97) building blocks embedded in larger organizational structures (Parmigiani & Howard-Grenville, 2011; Salvato & Rerup, 2011).

In view of these considerations we conceive of administrative styles as rather 'sticky', but not static features of an organization. Stickiness does not completely exclude the possibility of change. We rather assume that changes in administrative styles are less likely than for less institutionalized features of an organization, and only unfold over longer periods of time along with changes in the internal and external challenges an IPA is facing. In this book, our central interest lies in comparing administrative styles and their underlying causes across different IPAs for a given period of time. While this approach rests on the stickiness assumption of administrative styles, our empirical findings indicate that in some cases these styles may display slow variation over time. Although the systematic analysis of the historical evolution of administrative styles is beyond the focus of this book (in particular because of the methodological challenges of empirically measuring administrative styles for periods in the more distant past), anecdotic evidence of changes in administrative styles over time is well in line with our theoretical argument; i.e. changes in the internal and external challenges an IPA is facing result in corresponding changes in organizational routines over time (see, for instance, Chapter 4 on the IMF).

2.1.4 Administrative Styles a Distinctive Dimension of Organizational Culture

We have seen that administrative styles are sticky and of an informal, routinized, deeply embedded nature, which intuitively brings to mind the wider notion of 'organizational culture'. Indeed, administrative styles are closely related to this more encompassing concept, which can very broadly be defined as stable pattern of 'basic assumptions' about the 'correct way to perceive, think, and feel' within an organization (Schein, 1990, p. 111). These 'basic assumptions' can be further broken down into different facets, or components, such as the 'ideologies, norms, and routines' governing an IPA (Weaver & Leiteritz, 2005, p. 370). In organizational routines, such as styles, we can observe the more abstract components of culture, e.g. norms and ideologies, translated and integrated in actual, tangible behaviour (Weaver, 2008, p. 37). Administrative styles thus constitute a distinct component of organizational culture, which can be viewed as a manifestation of the respective IO's wider culture.

The different components of organizational culture are generally studied at three different analytical levels (Jann, 2002): the micro-level, including the values, roles, and behaviours of individual members of the administration, as well as the attitudes of the general public towards administrations (e.g. Chwieroth, 2011; Hooghe, 2001; Xu & Weller, 2008; Zürn & Checkel, 2005); the macro-level of administrative traditions that refer to overall basic understandings and historical evolution of administrative systems (Barnett & Finnemore, 2004; Chwieroth, 2010; Momani, 2005); and the meso-level of administrative styles, understood as the standard operating procedures of administrative behaviour and decision making. Administrative styles add this hitherto lesser explored analytical meso-level of behavioural routines to the literature.

Whereas administrative styles are thus congenial to notions of administrative culture, they should not be confused with organizational pathologies. The classic pathologies of administrations refer to problems that administrations face by virtue of being bureaucracies (Dunleavy, 1991; Niskanen, 1971). To give just one example, building on Weber's arguments about domestic bureaucracies, Barnett and Finnemore (1999, 2004) draw on the concept of bureaucracy in the classical Weberian sense: organizations characterized by formal structures, hierarchy, expertise, and moral authority. IOs are 'social creatures' that use their authority, knowledge, and rules to act autonomously in ways that may or may not reflect the interests and mandates of states because their bureaucracies have legitimate authority and control over expertise. In essence, the core argument is that IOs' actions (and pathologies) are written into their bureaucratic structures. Through the 'irrationality of rationalization', rules become ends in themselves, 'bureaucratic universalism' propels general, one-size-fits-all solutions, 'insulation' hinders organizational learning, and 'cultural contestation' leads to turf wars (Barnett and Finnemore, 2004: 39–41). IOs, therefore, are all more or less pathological depending on how 'bureaucratically' they are organized and how deeply this logic is already inscribed in their culture and routines. Administrative styles, by contrast, vary. Not all IPAs will be giants, not all of them dwarfs. Moreover, as we discuss in detail in the Section 2.2, they emerge not as a product of endogenous factors alone but also as sensitive to external developments.

We consider organizational fragmentation, similar to the endogenous dynamics within organizations, not as a given but as a varying factor that has profound implications for IPA agency. The concept of administrative styles – by definition – conceives of bureaucratic bodies as rather homogenous units in terms of shared orientations and routines. However, we conceive of them as unitary actors only insofar as the 'style' is concerned while at the same time acknowledging the idea that IPAs can be more or less internally fragmented (Barnett & Finnemore, 2004; Graham, 2014). While the structural dimension of fragmentation is of lesser relevance for administrative styles, since we are interested in informal features only, we include actor-based fragmentation (Graham, 2014, p. 370), especially in epistemic terms, as an explanatory factor that may account for the emergence of a particular administrative style (see Section 2.4, below).

In light of the considerations above, administrative styles can thus be generally defined as stable informal patterns that characterize the behaviour and activities of public administrations in the policy-making process (Knill, 2001; Knill & Grohs, 2015). In this book, we concentrate on those characteristics and behaviours that are associated with IPAs' ambitions to influence IO policies. The focus on informality allows us to go beyond structural features of bureaucracies, such as their mandate, political autonomy, size, organizational structure and differentiation, resources, tasks, and staff composition. Thereby, the extent to which IPAs seek to influence the policy process becomes comparable across a vast array of organizations, which otherwise could not be compared due to structural idiosyncrasies. By scrutinizing whether an IPA regularly exceeds the formal requirements and rules or rather adheres to them closely, the underlying legal arrangements fade from the spotlight without being rendered irrelevant.

2.2 Positional and Functional Orientations in Administrative Styles

Administrative styles can encompass many different elements. Which of these elements are considered as analytically relevant strongly depends on the underlying research interest. For national administrations, for instance, styles have been discussed in particular through the analytical lens of state-society relationships (Knill, 2001; Richardson, Gustafsson, & Jordan, 1982; Vogel, 1986). The styles concept has been used primarily to describe basic features of administrative behaviour in the interaction between public authorities and society (e.g. anticipatory versus reactive, legalistic versus pragmatic, interventionist versus mediating patterns of intervention, or open versus closed, consensual versus adversarial relationships between public and private actors). With the exception of Richardson et al. (1982), who additionally include the dimension of problem-solving approaches, the above concepts are essentially restricted to defining styles on the basis of governmental intervention patterns and administrative interest intermediation. In contrast to these national style typologies, we are less interested in the interaction between IPAs and societal actors and more interested in focusing on style elements that capture the bureaucracy's potential to exert policy influence. This does not mean that we completely exclude interactions with societal actors. Rather, we consider them only insofar as they matter for an IPA's policy influence. At the same time, this way we avoid potential problems of conceptually over-stretching the styles concept as it has been developed for the analysis national administrations so far. By focusing on style features related to the politico-administrative nexus, we introduce a new conceptual dimension that might stimulate new research on national administrative styles (Bayerlein & Knill, 2019).

With a view to the potential policy influence of an IPA, we analytically distinguish between two distinctive orientations underpinning administrative styles, namely the positional and the functional orientation. The prevalence of these abstract orientations allows us to answer two central research questions underlying this book. First, we argue that the stronger the prevalence of these orientations in administrative styles, the more an IPA intends to influence the policies adopted and implemented by its organization. Second, this influence can unfold in different ways as it can be guided by institutional consolidation or policy effectiveness. To identify these different motivations underlying administrative behaviour, we focus on behavioural patterns during all central stages of policy making – policy initiation, policy drafting, and implementation.

Positional Orientation: If administrative styles are shaped by a positional orientation, the central objective behind administrative routines is determining how a certain policy will affect the autonomy and legitimacy of the IPA. Positional administrative routines are directed towards influencing the institutional conditions under which IPAs operate when interacting with their organizational environment and political principals (Knill & Bauer, 2016, p. 951). The provision of effective solutions to policy problems is less important than positional improvements or – in the extreme – safeguarding an organization's raison d'être. Effective problem solving is thus not a dominant orientation per se but is mostly considered as a means to the end of positional achievements. The positional orientation of an IPA includes all behavioural aspects that aim at stabilizing or enhancing the political support for the organization, be it from its political principals (i.e. the member states), important societal actors, NGOs, or any other actor whose political support may be valuable to the IPA.

Functional Orientation: A functional orientation becomes manifest in the extent to which IPAs' behaviour is directed at constantly advancing the policy performance of an IO. The dominant focus is on optimizing internal structures and processes to facilitate the initiation, drafting, and effective implementation of well-designed policies (Meyer, Egger-Peitler, Höllerer, & Hammerschmid, 2014). IPAs' routines and standard operating procedures are directed towards effective problem solving; behavioural elements ensuring functionality are more pronounced than elements directed towards positional achievements. This does not mean that positional orientations are completely absent. However, they are less emphasized, and they are important to the IPA insofar as they help to improve policy effectiveness.

2.3 Four Ideal Types of Administrative Styles

Based on the distinction and prevalence of positional and functional orientations in IPAs' behavioural patterns, we suggest an ideal-typical distinction of administrative styles that apply to administrative routines of shaping the policy-making process. To begin with, we differentiate between servants, which do not seek to exert autonomous influence on the IO's policies, and three types of more influence-orientated IPAs. IPA influence can be driven by positional or functional orientations. We thus further specify the three influence-orientated types depending on the extent to which their activities are routinely targeted to influence the IPA's position within the organization and towards their principals (positional orientation), or the substantial policy output of their organization in terms of quality and effectiveness (functional orientation), or both. By way of cross-tabulating positional and functional orientations, we arrive at four ideal-typical administrative styles: advocates, consolidators, entrepreneurs, and servants.

Advocates: Advocates focus their activities on influencing those aspects that are directly related to the quality, internal consistency, and effectiveness of their policies. Such bureaucracies will place less emphasis on behavioural patterns directed at safeguarding or advancing their institutional position but will advocate for their approach to advance the problem-solving capacity of their IO.

Advocates are driven primarily by a functional orientation. Their behavioural patterns come close to those of a policy entrepreneur (Kingdon, 1984; Mintrom & Norman, 2009). They are not satisfied with merely promoting their positional interests within institutions that others have established. Rather, they are driven by the goal of constantly improving policy outcomes. They use and invest their resources to develop and promote new policy ideas, to attach the solutions they developed to new policy problems, and to adjust managerial processes in order to optimize their capacities to develop, implement, and evaluate innovative policy approaches.

Consolidators: Exactly the opposite scenario applies to what we refer to as a consolidating administrative style. Consolidators concentrate primarily on strengthening or safeguarding their political autonomy, status, size, and competencies. Their main interest lies with the increase of competencies as such: in other words, the growth of the policy portfolio (within and beyond the mandate of the IPA) is given priority over policy consistency. Consolidators are hence driven primarily by positional rather than functional orientations.

Rather than displaying features of policy entrepreneurship (as is the case for advocates), consolidators can be characterized as institutional entrepreneurs. Institutional entrepreneurship describes 'activities of actors who have an interest in particular institutional arrangements and who leverage resources to create new institutions or to transform existing ones' (Maguire, Hardy, & Lawrence, 2004, p. 657; see also Battilana, Leca, & Boxenbaum, 2009). According to this perspective, IPAs 'secure and advance their position through the promotion of institutional change that arises when organized actors with sufficient resources see in them an opportunity to realize interests that they value highly' (DiMaggio, 1988, p. 14). When IPAs pursue a consolidating administrative style, they place stronger emphasis on institutional changes than on improving the policy effectiveness of their organizations. For advocates, by contrast, the pattern is the exact opposite.

Entrepreneurs: An entrepreneurial style is the combination of the previous two types (advocate and consolidator) and thus presupposes administrative routines that entail intensive bureaucratic advocacy in substantial policy making and a strong orientation towards institutional consolidation to strengthen the administration's position. This, however, does not imply that this style is superior to the other types in terms of administrative performance. Generally, we do not attach any normative connotation to a particular style per se.

Servants: Finally, a servant administration presumes a rather reactive and instrumental role. In terms of influence, IPAs of this type are the opposite of the three above. The administration refrains from any attempt to intervene with politics beyond its formal duties and does not attempt to influence the policy process. In this case, the bureaucracy follows a routine pattern of operating by the book, strictly adhering to the formal procedural and legal arrangements that define its tasks and functions. The distinctive feature of a servant style is that behavioural patterns related to positional and functional orientations are for the most part absent.[2]

That servant-style IPAs do not intend to influence the policy process must not necessarily be equated with suboptimal performance or the absence of (intentional) action per se. It is quite possible that a servant-style IPA conceives of itself as a good and faithful servant to its political principal and acts accordingly (Boyne & Walker, 2004, p. 240; Rainey, 2009). As with other administrations, a servant is charged with drafting and implementing policies. However, servant-style IPAs do not strive to exert influence of their own on IO policy making, since they do not attempt to realize their own interests.

Also, it may be that an influence-oriented IPA conceals its positional or functional goals and instead pretends to be a mere servant. There might be constellations in which an IPA pretends to act in a servant manner, constituting a 'veil of instrumentality' that allows the administration to exert considerable policy influence that goes unnoticed by its principals. However, we are less interested in the ways IPAs sell and convey their actions to their principals than in their actual day-to-day doings regardless of the framing. Thereby, IPAs pursuing this strategy do not fall into our servant type. The opposite is true: an IPA that makes an effort to cover up its influence cannot be a servant, since this type of style is defined by the lack of influence, and informal attempts to frame its own behaviour for the principals are genuinely political.

Regarding the three more influence-oriented styles, i.e. advocates, consolidators, and entrepreneurs, is important to highlight that despite some obvious resemblances we pointed out above, they should not be equated with what the literature conventionally labels policy (e.g. Palmer, 2015; Roberts & King, 1991; Zahariadis, 2003), institutional

---

[2] Others have referred to what we mean by servant IPAs as 'witless tools' (Cortell & Peterson, 2006, p. 255) and 'perfect handmaidens' (Gould, 2006, p. 281) or compared their behaviour to the movie character Forrest Gump (Hawkins & Jacoby, 2006, p. 201).

(e.g. Battilana, Leca, & Boxenbaum, 2009; DiMaggio, 1988; Maguire et al., 2004), or norm (e.g. Finnemore & Sikkink, 1998; Keck & Sikkink, 1999; Risse, Ropp, & Sikkink, 1999) entrepreneurs. This is because policy (as well as norm or institutional) entrepreneurship usually operates at the micro-level. The vast amount of different conceptualizations have in common that they focus on a highly motivated individual or team, exhibiting a 'high degree of entrepreneurial flare' (Mintrom & Norman, 2009, p. 649), trying to draw attention to a problem, presenting innovative solutions, and building support coalitions to secure policy action.

While policy (and institutional) entrepreneurship in this sense resonates especially with what we describe as IPA advocacy (and consolidation) the notions are distinct from each other. While policy entrepreneurs are typically single individuals or small groups pursuing one particular instance of policy change at a specific time, influence-orientated IPAs are collectively and routinely guided by a functional or positional orientation, theoretically irrespective of the policy at hand. There are thus two fundamental differences between the two concepts. The first lies at the analytical level, as one looks at organizations at the micro-level of influential individuals, while the other approaches organizational agency at the meso-level of IPAs' routine behaviour. The second key difference is that policy entrepreneurship usually constitutes a single process of attempting to change a concrete policy or institution, whereas an IPA's style describes a much more constant and permanent spirit. It could hence be in rare cases that we find individual entrepreneurs in IPAs, which are on the whole not characterized by a functional or positional orientation in their administrative style. This, however, should rather be an exception than the rule. It is theoretically plausible to assume that there is a higher probability to encounter individual entrepreneurs in an influence-orientated IPA as the overall orientation could both inspire and favour such singular undertakings. In general, however, we would argue that when interested in the organization as such and not so much a single policy or outcome, it is more fruitful to look at the IPAs' stance towards all policy that is made instead of cherry-picking single ones.

To sum up this section on our four ideal-typical styles, Table 2.1 displays how the different emphases in orientations relate to the respective administrative style. Since entrepreneurs, according to our definition, are driven by both policy effectiveness and institutional concerns,

Table 2.1 *Four ideal types of administrative styles*

		Functional Orientation	
		High	*Low*
Positional	*High*	Entrepreneur	Consolidator
Orientation	*Low*	Advocate	Servant

their styles will equally incorporate the functional and positional behavioural patterns specified above. Consolidators, by contrast, should
predominantly focus on the positional dimension because they are
mainly orientated towards safeguarding their position vis-à-vis their
principals and institutional environment. Exactly the opposite can be
expected for advocates who concentrate on the functional aspects of
optimizing their work to achieve substantial policy influence. A servant
IPA, finally, does not explicitly draw on any of these orientations, since
they all run counter to its reactive stance.

2.4 Explanations of Administrative Styles

Which factors can account for variation of administrative styles across
different organizations? Why are the routines and standard operating
procedures in some IPAs more entrepreneurial while others are more
servant-like, as will be shown in the chapters to come?

   To answer these questions, it seems tempting at first glance to resort
to structural factors, such as the polity of the organization, including its
mandate, decision rules, resources, size, and constituency, to explain
IPA influence (Bauer & Ege, 2013; Verhoest, Peters, Bouckaert, &
Verschuere, 2004). Indeed, studies focusing on these factors have
become increasingly prominent in the study of IPAs and IOs in recent
years (for an overview, see Eckhard & Ege, 2016). Yet for several
reasons, this strand of research cannot on its own be considered informative for explaining that administrative styles arise as a result of
informal influence. On the one hand, accounting for variation in
administrative styles is beyond the explanatory scope of these
approaches. These theories imply that IOs operating in comparatively
similar environments and structural arrangements will be equally influential and exhibit the same style. Since one of our main objectives is to

show how IPAs work their way around the by-the-book logic, this argument is rendered of limited use. On the other hand, and most importantly, we consider formal rules of procedure not as an explanation of styles but as the benchmark against which they manifest themselves. As emphasized in the previous section, we conceive of administrative styles as informal patterns relative to a given formal setting. It is the more subtle deviations from the rules that matter for the purpose of our study. The formal setting is hence a logical component of the phenomenon under study. Therefore, we contend that in order to explain styles, we must necessarily resort to factors that are external to our conception of the dependent variable (i.e. that are informal and not process-related).

Some authors have pointed to the structure and type of the problems addressed to account for an IPA's influence on certain policies (Eckhard & Ege, 2016). Yet this situational, output-centred approach stands in stark contrast to the relatively sticky procedural patterns of behaviour we interpret as styles. Although it is quite possible that attempts of influence are more or less successful depending on the policies in question, it does not explain the underlying orientation – that is, the administrative style. Although well suited for individual instances of bureaucratic influence, this situational emphasis also rules out explanations that focus exclusively on organizational crises (Broome & Seabrooke, 2012; Chorev, 2012) to explain IPAs' styles in a comparative fashion.

In contrast to the above-mentioned structural approaches, and inspired by contemporary institutional theory, we argue that IPAs are subject to external institutional challenges but at the same time may have the internal potential to actively influence their environment (Oliver, 1991). In the last decades, institutional theorists have moved towards bringing 'agency back into the institutional framework without denying the crucial importance of institutional embeddedness and thus move[d] beyond the vague notion of institutional pressures to investigate the dialectical interplay between actors' actions and institutional embeddedness' (Leca & Naccache, 2006, p. 643). Actions and behaviour are a product of the interplay of organizational agency (internal) and the demands of the surrounding institution, that is, the organizational environment (external). An IPA's experience with institutional demands varies depending on how external and internal pressures interact (Greenwood & Hinings, 1996). In these constellations, organizational routines form as

Table 2.2 *Determinants of administrative styles*

Determinant dimension	Indicators
External challenges	Perceived domain challenges
	Perceived political challenges
Internal challenges	Contested belief systems
	Restrictions on the IPA's cognitive slack

'natural product of action' (Feldman & Pentland, 2003, p. 98), when multiple actors face the challenge of solving similar and recurring tasks using coordinated interaction. Given that organizations avoid enacting 'routines with no attention to the purposes of the work' (Birnholtz, Cohen, & Hoch, 2007, p. 328), a number of factors enable some actions and constrain others, making it more likely that routine participants execute some actions while avoiding others (Faraj & Xiao, 2006). Over time, these style patterns, once formed, are assumed to display high stability.

In line with this thought, we argue that administrative styles vary along two dimensions, namely the external and internal challenges a bureaucracy is subject to. While the former refers to the perception of external political pressure faced by the administration, the latter captures the degree of cognitive slack and internal epistemic contestation of an IPA. The two determinants are described in more detail in Table 2.2 and below.

2.4.1 *External Challenges to the Bureaucracy*

External challenges are defined by the extent to which the IPA perceives its institutional status and operation as subject to intervention and exogenous pressures. In their behavioural routines, 'agents are not free-floating and unencumbered but rather operate within an institutional context that at least in part determines their behaviour' (Howlett, 2004, p. 16). It makes a difference for administrative styles whether a bureaucracy is saturated and stable or whether it deems its status to be effectively put into question. The external challenges dimension primarily affects the positional orientation of an IPA. In the absence of perceived political or domain challenges, we do not expect an IPA to pursue a strong positional orientation towards institutional consolidation. Strengthening the IPA's institutional position will be necessary only if its standing or existence is seen to be under threat. The more the status of an administration is subjectively under political scrutiny and the more its political support seems externally challenged, the bureaucracy must act in an increasingly consolidation-driven manner to improve or safeguard its institutional position.

Crucially, we contend that an IPA's perception of external challenges is better suited to explaining their style than merely considering factual structural features of their environment. While capturing relevant structural features of the field, this view accounts for the fact that organizational challenges cannot be expected to matter per se (i.e. unfiltered by the organization). As with all pressures, challenges need to be defined and acknowledged by the organization in order to have an effect. 'Conflicting institutional demands in a given field are not experienced in a similar way by all organizations since field level institutional processes are filtered and enacted differently by different organizations' (Pache & Santos, 2010, p. 11). Even when external pressures are similar, IPAs do not need to respond in exactly the same way (Greenwood & Hinings, 1996) as they perceive their environment and their own position in it differently.

Two kinds of perceived challenges are of importance in explaining administrative styles. First, external challenges are affected by the perception of dynamics within the organizational domain in which the administration is located. Within a given domain or jurisdiction, different organizations will compete for resources and competences. Failures to be innovative and to adapt may result in budget cuts and a loss of political attention, thus 'allowing some organizations to flourish and some to languish or, less frequently, to die' (Peters, 2010, p. 203; see also Adam, Bauer, Knill, & Studinger, 2007; Peters & Hogwood, 1988).

Second, bureaucratic vulnerability should increase with the extent to which an organization sees itself as politically challenged. On the one hand, the more an IPA perceives itself as being in the political spotlight – in a position highly salient on the agenda of its political principals and (global) civil society – the more the administration will try to consolidate its status. On the other hand, the more homogeneous the IPA considers expectations towards their activities and performance to be

(Hawkins et al., 2006; Lyne, Nielson, & Tierney, 2006), the more it has to fear political intervention. Conversely, a pronounced awareness of heterogeneous principal interests – such as between donor member states versus receiving member states, for example, or between democratic member states versus autocratic member states – offers the bureaucracy manifold opportunities to play political actors off against each other, thereby effectively 'making use of institutional complexity' (Vermeulen, Zietsma, Greenwood, & Langley, 2016).

2.4.2 Internal Challenges to Bureaucratic Policy Capability

The level of internal challenges a bureaucracy faces strongly affects its ability to pursue clear and consistent policy targets. We consider those IPAs internally challenged whose policy capabilities are limited by internal disparities or cognitive strait jackets. It makes a difference for administrative styles whether the bureaucracy is actually capable of developing an interest in the solution of certain policy problems or whether it is by default restricted to merely administrating these policies. We would expect bureaucracies with low internal challenges to display a more advocacy-orientated style during all stages of the policy cycle than bureaucracies facing higher internal challenges.[3]

In order to fully realize their informal potential, IPAs need to have sufficient cognitive slack, that is, time, space, and resources to communicate, think, and innovate. Similar to the preconditions for bureaucratic expertise and expert authority (Barnett & Finnemore, 2004; Busch, 2009; Dijkstra, 2008; Jinnah, 2010), cognitive resources refer to the degree to which an organization prioritizes research and emphasizes and values expertise in the given issue area and beyond. Cognitive slack also presupposes a sufficient amount of time available to professional staff to create and process specialized knowledge. The space to produce high-quality cognitive outputs is diminished the more principals control and interfere in the day-to-day work of the bureaucracy

---

[3] Let us emphasize again, that this does not mean that, conversely, high internal challenges exclude *any* possibility of entrepreneurship in the classical sense. Policy entrepreneurship by an individual or small group of staffers could still be possible – yet only as an exception to the rule. Instead of the IPA itself exhibiting entrepreneurial advocacy flair, it would only pertain to a few individuals under special circumstances. Advocacy then would not constitute a behavioural pattern, but a single instance.

(Boschken, 1988; Durant, 2009). Are policy products developed jointly with a high degree of exchange between bureaucrats and principal representatives, or is the role of political masters rather confined to placing an order and controlling the end result? This procedural discretion is not a matter of formal autonomy and delegation but rather reflects how much effort member states do invest de facto to oversee daily workflows and personnel within the IPA. Put simply, this relationship can be summarized as follows: the more informal control the principal is equipped to exert (Best, 2012), the more the IPA will be internally challenged with regard to its cognitive slack, that is, the capability and potential to initiate, design, and promote effective and sound policies for their IO.

   Second, we expect internal challenges to increase with the extent to which staff members' professional backgrounds are characterized by heterogeneous epistemic and normative beliefs (Kaufman, 1960; DiMaggio & Powell, 1983). The more staff members share the same professional background, for example in medicine or economics, the more we should expect a strong and consistent policy orientation (Broome & Seabrooke, 2012; Chwieroth, 2013). The same holds true for a strong esprit de corps. Conversely, internal heterogeneity can lead to internal contestation of belief systems, thereby impairing the IPA's ability to act concertedly and consistently.

2.4.3 Administrative Challenges and Administrative Styles

Based on the two explanatory dimensions of internal and external challenges to the bureaucracy, we can develop expectations regarding the prevalence of different administrative styles. First, we expect that the combination of low external and high internal challenges should come along with administrative routines that strongly resemble the servant ideal. When the administration's hands are tied and its position is deemed stable, it neither perceives the need for institutional consolidation nor commands the means to become active in terms of promoting more effective policies.

   Second, and by contrast, in constellations characterized by low internal challenges and high external challenges to the bureaucracy, we expect the opposite entrepreneurial style. While the low internal constraints provide the bureaucracy with broad leeway to advocate its policy goals and allow for a functional orientation, the perception of external challenges implies that this functionalist orientation is combined with routine patterns of institutional consolidation (positional orientation).

Third, bureaucracies pursuing an advocacy style do not face particularly pronounced challenges, either internal or external. They can be expected to focus their entrepreneurial activities solely on those aspects that are directly related to the quality, internal consistency, and effectiveness of their policies. By contrast, such bureaucracies will place less emphasis on behavioural patterns directed at safeguarding or advancing their institutional position, because the IPA is saturated and stable internally. Equipped with sufficient cognitive slack and unified belief systems, the IPA can substantially influence the IO's policies. Policy advocacy can unfold relatively unimpeded internally, and no external threat puts them into a position in which they must also consolidate themselves. For policy initiation, this means that internal policy development is attributed higher priority than support mobilization and mapping of political space. During drafting, aspects relating to policy quality and consistency will be more important than strategies of political anticipation. In the implementation stage, evaluation and policy promotion can be expected to be more relevant than policy promotion or the strategic use of enforcement powers.

Fourth, the emergence of a consolidating administrative style is favoured by the constellation of high internal and high external challenges. When external pressures are strong and the bureaucracy sees the status of the organization or its bureaucracy as being called into question, the IPA reacts and aims to stabilize its position by attempting to consolidate its institutional standing. Since internal challenges do not allow for substantive policy influence, the IPA will resort to making the best of its situation in institutional policy terms. Bureaucracies will concentrate their entrepreneurial activities primarily on strengthening their political autonomy, status, size, and competencies. In order to achieve these objectives, such bureaucracies will be rather eclectic with regard to the initiation and drafting of new policies. Their main interest is on the increase of competencies as such; that is, the growth of the policy portfolio is given priority over policy consistency. As a consequence, support mobilization and mapping of political space will be considered more important than the

Table 2.3 *Administrative styles and bureaucratic challenges*

		Internal Challenges	
		Low	*High*
External	*High*	Entrepreneur	Consolidator
Challenges	*Low*	Advocate	Servant

internal identification and definition of policy issues. At the same time, this implies the dominance of satisficing over optimizing routines during the drafting stage, i.e. we should see organizational routines that entail searching through the available alternatives until an acceptability threshold is met (Simon, 1997). Moreover, attempts to go beyond negative coordination to improve policy consistency cannot be expected. By contrast, much more emphasis will be placed on efforts of political anticipation. During the implementation stage, any attempts to enhance policy effectiveness through proper implementation, policy promotion, and evaluation, will be of minor importance, given the predominance of positional rather than policy interests of the bureaucracy. Table 2.3 summarizes how external and internal challenges to the bureaucracy relate to the different types of administrative styles.

2.5 Conclusion

This chapter opened with the observation that the growing involvement of international bureaucracies in policy making stands at odds with a lack of systematic knowledge of the role and agency of these administrative bodies. To address this issue, we departed from conventional accounts that merely focus on formal structures and policy outputs, and we directed our analytical interest at informal routines and practices that shape administrative behaviour and potential influence throughout the policy-making process.

To identify differences in bureaucratic routines of exerting influence, we developed the concept of administrative styles and analytically distinguished between four ideal-typical patterns: servant, advocate, consolidator, and entrepreneur. In addition to this concept, we offered a theoretical framework in order to account for variation in administrative styles across different organizations. The analytical use of the styles concept, its empirical manifestations, and the explanatory relevance of our theoretical argument will be demonstrated in the following chapters.

3 | Observing and Explaining Administrative Styles: From Concept to Empirical Analysis

In the previous chapter, we introduced our concept of administrative styles and the conditions that enable or constrain their evolution. Now we will demonstrate how these conceptual and theoretical considerations can be studied empirically. We start with a detailed overview of the operationalization of IPAs' administrative styles. We then present our empirical understanding of the explanatory factors which account for variation in administrative styles across different organizations. In a third step, we reflect on the rationale for case selection and briefly introduce the IPAs under study. Finally, we elaborate on our methodological approach to assess IPAs' informal bureaucratic routines.

3.1 Observing Administrative Styles

Administrative styles manifest themselves in distinct behavioural patterns. As laid out in the previous chapter, IPAs can be guided either by a positional orientation, working to safeguard their institutional standing, or by a functional orientation directed at constantly improving their IO's substantive policy performance. These latent orientations towards influencing the policy process become empirically visible in IPAs' day-to-day working procedures. But how can we empirically assess concepts as abstract as informal bureaucratic routines and standard operating procedures? In what ways do they manifest themselves in observable behavioural patterns throughout the central stages of policy making? And how can we make these patterns comparable across different IPAs dealing with various issues in quite different organizational environments?

To address these questions, we start from a basic distinction between three different stages of the policy process in which IPAs might be involved, namely the initiation of IO policies, the drafting of policy proposals, and the subsequent implementation of the policies themselves. During the stage of policy initiation, the analytical focus is typically on the identification and definition of new policy problems and the prioritization of these issues on the IO's agenda. These processes typically involve a wide spectrum of public and private actors at different institutional levels, all of whom might have specific and often highly diverse stakes in defining policies in a specific way and pushing them onto the political agenda. In light of our research interest, the central question is the extent to which IPAs have adopted informal routines of more or less active involvement at this stage. To assess these routines, we focus on three indicators: issue emergence, support mobilization, and mapping of political space.

Issue emergence: Issue emergence captures the origin of IO policies. As mentioned above, policy problems might be identified and defined by a broad range of actors. Focusing on IPAs, we are interested in the extent to which they have developed informal routines and procedures to actively identify new policy issues that should be addressed by their IO. IPAs might vary in their ambitions to come up with new policy items, implying that new policies of an IO might usually emerge from the outside (in the case of low ambitions) or from the inside, that is, from the IO bureaucracy.

Support mobilization: It is well acknowledged in the public policy literature that the mere identification of a policy problem does not necessarily mean that the issue makes it onto the political agenda. Due to limitations in political attention, there is fierce competition among different issue stakeholders for agenda space (Baumgartner & Jones, 2010). We assume that IPAs will differ strongly in routines directed at the mobilization of support for policy issues. They might display highly active patterns involving the building of coalitions with other actors in order to increase the external support for a certain issue, or they could work in a passive pattern where orientations towards mobilizing external support are completely absent.

Mapping of political space: Research on the European Commission has shown that bureaucracies can develop highly differentiated procedures for detecting the preferences of their political principals with regard to certain policy issues (Knill, Eckhard, & Grohs, 2016). This mapping of the political space in turn enables the bureaucracy to assess the political feasibility of different policy options. Again, we assume that IPAs' routines might incorporate such mapping activities to a different extent. While some IPAs might routinely seek to identify political preferences at a very early stage of the policy process, such patterns might be completely absent in other bureaucracies.

Assuming that a certain policy problem has been identified and has also made it onto the political agenda of the IO, we move to the stage of policy drafting, during which policy proposals and decisions are formulated. One of the most important sources of administrative influence is the drafting of policy proposals by the bureaucracy. Although such drafts might undergo certain changes in the political decision-making process, they pre-structure the basic content and the instrumental design of a policy or programme. Yet we know from research on national and EU-level policy making that bureaucracies display strong differences in the ways they are engaged in this process. To capture this variation, existing research points to the indicators of solution search, internal coordination, and political anticipation (Hood & Lodge, 2006; Knill, 2001; Page, 1985; Peters & Pierre, 2004).

Solution search: Administrations can rely on different routine procedures in the development of their proposals. More specifically, they can either follow a pattern of incremental adjustment or pursue more synoptic strategies of rational solution search. In the former case, administrations will strongly adhere to the logic of satisficing. Rather than aiming for the most effective policy solution, existing policies will be perpetuated and incrementally adjusted in response to new developments. In the latter case, by contrast, they will apply more sophisticated techniques of systematically assessing underlying problems and evaluating different solutions (Balla & Gormley, 2018).

Internal coordination: While solution search defines the ambitions of administrative divisions or units in charge of a certain issue area to engage in the development of more or less optimal policy solutions, internal coordination refers to the procedures of addressing horizontal policy externalities. To what extent are IPAs trying to effectively address potential interferences between policy proposals that are developed in different organization units? In this regard, two basic modes can be distinguished (Scharpf, 1994). Negative coordination represents the standard model of administrative coordination. Administrative units are typically concentrated almost exclusively on their own issues and only really become involved in the drafting process of other units when they see that a circulated draft proposal interferes with their work or objectives. By contrast, in positively coordinated organizations, drafts are circulated at much earlier stages and various administrative units engage in simultaneous joint problem-solving activities from the very start.

Political anticipation: In drafting policy proposals, bureaucracies can strongly vary in the extent to which they are responsive to political preferences. In the public administration literature, this variation in the anticipation of political preferences is discussed under the heading of functional politicization. Functional politicization captures political responsiveness and refers to the bureaucracy anticipating and integrating politically relevant aspects in their day-to-day functions (Aberbach, Putnam, & Rockman, 1981; Mayntz & Derlien, 1989). In the drafting of policy proposals, IPAs then either leave out politically sensitive issues, add certain details according to anticipated preferences, frame or re-frame the issue, or simply formulate a given proposal such that it will likely not touch upon too many sensitivities (Hustedt & Salomonsen, 2014; Acs, 2018).

Finally, informal routines and administrative procedures might vary when it comes to IPA involvement in post-decisional politics. With regard to the implementation stage, we consider three indicators to capture variation in administrative styles: the way in which IPAs routinely make use of their formal control and sanctioning power, their engagement in policy evaluation, and their ambitions to promote IO policies in their organizational environment.

Use of formal powers: Although the enforcement powers of most IPAs are relatively weak compared to their national counterparts, they can pursue two rather different approaches to ensure more or less effective compliance with international policies. On the one hand, we might observe patterns in which IPAs simply adhere to standard templates in applying their rules. This can be in an attempt to implement and sanction international policies as much as possible by relying on their own resources (Lavenex, 2016) or simply because the IPA sees no need for strategic considerations about possible repercussions. On the other hand, IPAs might regularly rely on much more cautious procedures in order to avoid open conflicts with member states, as this might undermine the member states' support for the delegation of further policy competencies to the IO (Knill et al., 2019). This does not preclude the possibility of the IPA putting its powers to full use where it sees fit. Rather, decisions about how to approach implementation are regularly made highly strategically with a view to possible conflict with member states.

Evaluation efforts: The implementation stage not only captures monitoring and enforcement, but also relates to activities of policy evaluation. The goal of evaluations is to systematically assess whether a given policy has achieved its intended objectives in terms of behavioural changes of policy addressees (policy outcomes) and the reduction or solution of relevant policy problems (policy impacts). Yet administrative capacities for systematic evaluation efforts display considerable variation across countries (del Río, 2014; Adam, Steinebach, & Knill, 2018). We assume that such variation in formal and informal evaluation routines can also be observed for IPAs.

Policy promotion: In addition to enforcement and evaluation activities, IPAs can rely on alternative ways to strengthen the overall impact of their policies. In particular, they can systematically try to promote their policies through various channels: for example by setting up close relationships with involved stakeholders, interest groups, national administrations, or external experts. IPAs can also strive to mobilize societal pressure 'from below' by disseminating information on national implementation performance (Knill & Lenschow, 2005). In this context, IPAs could also engage in orchestration by enlisting intermediaries, such as transnational NGOs, on a voluntary basis to, for instance, advocate for their policy targets (Abbott, Genschel, Snidal, & Zangl, 2015).

Overall, we thus rely on nine indicators – three for each stage of the policy cycle – in which IPAs regularly have room to manoeuvre and are therefore able to exert informal influence. We suggest that all indicators are equally important for the assessment of an IPA's orientation. Depending on the emphasis IPAs place on each of these aspects, they can be classified as either position-orientated, function-orientated, both, or neither.

Position-orientated IPAs are expected to put a strong emphasis on the mapping of the political space, the mobilization of support, political anticipation, and the strategic use of formal power. First and foremost, during the stage of policy initiation, the positional aspects of administrative behaviour entail patterns of anticipation. In the policy-initiation phase, 'mapping of the political space' – the anticipation of the political feasibility of an issue – is key to guaranteeing alignment with political interests of the principals at an early stage (Aberbach et al., 1981; Mayntz & Derlien, 1989). The prevalence of political anticipation is further relevant when it comes to policy formulation. In order to prevent political rejection by member states later on, in the interest of their positional orientation, IPAs proactively anticipate political 'red lines' and make use of political facilitation mechanisms during the drafting procedure. A third element to strengthen an IPA's institutional position is to mobilize political or societal support. In this case, administrations are involved in frequent communicative efforts with a broad range of external actors like interest groups, NGOs, policy networks, and the media (Stone, 2008). Lastly, to not endanger their organizational standing, in the positional spirit, IPAs try to strategically circumvent conflict in the use of their formal powers in policy implementation. Enforcement and monitoring routines are guided by strategic considerations, either by trying to settle issues quietly or by deliberately shying away from using their powers to the fullest, if at all.

By contrast, in the *function-orientated spirit*, we expect IPAs to focus rather on the development of their own policy ideas and proposals, solution search, internal coordination, policy promotion, and evaluation of their policies. First, to enhance policy effectiveness, IPAs identify policy problems and initiate policy developments from the inside by accumulating policy-related knowledge. They focus on investing internal resources for the identification of issues worth addressing. Second, with regard to policy quality and content, administrators engage in optimizing strategies of solution search when drafting proposals. In the optimizing mode, IPAs evaluate a large number of different alternatives and go with the solution they deem best, which may not necessarily be the easiest one. This strategy differs from the satisficing mode, which would merely require the routine use of simple heuristics and rules of thumb (Simon, 1997). Third, to be truly able to work in a functionally orientated manner, IPAs should have well-functioning internal coordination mechanisms. Optimizing routines, for instance, demand a higher degree of horizontal coordination mechanisms within administrations and thus require a departure from the default patterns of negative coordination, which are characterized by a highly fragmented drafting process (Scharpf, 1994). Fourth, IPAs orientated towards influencing

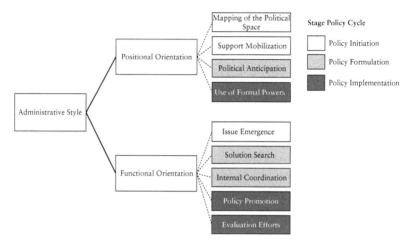

Figure 3.1 Indicators of administrative styles

their IO's policies should ambitiously use all conceivable means to evaluate their policies and improve their knowledge management beyond the data that is formally required to do so. Finally, in the interest of functionality, administrations might engage not only in monitoring and enforcement but also in enhancing the impact and effectiveness of their programmes through strategies of capacity building and policy promotion (Finnemore, 1993). IPAs mobilize all available means to strengthen the implementation capacities of the relevant actors and rely on a very proactive form of communicative engagement with member states that goes well beyond their formal duties. Figure 3.1 summarizes our nine indicators associated with the respective orientation and the policy cycle stage to which they are linked.[1]

In their informal practices and routines, an IPA's underlying orientation will determine both the relative emphasis it places on the respective indicator's practices and the amount of effort it exerts in performing those activities. To allow for a systematic comparison of the different

---

[1] We are aware of the fact that policy cycles are continuous, i.e. that in reality the different stages of the policy cycle are intrinsically interconnected. For instance, evaluation activities ideally feed back into the policy initiation and the formulation phase. For the purpose of this study, however, we consider the policy cycle to 'end' at the evaluation stage and thus assess each stage of the cycle separately. By sticking to this simplified 'stages' heuristic, we are able to look for both mutually reinforcing patterns of administrative behaviour as well as potential deviations along the policy cycle.

indicators, we denote IPAs' regular efforts as being either low or high when it comes to the execution of the different activities mentioned. This classification is based on whether certain behavioural patterns can be considered as regular features characterizing IPAs' informal administrative actions. In addition to this binary distinction, we add a residual medium category to capture those cases in which an IPA's behavioural pattern cannot be observed on a regular basis but rather occurs only occasionally. For instance, this applies to cases where a behavioural pattern is only observable to a limited extent and not much emphasis is placed on it or when an IPA has not yet developed standardized operating procedures across the organization.

While for almost all indicators there are no *formal* requirements that may predetermine how these activities are pursued, the extent to which IPAs evaluate their policies or make strategic use of formal powers obviously depends on more structural conditions, such as whether an IPA has a specialized evaluation division or does possess the statutory competences to sanction the IO's member states. In these cases, we use the formal conditions as a yardstick against which an IPA's informal routines are assessed. Regarding the strategic use of formal powers, for instance, the manifestation 'high' describes that an IPA does not simply stick to the rules but rather behaves 'politically'. This may include deliberately abstaining from using enforcement powers or even going beyond the formal duties. Tables 3.1 and 3.2 provide an overview of our nine indicators as well as their exact operationalization.

3.2 Identifying External and Internal Challenges of Bureaucracies

In the previous chapter we proposed a rather parsimonious theoretical explanation for the emergence of IPA administrative styles. Two types of challenges to the bureaucracy – external and internal – constitute the key explanatory factors accounting for the variation of administrative styles across different organizations. While the former refers to perceptions of external pressure, the latter captures whether IPAs can develop a consistent organizational objective and whether they are also able to pursue a goal of common interest.

With regard to the perception of external pressure, two questions are of particular importance. The first is whether an IPA considers

Table 3.1 *Positional orientation – indicators and their operationalization*

Orientation	Phase	Indicator	Operationalization
Positional Orientation	Policy Initiation	*Mapping of political space*	*Low*: Usually no mapping activities to investigate IPA's principals' preferences at an early stage *Medium*: No clear pattern: Occasional mapping activities to investigate IPA's principals' preferences at an early stage *High*: Usually strong mapping activities to investigate IPA's principals' preferences at an early stage
		Support mobilization	*Low*: Usually no mobilizations activities; no active coalition-building exercises to gain external support *Medium*: No clear pattern: Occasional mobilizations activities *High*: Usually strong mobilizations activities; active coalition-building exercises to gain external support
	Policy Drafting	*Political anticipation*	*Low*: Usually no functional politicization; IPA is routinely not sensitive to its political implications *Medium*: No clear pattern: Occasional functional politicization *High*: Usually strong functional politicization; IPA is routinely very sensitive to its political implications
	Policy Implementation	*Strategic use of formal powers*	*Low*: Usually IPA makes use of its formal powers without much strategic deliberation *Medium*: No clear pattern: Occasionally IPA acts strategically in avoiding conflict *High*: Usually IPA strategically refrains open conflicts

Table 3.2 Functional orientation – indicators and their operationalization

Orientation	Phase	Indicator	Operationalization
Functional Orientation	Policy Initiation	*Issue emergence*	*Low*: Usually outside the bureaucracy *Medium*: No clear pattern: Occasionally within the bureaucracy *High*: Usually within bureaucracy
	Policy Drafting	*Solution search*	*Low*: Usually pragmatic drafting with short-cuts or simple heuristics, settling for the first best solution *Medium*: No clear pattern: Occasionally systematic assessment of the underlying problems and a consideration of many alternatives *High*: Usually systematic assessment of the underlying problems and a consideration of many alternatives, settling for the optimal solution
		Internal coordination	*Low*: Usually no efforts to deviate from the default mode of negative coordination *Medium*: No clear pattern: Occasional efforts to deviate from the default mode of negative coordination *High*: Usually strong efforts to deviate from the default mode of negative coordination

Table 3.2 (*cont.*)

Orientation	Phase	Indicator	Operationalization
	Policy Implementation	*Policy promotion*	*Low:* Usually IPA takes no efforts to strengthen the impact of organizational outputs *Medium:* No clear pattern: Occasionally IPA takes efforts to strengthen the impact of organizational outputs *High:* Usually IPA takes strong efforts to strengthen the impact of organizational outputs in every possible way
		Evaluation efforts	*Low:* Usually IPA barely follows the formal evaluation guidelines or does not apply them properly *Medium:* No clear pattern: Occasionally IPA follows the formal evaluation guidelines *High:* Usually IPA strongly follows the formal evaluation guidelines and makes frequent use of the institutional evaluation mechanisms

its organizational domain to be particularly competitive and whether it reckons its positions within that domain to be threatened or safe. Other organizations, be they NGOs, IOs, multinational corporations, or something else, can be viewed as competitors for both funding and influence, as partners that strengthen the IPA's position in its organizational environment, or as being largely irrelevant. Similarly, the IO's position can be perceived as focal, as peripheral, or as threatened. Thus, the second question is whether an IPA regards its own actions as politically challenged. This kind of challenge touches upon the relationship of the IPA not to its broader organizational environment, but to its principals and civil society. It matters whether an IPA considers itself to be under constant political scrutiny or to be undisputed or even unrecognized by its principals. An IPA will be in the political spotlight when either the organization or the issues it works on are particularly salient and highly ranked on the agenda of its principals. Crucially then, the bureaucracy needs to be aware of the spotlight it finds itself in and the quarrels that might impede its work or standing. We consider both kinds of external challenges to be either high or low. In this context, 'high' denotes a pronounced awareness of these challenges, and 'low' stands for the challenges being of little or no relevance in the eyes of the IPA. A medium manifestation is assigned for the overall external challenges when either one of the perceived domains or political challenges is high while the other one is low.

Turning to the internal challenges, we posit that there are two central factors that must be taken into account. In order to assess if IPAs are able to develop and pursue a common and consistent organizational goal, we consider the extent to which their belief systems are homogenous and unified, as well as the restrictions on their cognitive slack. While the absence of the former can constrain an IPA's ability to act concertedly and coherently, the presence of the latter hampers the formation of its own organizational ideas and aims.

As previously mentioned (in Chapter 2, section 4.2), the term 'cognitive slack' denotes the resources, space, and time that enable IPAs to develop and formulate their own organizational ideas and aims. In this context, we operationalize resources by the extent to which IPAs can access and process information independently from their member states by relying on central in-house research bodies. Whether staff members have the space to produce high-quality outputs is determined by the extent to which the IPA's political principals control the day-to-day operations of the bureaucracy. Here, the crucial question is whether member states' representatives interfere with an IPA's work by tight mechanisms of procedural oversight and how much they are involved in the bureaucracies' internal working procedures. In contrast to these two factors, the time available to the IPA can hardly be assessed in general terms but varies strongly depending on the specific task to be carried out. Thus, instead of assessing the average time available, we consider the time factor only when time constraints are explicitly reported. We consider the set of factors to be jointly sufficient without being individually necessary. In other words, while we consider IPAs with adequate time, space, and resources not to exhibit a lack of cognitive slack (low), this does not necessarily imply that an IPA cannot pursue its goals if one of the factors is absent. By contrast, in cases where an IPA has inadequate time, space, and resources, we can safely assume that it lacks the scope necessary to develop and formulate an individual organizational stance on the issues it deals with (high).

The degree of epistemic heterogeneity influences whether an IPA can undertake a concerted joint effort towards achieving a common organizational goal. We evaluate the homogeneity of an IPA's staff in light of their educational or professional backgrounds. The more varied the staff members' educational backgrounds, the more difficult it is for them to commit to a shared objective. Thus, we consider the contestation of an IPA's belief system to be high in cases where there is no dominant academic discipline among the staff members or where the discipline itself is highly fragmented or disputed internally. By contrast, this internal challenge is considered low if staff members are largely recruited from candidates with the same educational background or when key managerial positions within the organization are traditionally held by specific professions, such as medical doctors or economists. Again, as in the case of external challenges, a medium manifestation is assigned for the overall internal challenges when only one of the two indicators (here: lack of cognitive slack or contested belief systems) can be considered 'high' while the other is 'low'. Table 3.3 provides an

Table 3.3 *External and internal challenges – indicators and their operationalization*

Variable	Indicator	Operationalization
External Challenges	*Perceived domain challenges*	*Low:* IPA considers its position within its organizational domain as focal or not challenged by other organizations *High:* IPA considers other actors in the organizational domain as competitors for funding and influence and its position as threatened
	Perceived political challenges	*Low:* IPA perceives its own actions to be rather undisputed or unrecognized by its principals *High:* IPA perceives its own actions to be under constant political scrutiny
Internal Challenges	*Lack of cognitive slack*	*Low:* IPA relies on central in-house research bodies, does not work under pronounced time constraints, and is not subject to strong procedural oversight *High:* IPA cannot or does not rely on central in-house research bodies; operates under pronounced time constraints; is subject to strong procedural oversight by its political principals
	Contested belief systems	*Low:* IPA staff members are recruited from the same educational or professional background or key managerial positions are traditionally held by a specific profession; there is a strong esprit de corps *High:* There is no dominant academic discipline among the IPA's staff members or the discipline itself is internally heterogeneous; there is no pronounced esprit de corps

overview of the operationalization of the key explanatory variables assessed.

3.3 The IPAs under Study: Combining a Diverse and a Most-Different Case Selection Technique

In the previous chapter, we developed an ideal-typical distinction of four administrative styles based on the prevalence of an IPA's positional and functional orientation. These four ideal-typical patterns are servants, consolidators, advocates, and entrepreneurs. These ideal types serve as analytical benchmarks to assess and compare administrative styles across different IPAs. Based on these considerations, our empirical analysis is guided by three objectives. First, we demonstrate that IPAs develop different administrative styles. Second, these styles differ in terms of their dominant orientations. Third, we explain the observed variation in administrative styles in light of our theoretical considerations developed in the previous chapter. In particular, we show that variation in administrative styles is caused by the external and internal challenges IPAs face rather than by the structural and formal features of an organization.

The logic of our case selection follows precisely these research objectives. First, we employ a diverse case selection strategy to capture the whole spectrum of administrative styles in our sample (Gerring, 2008). We thus intentionally select our cases based on the dependent variable. In the course of a larger research project on IPAs' role in policy making beyond the nation-state, we assessed the administrative styles of numerous IOs (see Bauer et al., 2017; Knill & Bauer, 2016), which were selected to capture variation in issue areas (migration, environment, security, economy), mandates (normative vs. non-normative/technical), scope (global vs. regional), and institutional context (UN agencies vs. treaty secretariats). We aimed to take into account primarily those IOs which have received at least modest scholarly attention in the recent past (Bauer & Ege, 2017; Ege, 2019) and which operate in a sufficiently established environment to allow for the emergence and consolidation of organizational routines. Accordingly, we deliberately excluded fast-evolving associations such as the G20 or the BRICS as well as 'experimentalist governance architecture[s]' (Sabel & Zeitlin, 2012) such as global and transnational public–private partnerships (see, e.g., Andonova, 2017;

Beisheim & Liese, 2014). This way, we arrived at a wider sample of *formal public intergovernmental organizations* (Karns, Mingst, & Stiles, 2004).

This broader sample also includes IOs such as the Organization for Economic Co-operation and Development (OECD), the Organization for Security and Co-operation in Europe (OSCE), the Bank for International Settlement (BIS), the European Commission, and the United Nations Educational, Scientific and Cultural Organization (UNESCO). While our theoretical framework holds in all these cases (Eckhard & Kern, 2017; Eckhard et al., 2016; Enkler, Schmidt, Eckhard, Knill, & Grohs, 2017; Knill et al., 2019; Knill et al., 2016), for the purpose of this book, we focus exclusively on the bureaucracies of eight task-specific IOs (Lenz et al., 2015); as mentioned in Chapter 1, these are the Food and Agriculture Organization of the United Nations (FAO), the International Labour Organization (ILO), the International Monetary Fund (IMF), the International Organization for Migration (IOM), the United Nations Environment Programme (UNEP), the United Nations High Commissioner for Refugees (UNHCR), the North Atlantic Treaty Organization (NATO), and the World Health Organization (WHO).

This way, next to our main objective of covering two IPAs of each style, this selection also enables us to demonstrate the applicability of our conceptual approach across highly different issue areas and beyond the UN family. The eight IPAs can be grouped in four pairs with administrative style patterns that come close to the four ideal types. Table 3.4 provides an overview of the administrative styles of the eight IPAs under study.[2] This overview is based on the summary of a thorough and in-depth assessment of the IPAs' administrative styles that is laid out in more detail in the case studies constituting the next four chapters of this book.

The variation in administrative styles becomes particularly apparent when comparing the bureaucracies of the ILO and NATO with those of the UNHCR and the IMF. While both the ILO and NATO secretariats refrain from almost any attempt to bring their own ideas and stances into the policy-making process, their counterparts at the

---

[2] For a horizontal overview of the values we obtained, as well as a brief summary of the discriminatory potential of each indicator please consult Appendix 1 and 2.

Table 3.4 *IPAs' behavioural patterns across different organizational activities during the policy cycle*

Orientation	Indicator	Servant		Consolidator		Advocate		Entrepreneur	
		ILO	NATO	IOM	FAO	WHO	UNEP	UNHCR	IMF
Positional Orientation	Support Mobilization	low	low	high	high	medium	medium	high	medium
	Mapping of the Political Space	low	medium	high	high	medium	high	high	high
	Political Anticipation	medium	high	high	high	high	high	high	high
	Strategic Use of Formal Powers	medium	low	high	high	low	medium	high	high
Functional Orientation	Issue Emergence	low	low	low	medium	low	high	high	high
	Solution Search	low	low	low	low	high	high	medium	high
	Internal Coordination	low	medium	low	low	medium	medium	medium	medium
	Policy Promotion	low	low	low	medium	high	high	high	high
	Evaluation	medium	low	medium	medium	high	medium	high	high

UNHCR and the IMF do so extensively. The bureaucracies of the FAO and the IOM, in turn, put a strong emphasis on activities that relate to the political aspects of their day-to-day work while being far less ambitious when it comes to activities aimed at enhancing the quality and effectiveness of their policies. The picture is slightly less clear when turning to the two remaining IPAs, namely those of the WHO and UNEP. Both the WHO and UNEP secretariats invest considerable effort in constantly advancing their policy performance while at the same time still somewhat intending to shape the institutional conditions under which the IPAs operate. Given their common behavioural patterns, we discuss the bureaucracies of the ILO and NATO as empirical examples of a servant style, those of the FAO and the IOM as consolidators, and those of the UNHCR and the IMF as entrepreneurs. Even though the WHO and UNEP are not as archetypical as the other IPAs assessed, the behavioural patterns of their secretariats come closest to the notion of an advocate. Second, for the IPAs analysed, we employ a most-different system design logic. We choose pairs of IPAs that share a similar administrative style but differ in other relevant structural and formal organizational features that may otherwise serve as a potential explanation for the outcome (Peters, 2013). To ensure that the different administrative styles do not simply mirror IOs' formal organizational features, each pair differs with regard to other potentially relevant organizational features – in particular when it comes to those that might have an immediate influence on the underlying administrative behaviour and orientation.

As will be shown in Chapter 4 on administrative styles in the IMF and the UNHCR, a common entrepreneurial style in both IPAs comes along with pronounced differences in the formal features of the two organizations. While the IMF secretariat enjoys a very high level of formal autonomy, administrative discretion is formally much more circumscribed for the UNHCR. If formal autonomy mattered in this case, the IMF bureaucracy should, we suggest, be much more entrepreneurial than its UNHCR counterpart. This expectation is reinforced when looking at other structural features, in particular organizational size and budget. In both indicators, the UNHCR reveals a much more dynamic development, while relevant figures for the IMF basically indicate a pattern of stagnation. Consequently, the UNHCR bureaucracy could afford to push much less given its standing (its comfortable growth and saturation), while stagnating developments should induce more entrepreneurial spirit in the IMF bureaucracy. In short, we are left with the puzzle of a similar entrepreneurship despite stark formal and structural differences across the two IPAs.

In Chapter 5, on the IOM and the FAO, we see that budget challenges and the struggle for organizational survival alone do not make for a consolidator style. The FAO has been substantially challenged for survival over recent decades, resulting in steep cuts in budget and personnel. After a sustained period of turmoil, it makes intuitive sense to consider the oldest permanent specialized UN agency in need of consolidation. However, the same cannot be said for the IOM. The organization has grown remarkably in size, budget, and membership over the same time period, which, from a perspective of organizational ecology, renders the IOM highly successful (Abbott, Green, & Keohane, 2016). If organizational survival were to be the sole predictor of administrative style, we could not convincingly explain the behaviours of staffers in the IOM. In addition, the two IPAs differ in their proximity to the UN system and the degree to which their mandates are purely operational. Whereas the absence of a pronounced functional orientation does not come as much of a surprise at the IOM given its purely operational mandate, it appears more puzzling when considering the FAO's normative focus. Again, these two IPAs leave us with a similar style that, taken on their own, neither their budgets and organizational success and failure nor their mandates can convincingly explain.

Chapter 6, on the WHO and UNEP, again shows that bureaucracies might develop a similar advocacy-orientated administrative style even when facing very different structural parameters. The WHO is almost omnipresent around the globe. The broad network of regional representations and country offices allows the IPA to easily acquire information from the local context and to advocate for its policies. In contrast to the WHO, UNEP has little to no operational presence at the country level. From a mere formal perspective, it is thus much more difficult for UNEP to directly exchange with member states' administrative staff, to gather information, and to push for action in its area of concern. Moreover, the location of UNEP's headquarters in Nairobi, Kenya, spatially bars the IPA from most international affairs and face-to-face interactions with peers from other IOs. In other words, if it were only about the opportunity structure of becoming an advocate, we could easily explain the administrative style present in the WHO but not in UNEP.

Chapter 7 deals with the ILO and NATO secretariats, which despite profound differences can both be considered servants. When it comes to delegation, the ILO has been extensively empowered by its tripartite principals, while very little competence has been transferred to the decision-making bodies of NATO (Hooghe et al., 2017). NATO has also been described as enjoying less institutional autonomy than the ILO (Reinalda, 1998; S. Mayer, 2014). As in Chapter 4, we thus see that administrative styles do not appear to be fully determined by formal autonomy or authority. Moreover, the two cases clearly show that neither the nature of the mandate nor of the policy field make for decisive factors in explaining styles. NATO operates in the realm of high politics, which has frequently been associated with low levels of IPA influence and independence (Snidal, 1990). While their servant style fits with such hypotheses, the ILO's servant style in low politics shows that the nature and domestic significance of the issue area, too, are not entirely accurate predictors for informal agency. Lastly, functionalist and neo-functionalist arguments about IOs' intended purposes do not seem to yield much explanatory power, given that NATO and the ILO differ in their 'service functions' (Keohane, 2005; Koremenos, Lipson, & Snidal, 2001).

By contrasting these four most-different pairs of IPAs, we highlighted that a number of commonly assumed formal explanatory factors cannot consistently explain why an IPA develops one style and not another. It became apparent that the eight organizations compared substantially differ in several exemplary structural aspects, such as the policy area covered, the personnel and financial resources available, geographical location and decentralization, institutional embeddedness, formal autonomy and authority, and their formal competencies and mandates. Having excluded these aspects as potential singular explanations for the outcome, in the following chapters we demonstrate that the IPAs' informal bureaucratic routines do emerge as a direct response to the conjunction of perceived external and internal challenges that a bureaucracy faces.

3.4 Methodological Approach

There are two especially profound methodological challenges in assessing administrative styles and organizational culture more broadly: informality and intra-organizational diversity. In setting forth our methodological approach, we thus put special emphasis on how we intended to approach several problems associated with these two factors.

First, to assess informal administrative styles, it is of limited use to study merely the formal discretion of IPAs. Rather, we need information about factual behavioural patterns that characterize daily bureaucratic routines. Informal routines are often so deeply institutionalized that an individual bureaucrat may be unaware of her own behaviour. Moreover, as collective patterns of behaviour, these informal routines necessarily have to be assessed by considering and combining different intra-organizational perspectives (Enticott, 2004). Having considered several alternative research strategies, we assessed IPAs' administrative styles by means of semi-structured expert interviews.[3]

In comparison to other methodological approaches, we consider the above-mentioned approach of data collection through semi-structured interviews as most suitable in light of our research focus. We rejected alternative methods such as surveys or participatory observations for several reasons. Survey research usually requires a high response rate to allow for meaningful interpretation: given the highly restricted access to IOs, we could not guarantee a sufficiently high number of participants. Moreover, especially in hierarchical organizations such as in public bureaucracies, participation in a survey is often not random (Lee, Benoit-Bryan, & Johnson, 2012). We were thus concerned that only specific positions within the organization would take part in the survey and that as a consequence, we would have been unable to derive a holistic picture of the organization under study from the data gathered. Most importantly, face-to-face interviewing allowed us to gather nuances that would have gone unnoticed in a survey, which is necessarily limited in number of questions and in opportunities for participants to clarify or communicate beyond the written word. Given the necessity of personal

---

[3] Interviews are cited in the text using the name of the IO followed by the interview number, e.g. IMF 1.

contact, another option would have been ethnographic methods (Rhodes, Hart, Noordegraaf, & Hart, 2007). However, while this method certainly would have yielded the most in-depth picture of bureaucratic routines, we decided against it because of the comparative nature of the project, the method's resource intensity, and – above all – restricted access to some of the IOs.

In the interviews, we asked various questions about the internal operating procedures to capture the latent concept of administrative styles. Some of the indicators presented above could be assessed by direct questions. For others, we had to rely on a more indirect approach, which would have been impossible with a survey approach. For instance, to capture how IPAs engage in solution search and internal coordination, we usually identified a number of organizational publications to which our interview partners had contributed and asked them to elaborate on the exact drafting procedure. Where applicable, we substantiated the interviewees' information with existing scholarly literature, which also served as background during the interviews, although it must be noted that the development of a scholarly state of the art varies greatly between the chosen IOs (Eckhard & Ege, 2016; Ege, 2019). In total, we conducted 131 semi-structured expert interviews of around forty-five minutes each, ranging from a minimum of eleven to a maximum of twenty-three interviews per organization under scrutiny (see Table 3.5). Collecting the views of multiple officials and triangulating them with scholarly accounts and government documents allowed us to identify intra-organizational consensus while cross-validating the information provided and checking for internal consistency. To ensure the reliability of the information gathered, we opted for a 'negotiated agreement approach' (Campbell et al., 2013, p. 305). This means that at least two coders had to engage with the transcribed interviews and assess the IPAs with regard to the nine central indicators. In a second step, the coders were asked compare their assessment and, in the case of disagreement, discuss their coding to arrive at a final version in which most discrepancies were resolved. In case of a continuing disagreement, an additional coder was involved. It is important to note that intercoder agreement is not the same as intercoder reliability because the latter does provide an indication of the degree of consensus reached when the coding is done in complete isolation (ibid.). We therefore went through all

Table 3.5 *Overview of interviewees by IO and position*

IO	Top managers	Middle managers	Policy analysts/ Technical officer	Total
FAO	3	1	19	23
ILO	1	3	12	16
IMF	1	6	8	15
IOM	1	3	12	16
UNEP	3	4	15	22
UNHCR	0	4	12	16
NATO	2	5	5	12
WHO	4	4	3	11

Note: 'Top managers' refers to the level of secretary general, directors, their deputies or equivalents; 'Middle managers' are heads of unit, team leaders, or equivalents; the remaining category embraces all types of issue specialists such as 'policy analysts' or 'technical officers', etc.

cases of negotiated agreements and checked for the accuracy of the final coding.

The second set of issues revolves around intra-organizational diversity across departments, hierarchical echelons, and locations. In assessing administrative styles, we conceive of bureaucratic bodies as rather homogenous units in terms of the shared orientations and informal routines. Yet in many instances, international bureaucracies are exactly the opposite, consisting of different departments, positions, and (field) offices with highly distinctive features (Morth, 2000). Regarding different positions, we aimed to obtain as much balance as possible by interviewing staffers from three different hierarchical levels in each IO (see Table 3.5). We also routinely asked for patterns beyond the staffer's own level within the hierarchy and cross-checked answers for consistency. While we did not get the opportunity to talk in the same way with many higher-ranked officials in all IPAs, we are confident that we captured potential differences across echelons. The fact that policy analysts and middle managers are overrepresented in our sample is not particularly problematic for our analysis. It might well be the case that the common staffer's experiences may be somewhat different from those of higher levels in the hierarchy, but we consider these differences to be rather constant across organizations and thus level out when engaging in comparative analysis.

To cope with the problem of intra-organizational diversity across issue areas, we concentrate on specialized agencies or task-specific organizations rather than large multi-purpose organizations, such as the OECD or the EU (Lenz et al., 2015).[4] Yet especially in strongly pillarized organizations such as the FAO or the WHO, we still find silos, bureaucratic entities that often work separately from one another. We account for this problem in two ways. First, silo thinking per se is not an analytical problem but a finding. In the FAO, for instance, we found that silos hamper coordination across the board and contribute to a lack of cognitive slack. In other words, the effects of strong vertical compartmentalization can be seen in the whole organization, which then factors into their common style. Second, to arrive at such a conclusion, one needs to select interviewees across the departments. We thus interviewed staff members from different parts of the organizations, with a slight focus on staffers in policy divisions flowing from our interest in how policy is actually made. In the empirical chapters, we report instances in which we found significant differences across departments and factor this into our overall style assessment (usually by assigning 'medium' values). To check for internal consistency, we conducted interviews with several staff members who had worked in the same division or on the same organizational outputs, such as country reports or policy guidelines, to further allow for cross-validating statements.

In terms of spatial differentiation, we restrict ourselves to the analysis of the IOs' headquarters. Where possible, we interviewed staffers who have been rotating in and out of the field, and in the empirical chapters, we tentatively suggest potential differences of field offices in style, where they have been explicitly reported. While we thus

---

[4] In such large, general purpose organizations, different administrative styles could theoretically coexist. This is mainly because external challenges could be perceived very differently. When working on entirely disparate issues, naturally, a multipurpose organization finds itself in several, possibly overlapping but distinct organizational environments and domains, but will likely not occupy the same position in all of them. Therefore, it could perceive itself focal in one and peripheral in another, which should lead to varying emphases on positional routines across the different sector's departments within the same IPA. Administrative routines in multi-purpose IOs certainly constitute a promising research agenda, yet one we deliberately do not cover in this book for the sake of clarity, consistency, and scope.

acknowledge that staffers in headquarters might work differently from their colleagues in the field, we still consider this approach viable for our purposes. Apart from obvious practical and logistical issues with interviewing staffers from several field offices per IO, there are conceptual reasons for this choice. Not unlike the point made about silos above, we do not necessarily consider decentralization as an analytical problem, but a factor that contributes to certain elements of administrative styles. Again, we would hold that the effects of decentralization should affect all members of the organizations. In line with research on administrative styles and behaviour on the national level, we assume that headquarters are more concerned with the shared, overall organizational goals and policies than are their regional counterparts, while still being involved in the planning and monitoring of field missions (Howlett, 2003; Kaufman, 1960; Knill, 2001). Analytically, this focus thus makes sense, since by definition of the styles concept, we are interested in bureaucratic routines with regard to actual policy making and IPAs' influence potential therein.

3.5 Conclusion

In this chapter, we empirically clarified how we study IPAs' administrative styles and their key explanatory factors. In translating the abstract concept of administrative styles into observable indicators, we identified nine different activities along the policy cycle that reflect an IPA's administrative style and its underlying orientations. Moreover, we specified our empirical understanding of the external and internal challenges that IPAs must cope with and which we consider crucial for the administrative style that an IPA develops. By combining a diverse and a most-different case selection strategy, we selected eight specialized international organizations that can be categorized into four pairs, each pair resembling one of the four ideal types proposed. While the pairs of IPAs share the same administrative style, they differ in most of their structural and formal organizational features. Using this two-step case-selection strategy, we are able to demonstrate first that IPAs do indeed develop very different administrative styles; and second, that there are actually no formal features that can singularly account for the evolvement of a specific style. In methodological terms, we argued that informal bureaucratic routines can only be captured comprehensively by means of semi-structured interviews with multiple proficient experts employed by the organizations under analysis. This approach allows us both to identify consensus across the organization and to cross-validate the information gathered.

In the four chapters to follow, we have two major aims. First, we show how exactly the administrative styles manifest themselves in the eight organizations under study. Second, we provide evidence that IPAs' informal routines do *not* result from single formal and structural features of an organization, such as their formal competencies and autonomy, but rather that they emerge as a response to the external and internal challenges IPAs must cope with.

4 | The IMF and the UNHCR
Entrepreneurial Administrations with Different Levels of Formal Autonomy

Nowadays, most observers would probably subscribe to the characterization of the IMF secretariat as an entrepreneurial bureaucracy. In many instances, this perception might be supported by the prominent role of the IMF during the financial and economic crisis that unfolded from 2007 onwards and the extensive media coverage of the organization that ensued. The case to assume a highly entrepreneurial role of the IMF administration becomes even clearer when considering its formal autonomy, which far exceeds the respective levels of any other IPA covered in this book. At first glance, it seems straightforward to expect that high formal autonomy (in terms of the number of delegated competencies, powers, and resources) should come along with more entrepreneurial patterns of administrative styles. From this perspective, the IMF should be a most-likely case of an entrepreneurial IPA. And indeed, our findings support this expectation impressively. The IMF secretariat scores as entrepreneur on all indicators with regard to both dominant functional and dominant positional orientations.

Yet concluding from this finding that the level of formal autonomy determines administrative styles quickly turns out to be a fallacy when we take a closer look at the UNHCR. The UNHCR secretariat displays a similarly entrepreneurial style, although its formal autonomy is much lower than is the case for the IMF. Evidently, formal and informal organizational patterns constitute distinct phenomena that do not directly relate to one another. This is reinforced by the fact that the emergence and shape of formal and informal arrangements are usually explained by different causal factors. In addition, the role of formal autonomy in determining administrative styles can also be fundamentally questioned when taking a closer look at the developments in the

IMF over time. While today, the Fund displays all features of an entrepreneurial style, this could not be said prior to the financial crisis of 2007. It was only after fundamental challenges to the Fund in the aftermath of the Asian financial crisis of 1997, that entrepreneurial administrative routines evolved.

While formal autonomy is primarily explained against the background of principals' preferences, institutional path dependencies, or functionalist reasoning (Ege, 2017; Hawkins et al., 2006; Pierson, 2000), informal patterns like administrative styles have their roots – as we argue in this book – in factors like cognitive capacity, common professional backgrounds, or administrative perceptions, as well as in narratives of external challenges through competition in organizational fields or political threat (see also Knill, 2001; Knill et al., 2019). In short, the fact that different variables account for variation in formal and informal arrangements should lead us to conceive of both elements as phenomena not determined by each other. As a consequence, a highly autonomous IPA does not necessarily need to adopt an entrepreneurial style, while an IPA with low autonomy may not automatically display a servant style.

The two IPAs studied in this chapter perfectly support this argument. In terms of their formal features, they can be characterized as most-different cases. The secretariats of the IMF and the UNHCR vary strongly not only in their formal autonomy but also with regard to other structural aspects. What they have in common, however, is their perception of similar levels of high external and low internal challenges to their organizations. We argue in this chapter that it is exactly this constellation that led to the emergence of similar behavioural routines. Both IPAs can be characterized as entrepreneurs: they combine strong policy advocacy with pronounced routines directed towards institutional consolidation.

As we have discussed in Chapter 2, the emergence of an entrepreneurial style presupposes that quite demanding conditions have been fulfilled, which should render an entrepreneurial style an exception rather than the rule. What are the specific conditions that drive (structurally highly diverse) IPAs to develop entrepreneurial routines? To account for this phenomenon, we investigate the explanatory power of two determinants: the constellation of internal and external challenges perceived by the IPA in question.

4.1 A Most-Likely and a Least-Likely Case for an Entrepreneurial Style? The Structural Diversity of the IMF and the UNHCR

As already indicated above, in many ways, a look at the structural features of the IMF suggests that this IPA has everything it needs to develop entrepreneurial bureaucratic routines. Exactly the opposite is the case when turning to the UNHCR. In this case, a mere look at the structural arrangements of the IPA favours the expectation of servant style while entrepreneurial orientations seem highly unlikely. The most central features suggesting such are their strongly different levels of formal autonomy. In addition, the two IPAs display strong variation in their functions as well as in their resource dependence.

While both organizations operate under the umbrella of the United Nations and were founded in the early post-World War II era, their secretariats display striking differences in their levels of formal autonomy. A recent taxonomy on the formal autonomy of IPAs rated the IMF in the highest and the UNHCR in the lowest quartile of its sample (Bauer & Ege, 2017, p. 29).

Although refugees can be considered a constant in history, it was only in the post-war period, when countries in Europe were overwhelmed with displaced persons and refugees, that formal organizational structures were established at the international level. In 1950, the UNHCR was created by the General Assembly of the UN in response to this problem. Its statute provides the organization with a mandate that covers two central roles: to provide protection to refugees and to find solutions to their plight. Yet the secretariat was given few responsibilities and little autonomy. To limit the authority and autonomous ability of the UNHCR secretariat, member states created mechanisms and procedures to restrain its action.

First, member states set up an executive and advisory mechanism, the Executive Committee of the High Commissioner's Programme (ExCom). ExCom approves the UNHCR's programmes and budgets, makes conclusions on policy issues pertaining to international refugee protection, and offers guidance on the IPA's internal workings and priorities. Membership in ExCom, appointed by the General Assembly, is open to member states pending a selection process (Gordenker, 1987). Membership has grown since its establishment in 1958, and a few powerful donor countries have tried to preserve their dominant influence over policy issues and UNHCR programming and priorities.[1] Second, member states gave the IPA a temporary mandate through which operations can only be renewed and extended by the General Assembly. Third, while the UNHCR acts under the authority of the General Assembly and fulfils its mandate under the auspices of the UN, it is ultimately dependent on member states for authorization and funding. The funding structure of the UNHCR implies that only administrative expenditures will be financed through the budget of the UN while all other expenses relating to the activities of the secretariat must be financed by voluntary contributions (originally only from member states). While the UNHCR was born with charitable ideas, funds provided by donor states generally depended on how states viewed the relevance of the IPA and specific refugee situations in relation to their own national interests (Loescher, 2001; McKittrick, 2008).

In contrast to these profound limitations, the IMF secretariat disposes of much more autonomy and discretion in its day-to-day operations. The IMF, with its 189 member countries, is responsible for overseeing and safeguarding the stability of the international monetary and financial system.[2] Founded in 1944 at the Bretton Woods Conference, its mandate includes the monitoring of the system of exchange rates and international payments, research and analysis on individual member countries' economies in the form of so-called Article IV surveillance reports, and dealing with cross-country macroeconomic and financial sector issues that bear on global stability.

Compared to the UNHCR, the IMF is more loosely coupled to the UN system. First, its secretariat enjoys much more formal independence (Bauer & Ege, 2017). Its internal decision-making process does not reflect the UN General Assembly's 'one-country, one-vote system'. Rather, the board of governors permanently delegates its powers to the executive board, on which twenty-four executive directors represent countries or groups of countries with voting rights based on their

---

[1] As a subsidiary organ to the UN, the UNHCR has no membership of its own. However, as the members of ExCom are the ones most heavily involved in the governance of the UNHCR, we deem it best to use the number of ExCom member states as of 2020, 106 (see: 'UNHCR Executive Committee of the High Commissioner's Programme', retrieved 19 March 2020 from www.unhcr.org/e xcom/scaf/5bbc66644/excom-composition-period-october-2019-october-2020. html).

[2] See: 'About the IMF', retrieved 20 August 2018, from www.imf.org/en/About.

relative position in the world economy. For instance, while the United States, as the largest economy in the world, is represented by a single executive director and wields 17.46 per cent of the total votes (which constitutes a blocking minority when altering the Fund's articles of agreement, which require 85 per cent of the votes), Bangladesh, Bhutan, India, and Sri Lanka share one director who has merely 3.05 percent of the voting rights.[3] Second, the fixed-quota system of financial contributions to the IMF puts the IPA in a rather comfortable financial situation. Third, member states typically restrict their steering activities to rare high-politics events with geopolitical implications. By contrast, the vast majority of daily decisions are made by staff with bureaucratic discretion and then approved merely ex post by the executive board (Chwieroth, 2009).

In sum, assuming that the degree of formal autonomy matters for administrative routines, the highly autonomous IMF secretariat should display an entrepreneurial style, whereas its counterpart at the UNHCR should come closer to a servant style, given its much more constrained discretion and hence room for independent agency.

This expectation is reinforced when considering further structural features along which these IPAs differ, namely size and budget. A glance at both indicators reveals much more dynamic developments for the UNHCR than for the IMF. With regard to organizational size, the UNHCR has more than four times as many employees as the IMF, with 10,800 staff in 128 countries and with 87 per cent of the staff working in the field. By contrast, the IMF fares with a much smaller work force of 2,400.[4] The budgets of the IPAs reflect these differences: while the IMF had an administrative budget of USD 1.1 billion in 2016,[5] UNHCR had USD 7.5 billion to spend in the same year.[6] Whereas the IMF's budget has been relatively stable (with the exception of increases after the world financial crisis of 2008), the UNHCR's funding for its operations has continuously increased. This has been a result of its changing environment: more and more people are being

---

[3] See 'About the IMF', retrieved 10 June 2019, from www.imf.org/en/About.
[4] See 'Figures at a glance', retrieved 3 July 2018, from www.unhcr.org/figures-at
    -a-glance.html and 'About the IMF', retrieved 20 August 2018, from www
    .imf.org/en/About.
[5] See 'Finances, Organization, and Accountability', retrieved 7 July 2018, from
    www.imf.org/external/pubs/ft/ar/2016/eng/fin-budget-income.htm.
[6] See 'UNHCR: Figures at a glance', retrieved 3 July 2018, from www.unhcr.org
    /figures-at-a-glance.html.

displaced around the world as a result of armed conflicts and other events, reaching an unprecedented 65.3 million people.[7] This has had considerable consequences for the organization, as one staff member pointed out: 'What is bad for many people around the world ironically is not bad for our business. Because the services we provide are more in need than ever' (UNHCR 13).

From its humble beginnings as a small organization with a narrow purpose and mandate, the UNHCR has grown considerably in size and scope to become 'one of the premier UN agencies' (Barnett & Finnemore, 2004, p. 118; see also Betts, 2012). Despite the UNHCR's more circumscribed mandate, its size and resources were subject to a highly dynamic development, while for the IMF, both indicators reveal a pattern of stability. From the outset, the UNHCR secretariat can thus be considered a much more likely candidate for a servant style than can its IMF counterpart.

To conclude, we have seen that the IMF and UNHCR bureaucracies can be treated as most-different cases regarding their structural features, including, in particular, their formal autonomy, mandate, size, and budget development. If these structural indicators were to matter for administrative styles, we should observe highly pronounced differences in administrative styles across both organizations. While the IMF would then be a most likely case for an entrepreneurial style, conversely, a least likely scenario would be expected for the UNHCR, as it should rather resemble a servant. Yet as will be shown in the following section, not only does the IMF pursue an entrepreneurial style, the UNHCR bureaucracy does as well. As will become clear, structural explanations fall short in capturing variation in informal bureaucratic behaviour across different organizations.

4.2 Administrative Styles in the IMF and the UNHCR: Entrepreneurs Despite Structural Diversity

Our concept of administrative styles distinguishes between two basic orientations, functional and positional. While the functional orientation of IPAs captures the extent to which administrative routines are driven by policy advocacy – that is, the motivation to constantly

---

[7] See 'UNHCR: Figures at a glance', retrieved 3 July 2018, from www.unhcr.org /figures-at-a-glance.html.

improve the policy effectiveness of their IO – the positional orientation reflects the prevalence of administrative routines guided towards institutional consolidation of the bureaucracy's internal and external standing. When analysing the different indicators for these dimensions for the two IPAs under study, we find that both the IMF and the UNHCR bureaucracies are characterized by administrative styles that come very close to the entrepreneurial ideal type. In both IPAs, we find administrative routines that strongly reflect orientations towards advocacy and consolidation. As can be observed from the overview provided in Table 3.2, both IPAs stand out as being by far the most active with regard to both orientations.

4.2.1 *Functional Orientations: The Prevalence of Advocacy Routines*

In both IPAs, the pronounced functional orientation towards policy advocacy is visible immediately from the fact that bureaucratic routines are strongly geared towards the *identification of new policy issues*. In the IMF, the two dominant approaches are either to set the agenda by developing original policy proposals and research that support these efforts or, alternatively, to react to upcoming issues as early as possible to be able to shape the discussion at the very beginning of a policy debate (IMF 1). The latter tends to be the case for globally relevant issues that enter the agenda unexpectedly, such as a sudden economic slowdown in a given country or sector, an important monetary policy decision by a major central bank, or other current events making headline news. IMF staff permanently monitor these events to ensure that no major issue will be overlooked; the area departments cover all regions and countries, while the functional departments cover all policy fields that are relevant to the fund. Once IMF staff conclude that an issue is going to be relevant, they even secure managerial support for internal resources to be mobilized to react to it, for example, by creating a task force or a temporary working group (IMF 2).

For the analytical work, we here have an own agenda and that is typically easier for structural and long-term issues; whereas in cross-country work, the agenda is set more centrally by issues that arise contextually, for instance the current refugee crisis in Europe. Everyone in the fund is aware that there is an issue there, so then it's more centrally driven. So the short-term agenda is often driven by events in the world. (IMF 7)

Similar entrepreneurial routines in identifying and defining new policy issues shape the administrative style of the UNHCR. Many officials see its bureaucracy as a highly innovative organization (UNHCR 7, 8) that is always looking out for future problems and developments: 'There is something about the DNA of UNHCR which is always to be looking beyond the horizon. We have today's problems, but we also have glimpses of the future' (UNHCR 1). Or, as academic observers like Weiss and Pasic (1997, p. 50) put it: 'Today's UNHCR is regarded by most observers as being at the top of the UN scale of performance – competent, well-managed, purposeful, disciplined.'

In line with this, the emergence of new issues is strongly driven from within the organization. This is seen, on the one hand, as a result of the specific position of the High Commissioner, who is supposed to be mainly guided by the protection needs of refugees and other people of concern (UNHCR 3). Yet also on the staff level, the UNHCR bureaucracy continuously monitors emerging issues and needs in its policy area by using its decentralized structure and strong field presence (UNHCR 4, 10, 11). Accordingly, the budget presented to ExCom is developed in a bottom-up fashion and informed by the field and the operational needs:

We develop a needs-based budget. So it starts with an assessment at the field level of what we think the people we serve need, to have their protection, basic assistance and solution needs met. Based on that, at the field level, we roll up something that is called the comprehensive needs assessment and it reflects what we should do and the resources required to make sure we can deliver for the people we serve according to the humanitarian standards that we promote. And that is qualified only by the fact that it should be feasible, implementable and realistic ... And then all of that is rolled up into a budget document, which is primarily a financial information but also gives a narrative description of what we plan to do. (UNHCR 3)

In addition to the field level, another important source for new issues is the global level and the larger UN family, with which the UNHCR is strongly interlinked (UNHCR 9, 10).

Entrepreneurial routines also shape the process of policy drafting. In both IPAs, we find administrative routines that reflect the motivation to go beyond the development of merely satisficing solutions, by working towards policy optimization. The IMF takes a very coherent and rigid course of action with regard to *solution search*. Although it is not a think tank or academic institution, the production of its flagship publications, such as the World Economic Outlook or the Global Financial Stability Report, adhere to standards similar to those of academia, especially when it comes to the methodological rigidity of how topics are researched and the choice of policy items that are recommended (IMF 3).

When you produce a draft, it gets corrected by your immediate supervisor, and then above, and another above – at least four or five steps, often all the way to the top and back down. So it's a very time-consuming process. It also goes horizontally because there is a very entrenched process of peer-review across departments, so any policy relevant paper goes to a lot of people and a lot of different departments, and they comment fiercely on the work of the other departments. There is a lot of competition and emulation. You spend a lot of time adjusting the text and the feedback of others until finally it goes to the board and then it basically rubber-stamps it most of the time ... At the IMF, staff are supposed to produce the perfect product. (IMF 1)

In contrast to this very rigid procedure at the IMF, because of the large size and wide array of different tasks of the organization, solution search in the UNHCR bureaucracy is much more dependent on the kind of output and the individuals tasked with its development. The UNHCR secretariat issues many studies and provides a lot of data or collaborates with academia on important matters of refugee research and the work of the organization. Accordingly, many staff members mentioned quite heavy research activities and thorough information gathering in preparing a policy or position paper (UNHCR 1, 5).

Furthermore, the UNHCR bureaucracy makes strong use of classical management tools, such as cost-benefit analysis, log frames, and risk assessments, in order to optimize decision making (UNHCR 10). Again, its decentralized structure allows the IPA to 'capitalize on field experience' (UNHCR 4), and at times there is a sort of pre-test in specific countries that feeds back into the final document (UNHCR 9). Policy development is decentralized and happens in the units most involved with the topic of concern (UNHCR 10). Thus, because much depends on the involved departments and individuals and because the UNHCR often operates in emergency situations, processes can at times be a bit ad hoc (UNHCR 11). In these instances, decision making is often limited by time constraints (UNHCR 4) and the need to react in a 'quick and un-bureaucratic way' (UNHCR 10). In view of these considerations, the prevalence of optimizing routines is somewhat lower in the UNHCR bureaucracy than is the case for the IMF, where such routines can be observed in their purest form.

Administrative routines in both organizations involve pronounced efforts to foster *internal coordination*. Due to the differences in size and structure, these routines are more developed and pronounced for the IMF. In the IMF case, we find an institutionalized, well-managed process of positive coordination. The IPA has developed a sophisticated internal system to complement this open style of coordination, which consists of a formal and an informal component. The formal component mainly concerns the coordination and steering activities of the Strategy, Policy, and Review Department (SPR), while an informal mechanism is sought to settle internal debates before they reach top management and/or the executive board (IMF 4).

There is a consensus-building exercise. Work circulates from one department to the next for commenting and review. For example, in the case of a country surveillance report, the respective area department starts with a document, which circulates to all the other departments involved. Then there is a policy consultation meeting where all the stake-holding departments meet and discuss the terms of reference for the mission. In this meeting, we try to build a consensus for the report. So there's quite a bit of coordination involved and it takes quite a bit of time between departments and with management. (IMF 2)

While the above clearly indicates a high degree of positive internal coordination at the IMF, the picture at the UNHCR is less clear cut. On the one hand, despite the size and decentralized structure of the UNHCR, many interviewed staff members described their internal coordination procedures as quite extensive (UNHCR 6, 8, 9). There are different task forces and working groups bringing together people from different departments in order to provide a platform for exchange on cross-cutting issues (UNHCR 8). Moreover, there is a codified system for policy approval, and if a policy is to be issued, the responsible unit has to provide a due-diligence memo showing that all the relevant stakeholders have been consulted (UNHCR 6). This system seems to work quite well:

When it goes to the top management, they can be sure that it has been properly reviewed and that enough consultations have taken place and that all the people that need to be involved and associated and consulted have been. And that therefore the final product is a mature reflection and expression of the state of information and art on a particular subject. (UNHCR 13)

On the other hand, due to its strongly decentralized structure, the organization has to deal with silo effects between different departments or country offices (UNHCR 10, 4, 12). The stronger offices at the field level, especially, tend to emphasize the interests of their operation at times, thus 'failing to forge a regional strategy that is mutually beneficial to all offices' (Gottwald, 2010, p. 22). However, the strict rotation system and informal exchange often help overcome such silo thinking (UNHCR 4, 10). Overall, the UNHCR case shows a mixed type of internal coordination that oscillates between positive and negative coordination depending on the actors and units involved.

These slight differences in solution search and coordination notwithstanding, both IMF and UNHCR bureaucracies show a pronounced entrepreneurial pattern in the active *promotion of their policies*. The IMF administration has established a large public relations team, which systematically accompanies the release of new publications or reports system with regular press briefings at the IMF headquarters in Washington, DC (Ecker-Ehrhardt, 2018). Another important venue to enhance its policy implementation capacities is to link departments with few to no implementation opportunities to the ones that are more deeply engaged with implementing policies. One example is the spread of new regulatory approaches from internal research to the outside world:

The Monetary and Capital Markets Department's way to foster implementation is to inform the area departments in charge of missions about macro prudential tools and how to use them. This type of knowledge transfer is very important for us. (IMF 5)

Yet outreach activities are limited by the extent of spare time that staff have, and in turbulent times, the first type of activity to get cut are extra efforts, such as policy promotion, as another staff member explains: 'Since there is such a large workload, within this division there is not a lot of time to publish things such as working papers on the side, that is more the responsibility of the research department' (IMF 4). Nevertheless, the IMF bureaucracy enjoys a high level of expert authority (Busch & Liese, 2017) and its publications and policy recommendations are well received by different stakeholders (IMF 15).

Turning to the UNHCR, administrative routines of policy promotion typically vary with the type of output. While an internal policy is mostly presented to member states and UNHCR partners (UNHCR 9), other outputs might be publicized to specialized circles (UNHCR 4). On top of these more specialized outputs, the organization also promotes its work to the larger public:

I would [probably] refer you to the core documents, which are the global appeal and our global report. But of course, on top of that we have a very strong media presence. If you look at events like World Refugee Day and the sort of advocacy campaigns that revolve around that, I think we are quite professional and effective. (UNHCR 3)

Due to its reputation as a 'reliable provider of information and statistics', the UNHCR gets cited a lot by the media (UNHCR 11). While one official stated that other organizations sometimes display a more aggressive marketing style, the IPA also seems quite strategic in the way it promotes its work, which it does by carefully choosing the right message for each environment and balancing these different messages in order to send out a coherent picture of the organization (UNHCR 10).

Both IPAs also display an entrepreneurial style with regard to *policy evaluation* and have adopted routines to further strengthen their evaluation function, which even goes beyond their member states' explicit demands. Both IPAs display administrative routines that are directed towards systematic learning from their experience with previous policies. Although the internal evaluation mechanism in the IMF initially faced considerable opposition on the part of the staff, it appears to be well accepted by now (Weaver, 2010). The Strategy, Policy, and Review Department is in charge of streamlining internal policy positions and ensuring coherence. Furthermore, it supports the triennial surveillance reviews (TSR), an institutionalized evaluation mechanism to judge the effectiveness of the fund's policy advice. These evaluations critically assess the IMF's performance, identify potential blind spots, and are presented to the board of executives (IMF 5). For instance, the 2011 TSR found that IMF surveillance was still too fragmented, and its risks assessment analyses needed a stronger focus on financial interconnections and transmission of shocks, which were key aspects in the run-up to the global financial crisis. The Independent Evaluation Office (IEO) is another unit responsible for evaluation activities and a permanent and institutionalized initiative of organizational learning in the IMF (IMF 6). While the TSR focuses on policy effectiveness, the IEO's mission scrutinizes the organizational effectiveness of the IMF. Both the TSR and the IEO ensure that the IMF bureaucracy takes strong measures to constantly evaluate the impact of its policies, as well as itself as an organization, in order to improve and institutionalize organizational learning.

Just like the IMF, the UNHCR secretariat has an effective evaluation system in place (DFID, 2011c). In 2010, the UNHCR implemented a comprehensive results framework, which – according to staff members – was 'a great step forward' (UNHCR 7). While one official stated that evaluation used to be 'cutting edge' and has lost a little bit of its effectiveness in recent years as a result of an overload of evaluation and monitoring requests (UNHCR 10), overall, the IPA seems committed to further strengthening and streamlining its evaluation function by having introduced a new evaluation policy in 2016 that is orientated towards the wider UN standards (UNHCR 2017c). As one interviewee pointed out in relation to the evaluation, 'I think that the organization has been adapting to all of the different field operations and done everything that can be done' (UNHCR 7). Moreover, some units developed special indicators more apt to their specific tasks in order to allow for more precise evaluation and monitoring of their activities (UNHCR 12, UNHCR 7).

In sum, both IPAs have developed a range of behavioural routines that reveals a strong orientation towards policy advocacy. This functional orientation is partially even more pronounced than for the WHO or UNEP bureaucracies – two cases in our sample that we have identified as IPAs coming close to the advocate ideal type that will be discussed in Chapter 6.

4.2.2 Positional Orientations: The Prevalence of Consolidation Routines

Monetary and fiscal policy and the management of refugee-related affairs are two highly salient issues that immediately affect the member states. It is thus not surprising that both organizations are quite closely monitored by their member states and other nongovernmental stakeholders like

NGOs (Zürn et al., 2012). Due to the overall high external challenges that the IMF and the UNHCR are exposed to, we expect both organizations to show a strong positional orientation. To prevent escalating contestation, both organizations should engage strongly in coalition building and anticipatory approaches to the political space and offensively use their formal powers to assert their position.

In both IPAs, administrative routines of institutional consolidation first become apparent in strongly developed procedures to *mobilize support* for their activities. Especially in response to strong criticism of the Bretton Wood institutions from both developing countries and global civil society in the 1990s (e.g. Stiglitz, 2002), the IMF bureaucracy has adopted more open and transparent approaches not only towards member states but also to a broad range of other stakeholders, including notoriously critical ones like several NGOs. However, this has not always been the case, as states one senior IMF expert who has been working at the fund for more than twenty years:

> One big difference in this crisis was that we are much more engaged with the external world ... A lot of work now has to do with external communications with stakeholders – that has changed quite a bit. The communications department helps the country teams a lot in engaging with the press and stakeholders. In the past, the fund has been more of a confidential adviser to governments. But now we have a much more active communications strategy. (IMF 2)

Furthermore, IMF staff is informally linked to country desks around the world and thus well-informed of important local issues: 'We have a lot of informal contacts with mission chiefs around the world by email and also informal meetings, so we are always up-to-date and know what works and what doesn't work' (IMF 5). Hosted academic conferences about major economic trends, such as the 'Rethinking Macroeconomic Policy' series, and indirect outreach efforts of IMF staff organized through executive directors' offices complement these efforts (IMF 4). The IMF's enhanced openness to external actors has resulted in the inclusion of non-traditional topics, such as gender equality, climate change, and income inequality, into the IMF's work. Yet many economists within the IMF have a rather critical view of this:

> These [topics] are not our core business, this is more for the World Bank or the OECD. We sometimes ask ourselves as staff: 'Do we really have a comparative advantage to work on this?' But it counts for management;

they have their own political agenda. It's clearly not part of our IMF mission, which is financial stability of the world economy. (IMF 10)

In general, the extent to which this openness in the initiation stage of the policy cycle actively influences public opinion about the IMF remains uncertain. It seems that it is more of an exercise in awareness of external interests and views, on the one hand, and signalling general perceptiveness of key stakeholders' needs at an early stage, on the other hand. Despite recent efforts and given that the IMF's openness has indeed increased, but no more than in other IOs (Tallberg , Sommerer, Squatrito, & Jönsson, 2014), we assess the IPA's support mobilization efforts as medium.

The UNHCR secretariat is more strongly engaged with a wide range of partners, with whom it works very effectively (DFID, 2011): 'We work with a large number of partners. More than nine hundred partners, and those have common shared principles and they are in line with our strategy and objectives' (UNHCR 6). Many of these partners are regional NGOs, receiving funds or cooperating with UNHCR at the field level (UNHCR 6), but the UNHCR also participates in different humanitarian and migration fora as well as coordination clusters and strongly collaborates with different IOs within and outside the UN system: 'So from the ground level all the way up to the sister agency or inter-agency level, we involve others as much as possible' (UNHCR 7). Moreover, NGOs are important partners of the UNHCR bureaucracy in the development of programme priorities as well as policies, and there are formal consultations with NGOs immediately prior to the annual meetings of ExCom (Betts, 2012). These consultations have grown in size and importance in recent years:

They've gone from about three hundred participants in a given year, now this year we will be near six hundred. There is almost no conference room big enough in Geneva for a conference of this type. It shows two things. First of all, the growing interest in our work. But secondly, we use the consultations as an opportunity to unpack some of the concerns and issues that we have, first of all for these field-based NGOs to better understand the relationship between what they do at the field level and what's going on at the policy level. And it's a way of creating coalitions of like-minded people who can then go out and do their work. (UNHCR 1)

Alliance building and common advocacy is perceived as being very important for the IPA (UNHCR 3, 10) and, according to one staff member, in working on new topics, 'the objective is to have one voice talking to states' (UNHCR 5).

While both IPAs are hence rather open to external actors and have adopted administrative routines to rally support for their activities, they have also incorporated administrative procedures to mobilize internal political support. This *mapping of the political space* includes scanning the principals' (i.e. member states') policy preferences and sensitivities, filtering out issues or approaches unlikely to make it onto the organizational agenda, and focusing energy on the most promising initiatives. At the IMF, these three tasks come relatively close to a job description given by a senior IMF official with decades-long experience who reflected about his own role:

> The executive board formally approves the work programme for the next six months, but in terms of ideas there is this informal process where we all talk to one another. Sometimes national authorities pass through concerns via the executive directors. Most of the work of senior management is exactly that, to talk to colleagues, see what's on the radar, if there's anything we are missing, etc. (IMF 2)

These informal talks help smooth the preparation of important policy positions in that the IPA already clears the most important political aspects before it is too late to make changes to a draft. Even the medium-term policy agenda is not just the product of top management agreeing with member states on what staff ought to do but evolves in informal meetings during the spring and fall annual meetings, when member-state representatives assemble in Washington, DC, to discuss the most important policy challenges to engage with (IMF 13). These informal meetings also give IMF staff a chance to screen current developments and shifts in the overall political landscape, which they may want to take into account when strategically reflecting on the feasibility of their policy recommendations.

In the UNHCR secretariat, we find similarly developed administrative routines directed at mapping the political space for new policy initiatives. These routines are reflected in a rather careful approach to launching new policy initiatives:

> If we were to decide unilaterally to launch a new initiative . . . if we did not do our homework right, in terms of sounding out opinion, it would be most unwise. So of course, any major new policy initiative would have to be carefully prepared and the opinions properly sounded out first. (UNHCR 13)

Due to the many sensitivities surrounding the policy area of refugee and migration governance, the IPA has enhanced not only its knowledge about these subtleties, but also the ability to carefully manoeuvre the (sometimes) opposing interests of its member states (political anticipation). The bureaucracy carefully weighs out the different interests and their implications for its mandate and, depending on the topic of concern, decides tactically when and how to put it on the table (UNHCR 10). When the UNHCR secretariat decides to launch an issue, knowing of the sensitivities and the trouble it might cause, it is a decision the IPA makes 'with its eyes wide open' because the implications for the refugees or the interests of important member states simply outweigh them (UNHCR 10). Due to the UNHCR's strong dependence on voluntary contributions and the tendency to earmark more and more funds, it is especially the big donor states that are of major interest for the UNHCR. The secretariat keeps active contact and holds bilateral conversations with them once a year, giving the IPA the opportunity to monitor and, to a certain degree, to influence their interests (UNHCR 7). As one staff member put it:

> By now we have a well-established system. So, we've got basically the top ten donors who are funding most of us and with all of them we have a fairly regular working level dialogue. Then we have at least once a year a high-level discussion with donors. We present our particular needs and issues and they will also give theirs. So, we have a whole service that's devoted to that. By now it's pretty accurate we know what their behaviour will be, and we also do have some ability to influence their decisions. (UNHCR 11)

The IPA thus not only knows of these sensitivities but also actively tries to avoid interference with them by way of *political anticipation*, for instance by 'keeping a low profile' until states decide to support UNHCR involvement (UNHCR 5) or by actively framing issues in a specific way: 'There are always member states and other agencies saying, "Is this your mandate?" That is always a political discussion. If we frame it in a way that UNHCR is already doing the job, there is no question about our mandate' (UNHCR 2). Similarly, another staff member underlined the role of framing: 'I mean the point of advocacy is not only just to be right, but to be effective. So, you do need to speak in a language that governments will understand' (UNHCR 3). The same applies to the drafting phase. In order to avoid problems, the UNHCR keeps in close contact with important member states, such as major donors or refugee-hosting countries, and often involves them in the drafting of new outputs (UNHCR 8, 9). One staff member described it as 'normal good practice' to consult with the most-concerned member states while drafting a new policy:

It would be, in my view, pretty unlikely that we would develop a policy without sufficient consultations either internally or externally ... After all, we are dependent on the financing of some twenty countries around the world. You can't ignore your stakeholders. That is not to say that we would always agree with all of them, on how states are behaving and practising ... In the end all policies are designed to be implemented. So, the value of any given policy is the degree to which it can be successfully implemented. (UNHCR 13)

Again, the decentralized structure is perceived as a strength, since it enables a regular exchange with the different governments (UNHCR 4, 11). The danger of siding with the government of a country one works in and the burden of self-censorship that can accompany such potential conflicts of interest are avoided by the strict rotation system, which prohibits staff members from staying in one place for too long (UNHCR 11). Moreover, one official pointed out that taking part in different meetings in international fora allows one to hear 'the discussions and the different sensitivities. So then when you draft something, you are influenced by that' (UNHCR 5).

The IMF bureaucracy has likewise developed pronounced administrative routines for successfully anticipating political constraints. This anticipation of the political environment occurs both internally vis-à-vis the board and externally when dealing with member states in country surveillance or programme work.

It is the role of the senior management to know what can fly and what cannot fly. It is not at the level of staff. They don't need to be concerned about any sort of political influence. Sometimes the fund in general takes stances that are not popular in some member countries represented at the executive board; but when we talk to people from these countries before, we get a sense of what is realistic and what not. So, there is some kind of internal filter in place. (IMF 2)

From the perspective of the executive board and top management, the division and department heads display a high degree of ambition to push for their policy positions in the negotiations and the re-drafting sessions. Some say that this sometimes enhances 'agency slack':

One strategic move of staff is sometimes to deliver papers to the board later than they should about major policy issues. There have been complaints from executive directors about short circulation times of papers, which leads to tensions ... At the IMF, it is very different from my previous work at [a different international organization]. There we may not have liked the decisions the principals made, but we knew that was the place where the decisions were made. The way I see it here, staff think they could make the decisions themselves, so why should they trust the top management or the board to make the right decisions? (IMF 3)

Finally, both IPAs display a relatively entrepreneurial style when it comes to the *use of their implementation powers*. While the IMF bureaucracy does not shy away from making use of its formal powers for implementation, which sometimes leads to open conflict with member states, it is generally strategic about the degree of conflict it is willing to engage in. Civil servants are well aware of the different boundaries that exist for the implementation of policies in different countries with different veto powers; they would not push as aggressively for their own positions with a large, highly industrialized country compared to a small, low-income one (IMF 6). In addition, most IMF staff members (of whom many have an academic background) have a strong intrinsic motivation to have a real-life impact and to see their policy advice being implemented (IMF 3). At the same time, everyone seems to be aware of the constraints and potential pitfalls around many policies. For staff to have an impact, it is not enough just to do good analytical work based on sound economics. It is also necessary to present findings and recommendations in a way that makes them more likely to be accepted by a wide audience, which may consist of non-economists and people who are generally sceptical about the IMF's work. This is especially true for Article IV reports, which usually receive much attention in the respective countries' national media once they are published:

For surveillance, by nature it's the most difficult area to get traction because the only way to implement things is to convince the authorities that it is something good for them to do. We also try to build a consensus around certain policies, and if most countries are on board with it, we can tell the remaining ones, 'You are the only ones not doing this'. In other areas, we get traction doing cross-country analytical work, but at the end, there is no formal mechanisms in surveillance work to ensure implementation. There is, though, a monitoring mechanism in Article IV consultations; countries need to report on their progress. But that does not necessarily give you extra leverage. (IMF 2)

There is a general tension in most IMF outputs between single-country work (e.g. Article IV consultations) and cross-country surveys (e.g. the Global Financial Stability Report). The advantages of single-country work include the fact that this type of output is much more in-depth and policy advice can be adjusted to national or even subnational idiosyncrasies to prevent following a one-size-fits-all policy approach (IMF 13). On the other hand, many topics in Article IV reports can be off the table because of member states' unwillingness to address them. Certain issues can sometimes be discussed only in a cross-country way that does not name or shame any individual member state. The same logic applies to many studies on the soundness of individual financial centres and the likelihood of their collapse. At times, it is considered a more appropriate approach within the IMF bureaucracy to slowly build a cross-country consensus on certain policies until the countries that follow divergent paths can be openly criticized (IMF 6). As one senior manager put it, 'If you are too weak, you are getting nowhere with your policy advice. Just as if you are pounding your fist on the table, you are also getting nowhere' (IMF 13). Hence, the IMF's relaxing of conditionalities (now called 'benchmarks' in Fund parlance) is a trait of its lending.

In line with this argument, there are many anecdotes of the IMF relaxing conditions or continuing to extend credit to a country that has not fully complied with an IMF agreement. At the same time, noncompliance is often sanctioned, with the most obvious sanction imposed on a country being the restriction of access to an IMF loan (Vreeland, 2003, p. 64). Yet, the threat inherent to such restrictions has been reduced in the era of credit ratings for states, an increased ability to borrow from commercial banks, and to restructure national debts. Against this background, countries increasingly only come to the Fund when they have no other viable option, or where, as in the case of Greece, the funds required are more than the European Central Bank could handle.

Hence, overall, the IMF secretariat carefully assesses in which situations it might engage in open conflict with member states – an approach the IMF shares with the UNHCR. As the 'custodian over the international refugee regime' (McKittrick, 2008, p. 13), the

main duty of the UNHCR bureaucracy is to oversee the implementation of the 1951 Refugee Convention. While this gives the organization symbolic authority to address governments on refugee
matters, it has no formal powers to take action against a state that
does not fulfil its obligations (ibid.). Despite this lack of strong
formal means, the IPA displays a very active style in using its
remaining powers to push its policies. The organization does not
refrain from conflict with member states: 'We are not at all averse to
conflict. Our first orientation is towards our mandate. That is the
role that has been given to us and that we need to fulfil' (UNHCR
10). Despite this role as a 'counterweight' to its principals (Lavenex,
2016), in many cases the organization has to consider carefully the
potential consequences of having a conflict with a member state.
This is because the UNHCR requires the host government's consent
to work in a given country and always faces the risk of expulsion
(McKittrick, 2008): 'One always has to be very careful in the
calibration of what to say and what the risks and consequences
are' (UNHCR 13). Therefore, many times the IPA prefers behind-
the-scenes diplomacy before going public (UNHCR 11, 13). As one
staff member tellingly put it:

Much of our work goes on behind the scenes. When UNHCR makes a public
statement of criticism of a government, it's because we have exhausted each
and every level before arriving at that point. And I don't mean to be collo-
quial, but I always say it's a bit like playing poker. If you get a bad set of
cards, you don't throw them in the face of the adversary and say, 'I don't
want to play anymore'. We need to remain in the game in order to be able to
improve the situation of those we serve. The other thing is that it is true we
have bilateral relations with governments, which is a good way to discuss
problems and issues and try to resolve them, but we also work in strategic
partnership with many, many states and organizations. So, there may be
situations where we say, 'We will not say anything publicly', but we know
that this or that ally and friend will at that point in time make the public
statement. (UNHCR 1)

Here again, the aforementioned strong ties to certain member states as
well as NGOs and other international organizations allow the UNHCR
secretariat to use all the channels at different levels in order to pursue
state commitment to the obligations of the 1951 Refugee Convention
(UNHCR 3, 6, 11).

Overall, the two IPAs under study have developed pronounced administrative routines directed at safeguarding and further enhancing their institutional position. Both IPAs share an administrative style that emphasizes close contacts to external actors as well as their principals and allows for the early identification and anticipation of the different sensitivities in their respective policy fields. This is accompanied by administrative patterns reflecting a sometimes conflictive use of implementation powers.

The IMF and the UNHCR hence have developed administrative styles that come very close to the entrepreneurial ideal type. They have adopted administrative routines that combine strong functional orientation towards policy advocacy with a strong positional orientation towards institutional consolidation. While for the IMF case, this finding can be considered rather unsurprising in light of the structural variables discussed above, judging from a purely structural perspective, we would have expected exactly the opposite the scenario for the administrative style of the UNHCR. How can we explain that the two IPAs have developed a similarly entrepreneurial style despite their outstanding structural diversity? We address this puzzle in the following section.

4.3 The Common Causes of Entrepreneurship: Similar Internal and External Challenges

At the core of our theoretical considerations lies the expectation that the extent to which IPAs perceive internal and external challenges plays a crucial role in determining their informal behavioural orientations – in other words, the extent to which these orientations are more or less directed at policy advocacy or institutional consolidation. If we turn to our cases of the IMF and the UNHCR, we find that indeed, both IPAs perceived relatively high external pressures while internal challenges remained very low. Despite their pronounced structural differences, both IPAs are thus characterized by a similar configuration of challenges, which underlies the emergence of an entrepreneurial style.

4.3.1 Low Internal Challenges to Producing High-Quality Outputs

The internal challenges a bureaucracy faces are supposed to have direct implications for an IPA's capacity to develop and pursue clear and consistent policy targets. Internal challenges hence primarily affect the extent to which bureaucracies develop administrative routines of policy advocacy. Policy advocacy not only presumes that bureaucracies have sufficient time, resources, and space for generating innovative policy solutions (cognitive slack). It also requires a certain homogeneity in dominant belief systems and professional orientations across staff members (uncontested belief systems). As we will see in the following, both the IMF and the UNHCR administrations are confronted with very few challenges and restrictions with regard to their cognitive slack and their epistemic homogeneity. Both IPAs face low internal challenges and hence can develop administrative routines that point to a strong orientation towards policy advocacy.

In the case of the IMF, this first becomes apparent by the fact that compared to many other international bureaucracies, the level of cognitive slack is very high. The IMF bureaucracy – as a matter of fact – can typically rely on very well-equipped in-house capacities, given its mission as a global hub for knowledge on economic and financial issues. In other words, the generation of knowledge, new policy ideas, and instruments is in the very DNA of the fund. At the same time, the combination of homogenous staff backgrounds and a shared economic language results in a low level of epistemic contestation within the bureaucracy. The academic backgrounds of IMF staff are quite similar, with a dominance of highly qualified economists from the world's leading research universities trained in mainstream general equilibrium models (Seabrooke & Nilsson, 2015). Furthermore, due to the efforts to recruit young economists right after graduate school, the organization is able to create a rather homogeneous esprit de corps among its staff by socialization (IMF 6; Nelson, 2014). Although similar professional backgrounds do not necessarily mean that policy proposals are not contested internally, the common professional socialization strongly facilitates bureaucratic policy advocacy (Chwieroth, 2009).

Yet as shown by Moschella (2010, p. 156), policy advocacy of the IMF bureaucracy unidirectionally determines neither the policies and ideas emerging at the international level nor the ones eventually adopted. Rather, the activities of the IMF bureaucracy are subject to continuous transformation through the interaction with the organizational environment (i.e. the ecology in which they are floated). Moschella's insights, however, support rather than weaken our argument. The internal working conditions of the IMF bureaucracy facilitate and favour strong policy advocacy. The bureaucracy is driven by the internal routine of constantly developing new and improving existing policies. It is obvious – and also not the point we want to make in this book – that this kind of bureaucratic policy agency is subject to subsequent deflections and transformations in the political process. Yet the mere fact that the IMF bureaucracy is driven by a strong functional orientation implies that it can be assigned agency.

At first glance, the internal conditions given at the UNHCR indicate a less favourable environment for the emergence of strong functional orientations. Compared to the staff of the IMF, the UNHCR's staff composition is rather heterogeneous in terms of academic background. This follows from the multidisciplinary nature of the issue area (see also Chapter 5 on IOM). In the UNHCR bureaucracy, professional heterogeneity, however, comes along with strong normative homogeneity. The organization is characterized by a very strong commitment to its humanitarian mandate, which provides for a common mindset shared by the entire staff despite different epistemic backgrounds:

> Some people link it to a cult, others don't. I don't think that it is a cult; I just think that there is a very, very strong mandate. I think there is a very strong commitment by all of the staff within this building and more importantly in our field locations and everybody wants to do the right thing and achieve the best results for refugees. (UNHCR 7)

The normative homogeneity characterizing UNHCR staff emerges from the very nature of the IO as a normative organization. Its central legitimacy emerges from its moral legitimacy to oversee international refugee law. As argued by Hall (2013), staff in normative IOs are often strongly committed to the core treaty or the conventions, which give the organization its identity. This creates a common normative understanding that is resistant to changes that could weaken or undermine the organization's identity (Krasner, 1999, p. 5).

This common understanding at the same time affects the nature of bureaucratic policy advocacy. The development of new policies is driven by the orientation to extend the organization's moral authority to new spheres rather than simply adding activities that might bring in additional funds but would detract from the UNHCR's core mandate. This approach can be well observed in the way the UNHCR approaches, for instance, the new problem of climate-change-induced migration (Hall, 2013, p. 104).

Thus, a common belief system makes up for the UNHCR's staff heterogeneity and results in a low level of epistemic contestation. It also shows a high level of cognitive slack. While there is no distinct research unit, the well-staffed research function is embedded in the Policy Development and Evaluation Service and other divisions or units depending on the thematic focus. The organization gathers a large amount of data on refugees and provides a statistical database, meaning that the UNHCR is able to provide the states with selected aspects of reality. It can form the understanding of certain challenges and propose appropriate solutions, hence actively shaping the discourse on migration (Geiger & Pécoud, 2013, p. 876). Moreover, there is much cooperation with external researchers for UNHCR publications and in the drafting of new initiatives and policy papers (UNHCR 4). This provides the UNHCR with the resources to access and process relevant information independently from its member states. The IPA is also able to produce outputs without much interference from its principals. Over time, the organization has shown a significant degree of independence in defining its mandate and adapting itself to a changing environment (Weiss & Pasic, 1997; Barnett, 2001; Betts, 2012). While the UNHCR obviously has to deal with a certain degree of time pressure with regard to its crisis-related operations, much of its work is also based on longer-term projects and goals, giving the staff enough time to develop its own organizational stance on such issues. Overall, the UNHCR displays a high degree of cognitive slack and homogenous normative orientation.

In sum, both the IMF and the UNHCR have in common that they are not particularly challenged internally (in terms of both cognitive slack and low epistemic contestation). These features facilitate the emergence of pronounced bureaucratic routines directed at policy advocacy.

4.3.2 Subjectively High External Challenges Call for Institutional Consolidation

The extent to which an IPA perceives itself to be challenged externally strongly affects if and how it develops administrative routines directed towards institutional consolidation. External challenges can emerge from a variety of sources, including competition within the organizational domain in which an IPA operates and the salience, as well as the political contestation, of issues the organization is dealing with.

A closer look at these aspects reveals that both IPAs under study constantly perceived considerable external challenges. The IMF faces continual challenges to its epistemic foundations. It is under considerable political pressure from member states, societal groups, and the media (Zürn et al., 2012) and thus has to be very entrepreneurial both to safeguard its institutional interests and to promote its policy proposals and initiatives. Monetary and financial-sector policy is a very salient topic that attracts much attention. Although the IMF does not have direct competitors in its policy domain, there are other actors, such as the G20, the Bank for International Settlements, the OECD, and national governments, as well as central banks, that challenge the fund's economic analyses and policy prescriptions (Viola, 2015).

In particular from the late 1990s onwards, the IMF has been subject to fundamental criticism. Its reputation was seriously harmed after its disastrous response to the Asian Financial Crisis, and it was rapidly losing staff. This went so far as that its cousin, the World Bank, began to occupy the Fund's fast-emptying office spaces. In the Asian crisis of 1997, many countries, including Indonesia, Malaysia, and Thailand, were required by the IMF to pursue a tight monetary (higher interest rates) and fiscal policy to reduce their budget deficits and strengthen exchange rates. However, these policies caused what had been a minor slowdown to turn into a serious recession with very high levels of unemployment. In 2001, Argentina was forced into a similar policy of fiscal restraint. This led to a decline in investment in public services, which arguably damaged the economy. The IMF has also been criticized for its lack of accountability and its willingness to lend to countries with bad human rights records. Moreover, in the context of the global financial and economic crisis that unfolded in 2007 and the years following, predominant neoliberal ideas of economic governance, as advocated by the IMF, have been increasingly questioned by several national governments. There is evidence of a 'new world' now populated by increasingly autonomous states in the South, the normalization of capital controls, and fund conditionality programmes that are increasingly criticized for their lack of consistency (Grabel, 2011).

A further indication of these challenges to the IMF is the proposal and establishment of alternative organizations by different groups of

countries that conceive the policies of the IMF to be structurally repro-
ducing rather than reducing inequalities between developed and developing countries (Desai & Vreeland, 2011). In 2011, for instance, the
ministers of economy and finance of the African Union proposed the
establishment of an African Monetary Fund (Asongu, 2014). In 2014,
the BRICS countries (Brazil, Russia, India, China, and South Africa)
launched a Contingent Reserve Arrangement to provide liquidity in
response to actual or potential short-term balance-of-payments pressures (Eichengreen, 2014).

The UNHCR similarly perceives itself to be an organization highly
challenged by its environment. The policy issue of refugees is almost as
salient and politicized as financial and monetary policy, since it also
touches on nation-states' core interests. Hence, the UNHCR faces
much political pressure from its member states and other external
actors. Since its establishment, the UNHCR has been at the heart of
international debates about human rights and international responsibility (Loescher, 2001). The IPA is entirely aware of the many political
sensitivities it has to deal with:

Refugee situations are nothing if not political, that's the nature of it. Yet we
are a non-political humanitarian organization as defined by our statute,
which I think most of us know how to deal with quite well in the sense that
you always strike a balance. (UNHCR 11)

Moreover, the UNHCR is operating in a very competitive environment. Only 2 per cent of its budget is covered by assessed contributions,
and the remaining 98 per cent comprises voluntary contributions that
have to be raised by the UNHCR itself (UNHCR 3). Accordingly, the
organization is in strong competition with other organizations like the
IOM for funds and attention (Betts, 2009; Loescher, 2001; UNHCR 8),
a fact that most of the staff are very well aware of (UNHCR 10,
UNHCR 7). The boundaries between different issue areas and mandates (e.g. refugee issues and economic migration) are becoming
increasingly blurred, and the resulting regime complexity allows states
to engage in forum shopping or regime shifting to avoid the obligations
of the 1951 convention, thus posing new challenges on the organization (Betts, 2013).

UNHCR staff think of the IOM as its major competitor in the
migration policy domain. Both organizations were created in the
European historical context of the post-war period, when millions of

people were displaced all over the continent. While the UNHCR was responsible for refugee protection and asylum, the IOM primarily dealt with logistical and other practical services (see Chapter 5). The IOM should primarily facilitate emigration of Europeans to other world regions in order to avoid overpopulation. The latter was seen by Western states as an obstacle to the Marshall Plan and the reconstruction of Europe; it was also thought to facilitate communist influence (Parsanoglou, 2015). Over time, both organizations emerged as important global players in the field of migration. Although the IOM cooperates with UN agencies and is often perceived as part of the UN system, it is merely a 'related agency' (and that only since 2016) (Elie, 2010; Venturas, 2015; Pécoud, 2017).

Although their mandates are basically complementary rather than competitive, given the IOM's construction as the UNHCR's operational, US-controlled counterpart primarily responsible for the transportation of people rather than for their human rights protection, there are considerable tensions between the two IPAs. While in practice they have been cooperating (Elie, 2010; Koch, 2014), UNHCR staff perceive strong challenges that emerge from the IOM's highly active orientation towards the acquisition of new projects and competencies (see Chapter 5). This can be traced to the fact that the IOM's funding heavily depends on voluntary project contributions. Not unlike a private business, the IOM depends on its donors and projects to ensure its survival (Georgi, 2010).

The above discussion showed that both IPAs under study perceive considerable external challenges. These emerge not only from the fact that they typically deal with politically highly salient tasks, implying higher degrees of attention and scrutiny from their member-state governments. External challenges also have their roots in the rather competitive organizational domains in which the IPAs are operating. In addition to these external pressures, internally, both IPAs are rather unconstrained in their thinking and work routines.

4.4 Conclusion: What Makes IPAs 'Tick' Entrepreneurially?

Existing accounts of mapping IOs and their bureaucracies predominantly depart from systematic assessments of the formal authority of IPAs and, more broadly, their structural setup. We have seen in this chapter that a mere focus on these arrangements falls short of capturing similarities and differences in informal routines of these bodies, that is, the extent to which these bureaucracies – regardless of their formal authority – are driven by orientations towards policy advocacy and institutional consolidation. We saw in this chapter that IPAs might develop similar entrepreneurial administrative styles, notwithstanding fundamentally different structural features. While for the IMF a high degree of formal autonomy goes hand in hand with pronounced entrepreneurship, the UNHCR bureaucracy displays similar informal orientations despite its much more constrained formal discretion.

Departing from this puzzle, we argued that administrative styles are determined less by formal features than by the extent to which an IPA perceives itself to be challenged from the outside and the constraints to which it is subject internally. It is this configuration of challenges on which the IMF and the UNHCR display very similar scores, despite their marked structural diversity. More specifically, we showed that low internal challenges provide both IPAs with enough cognitive coherence and resources to effectively develop and advocate for new policies. Both bureaucracies are subject to only very limited constraints in terms of research capacities and epistemic and normative heterogeneity. These ingredients constitute a highly favourable environment for the development of administrative routines of actively initiating, drafting, and promoting new policies.

Despite this comfortable position for policy advocacy, both IPAs perceive themselves to be considerably challenged from outside. To some extent, this is the result of the substance of their tasks, which are subject to high politicization and salience. However, concluding from this that the nature of the policy field and its politicization were to be a suitable single predictor for administrative styles turns out to be spurious. NATO, for instance, which navigates a highly salient field, exhibits a servant style (see Chapter 7). Moreover, both IPAs face continual competition from other IPAs in their domain, which, in the case of the IMF, have further increased over the last years. As a consequence, neither IPA can afford to merely sit back and do nothing, as this could subjectively endanger their future survival and institutional prosperity. Rather, these challenges led to the development of pronounced positional orientations in their administrative styles. In sum, the configuration of low internal and high external challenges in both IPAs led to the emergence of a fully entrepreneurial style in which strong policy advocacy routines are coupled with routine patterns directed at constant institutional consolidation.

5 | The IOM and the FAO as Consolidators: Struggles of the Challenger and the Challenged

The notion that civil servants in the UN Food and Agricultural Organization (FAO) work towards consolidating their organization's institutional standing comes as no surprise. The FAO has been struggling for survival for more than half of its organizational lifetime (Freitas, 2013). It has been challenged to overcome failures in the past, was unable to establish itself as an uncontested authority in development aid, and was criticized for politicization and ineffectiveness (Shaw, 2007; McKeon, 2009). This led to a downward spiral with important contributors withdrawing money. Within ten years – from the mid-nineties onwards – the FAO's total resources fell by over 30 per cent, and the organization had to let go of a quarter of its staff (FAO, 2007; see also Shaw, 2009). Taking into account the stickiness of administrative styles, it is thus reasonable to assume a pronounced positional orientation. Despite the budget having stabilized somewhat over the last few years and notwithstanding profound recent reforms, the FAO still finds itself in a rather precarious position. Prioritizing the survival and expansion of its apparatus over substantive advocacy hence seems to be a perfectly reasonable reaction to the past decades' turmoil.

Nothing of this sort could be said about the International Organization for Migration (IOM). Quite to the contrary, the IOM's recent history is one of stellar organizational success (Loescher, 2001; Elie, 2010). In the course of the last twenty years, the organization has expanded dramatically in both size and budget. Its membership pool grew from only 67 member states in 1998 to a current 172 as of mid-2018.[1] The increase in budget is even more impressive: while the 1998 budget was USD 242.2 million, the projected total budget for 2018 is estimated at over USD 2 billion, which represents an eight-fold increase (Bradley, 2017; IOM, 2017a). From the outset, there thus seems to be

---

[1] See IOM (2017b).

no immediate need for the IPA to secure or safeguard the IOM's institutional position. Yet as we will show in this chapter, despite these successes, the IOM's IPA exhibits a positional orientation that is similar to the one we find at the FAO.

Both IPAs can thus be characterized as consolidators: they combine pronounced routines directed towards institutional consolidation with only weak policy advocacy. How can we make sense of this similarity in style? It appears that on their own, objectively endangered organizational survival and the associated bureaucratic struggles to maintain the organization do not make for a satisfactory explanation. In this chapter, we argue that in order to come to terms with informal bureaucratic routines in the FAO and the IOM, we need to move beyond single explanatory variables. We show that none of the prominent IPA features – size, budget, mandate, or organizational structure – can convincingly account both for the IPAs' pronounced positional orientation and their lack of functional orientation geared towards advocacy. Rather, as we have argued above, it is the respective IPA's perception of external challenges that make for an orientation towards safeguarding or advancing its institutional position. Where external challenges are paired with internal pressures, which impair policy advocacy from within, we should see IPAs act as consolidators. For the IOM and the FAO, it is exactly this constellation that led to the emergence of similar administrative routines.

In the following section, we show how a number of mostly structural variables are ill-suited to convincingly account for the two IPAs' similar administrative styles. We then go on to describe in more detail how the consolidator styles become visible in the IPAs' daily bureaucratic routines, before returning to the argument made above. Here, we show how the combination of pronounced internal and external challenges can account for the similarity of styles in these different organizations. In the last section, we conclude by reflecting on the broader lessons that can be drawn from this chapter.

5.1 Beyond Organizational Success and Failure: Comparing Structural Features of the IOM and the FAO

By directly comparing the FAO and the IOM in a number of key characteristics, such as their institutional context, their mandate, and their size, this section shows that the two organizations are indeed different, albeit slightly less so than others that are assessed in this book (see Chapter 3). However, we argue that in isolation, their similarities do not hold much explanatory potential with regard to administrative styles.

First, the FAO and the IOM differ in the scope of their mandates. Established in 1945, the FAO is the UN's specialized agency dedicated to the fight against global hunger and malnutrition. Its main aims are to raise agricultural productivity and nutrition levels worldwide, to improve living conditions of rural populations, and to contribute to the growth of the world economy (Shaw, 2009, p. 68). In the pursuit of these goals, it is tasked with the facilitation of international agreements in the area of food security and agriculture, the collection and dissemination of statistical data and information on agricultural trends and developments, and the implementation of country-based development programmes and projects. This comprehensive mandate defines the FAO's role not as an 'aid organisation but as a knowledge organisation with a normative focus working on global public goods'.[2]

The IOM has been established as an organization without an explicit normative mandate. Founded in 1951 as a small logistics organization and counterpart to the UNHCR (see Chapter 4) in order to aid the resettlement of refugees in the aftermath of World War II, it has maintained its focus on technical and operational tasks into the present day (Venturas, 2015). Having originally been consciously founded outside the UN system, the IOM became a UN 'related organization' in 2016. Notwithstanding this status, the IOM is not obliged to work under the UN human rights framework since it does not have a humanitarian protection mandate and is not a legally mandated, treaty- or convention-based organization (Elie, 2010; Pécoud, 2017). Rather, the IOM understands itself to be an operational organization providing services and advice to governments and migrants in four broad areas: migration and development, facilitating migration, regulating migration, and addressing forced migration. In addition to on-the-ground assistance, its activities include the promotion of international migration law, policy debate and guidance, and emergency response.

---

[2] See 'Swedish Assessment of Multilateral Organizations: The FAO', retrieved 3 August 2018, from www.government.se/contentassets/424997a24f644c2 b823bc0b456ec8a15/the-food-and-agriculture-organisation-fao.

One would intuitively expect that a normative mandate comes along with a more advocacy-orientated administrative style. As highlighted by Hall (2013, 2015), organizations with a normative mandate tend to focus on developing the best possible policy options within the scope of their mandate. More functional IOs, by contrast, often engage in policy issues in which they do not possess much expertise, with the sole aim of maximizing their organizations' finances and relevance. Yet we see little substantial advocacy at both the IOM and the FAO despite the latter having a clear normative mandate. Following that reasoning, the IOM's purely operational scope should serve as an explanation for the emergence of an administrative style that favours consolidation over policy advocacy (ibid.). However, this argument does not apply to the FAO. Despite having a more normative focus, the FAO's IPA similarly does not put much emphasis on enhancing the effectiveness of its policies, projects, and programmes but focuses on safeguarding its organizational standing and reputation. This implies that on its own, the type of the mandate does not sufficiently explain why a particular administrative style emerges.

Looking at the two organizations' sizes and budgets, the IOM's immense growth and the simultaneous reductions of the FAO have led to the IOM having almost double the FAO's budget at its disposal; whereas the IOM's total projected annual budget for 2018 is estimated to amount to around USD 2.15 billion (IOM, 2017a), the planned biannual FAO budget for 2018–19 is USD 2.6 billion.[3] After the IOM's surge in membership accessions, both IOs operate on a global scale with near universal membership of 194 countries in the FAO, and the IOM having 172 member states to date.[4] With around 10,000 staff members, the IOM is now approaching the size of the UNHCR (Bradley, 2017),[5] while in 2016 the FAO's administration consisted of only around 3,250 regularly employed professional and support staff and continues to face problems of understaffing (FAO, 2018).[6]

---

[3] See 'Who we are', retrieved 15 August 2018, from www.fao.org/about/who-we-are/en/.

[4] See 'Who we are', retrieved 15 August 2018, from www.fao.org/about/who-we-are/en/ and 'About IOM', retrieved 16 August 2018, from www.iom.int/about-iom.

[5] See 'IOM Snapshot', retrieved 16 August 2018, from www.iom.int/sites/default/files/about-iom/iom_snapshot_a5_en.pdf.

[6] See 'Who we are', retrieved 15 August 2018, from www.fao.org/about/who-we-are/en/.

Again, this difference is not reflected in the two IPAs' similar administrative styles. Although the FAO is in a considerably less comfortable position in terms of budget and personnel, staffers in the IOM, too, show a strong orientation towards positional consolidation in their quotidian work routines.

Both originations are highly dependent on voluntary contributions. In the 2018–19 biennium, 39 per cent of the FAO budget stems from the regular budget through contributions paid by member states, while 61 per cent is to be mobilized through voluntary contributions from member states and other partners of the organization (ibid.). The IOM's work is almost exclusively financed via voluntary contributions. More than 97 per cent of the funding comprises earmarked contributions for projects, with the remaining 3 per cent being the administrative budget, funded by member state core contributions (IOM, 2017a). Theoretically, the reliance on voluntary funding puts IOs under pressure, which should generally favour the emergence of consolidating routines (Graham, 2017). Yet solely considering the reliance on voluntary contributions explains neither the absence of functional orientation nor the emergence of a strong positional orientation, as is shown in the Chapter 6 with the case of UNEP (see also Chapter 4 on IMF).

The two organizations have a further commonality. Their dependence on voluntary contributions and, especially in the IOM, the associated projectization, factor into the structuring of the respective organizations. On the one hand, decentralization could impede the development of a strong functional orientation in that it adds complexity and complicates coherent approaches. On the other hand, decentralization could actually help the IPA have an ear on the ground, making advocacy more rather than less likely; we explore this second hypothesis further in Chapter 6. It is safe to say, however, that one way or the other, this aspect of organizational structure can be assumed to matter for how IPAs work. The two IOs are strongly decentralized, albeit to varying degrees. The IOM is clearly more decentralized than the FAO, both in terms of geographical coverage and personnel distribution. Besides its Geneva-based headquarters, the IOM runs two administrative centres in Manila and Panama as well as more than 400 offices in over 100 countries. More than 97 per cent of its staff are working in the field (Geiger & Pécoud, 2010).[7] The FAO possesses an

[7] See 'About IOM', retrieved 16 August 2018, from www.iom.int/about-iom.

only slightly less extensive country structure with a decentralized network of five regional offices, ten sub-regional offices, and eighty-five country offices. With regard to personnel distribution, currently, 57 per cent of staff are based at headquarters in Rome, making it clearly more centralized than the IOM (Fouilleux, 2009).[8] In their degrees of staff centralization, the two IPAs are clearly different, whereas in geographical terms they display similarly high levels of dispersion. We can hence exclude the former as a common cause of a consolidator style. Regarding the latter, the case of the WHO in Chapter 6 shows that geographical decentralization per se does not necessarily hamper the development of strong policy advocacy. Taken as singular independent variables, both kinds of decentralization seem not to be of much help.

In sum, it has become clear that despite exhibiting the same administrative style, the IOM and the FAO are rather dissimilar in some key structural features. In terms of size and budget, the IOM is certainly bigger and better funded than the FAO, which renders consolidating efforts less likely. Similarly, a focus on advocating for a specific policy approach and the quality and internal consistency of organizational outputs seems to not be fully determined by the normativeness of the mandate (see also Chapter 7 on the ILO). Where we do find similarities, they turn out to be spurious. Taking into account our findings from the other empirical chapters, both decentralization and funding structure turn out not to clearly predict the absence of functional orientations and the presence of political orientations. In light of this, we contend that instead of considering structural features on their own, we have to consider them in interplay. Moreover, we have argued in Chapter 2 that we need to bear in mind that objective, external challenges are filtered through staffers' perceptions. Before elaborating on how the IOM and the FAO illustrate these arguments, in the next Section, we first show how close the two IPAs come to the consolidator ideal type in the empirical reality of their daily routines.

---

[8] See 'Who we are', retrieved 15 August 2018, from www.fao.org/about/who-we-are/en/.

5.2 Consolidating and Gaining Ground: Administrative Styles in the IOM and the FAO

Consolidators are ideal-typically characterized by the prevalence of positional as opposed to functional orientations. Instead of concentrating on advocacy for their cause, consolidators are concerned with their organizational standing vis-à-vis their member states and institutional environments. This should visibly translate into bureaucratic routines. Analysing the IOM's and the FAO's IPAs standard operating procedures over our nine indictors, we see that both indeed come close to the consolidator ideal type. While functional behavioural routines are the exception rather than the rule, we find a number of default patterns reflecting positional orientations. Starting with the positional indictors, in the following we explore the IPAs' administrative styles in more detail.

5.2.1 Positional Orientations: Routinized Efforts to Safeguard the Organization

The IOM and the FAO display very active behavioural routines with regard to their positional orientation, putting strong emphasis on mapping the political space, support mobilization, political anticipation during the drafting stage, and the strategic use of formal powers.

Both IPAs are strongly engaged with other actors, *mobilizing support* for their work. Since the 1990s, the IOM has constantly intensified and broadened its relationships with other IOs, NGOs, and civil society organizations (DFID, 2013b; Georgi, 2010, pp. 56–9). By now, the importance of such collaboration is strongly entrenched in the organization and formally laid down in its constitution as well as in different strategic documents (IOM, 2013, 2016, 2017a).[9] Cooperation and support have been institutionalized in various fora, such as the International Migration Dialogue or the Geneva Migration Group and its successor, the Global Migration Group (GMG), to name just a few (Newland, 2010). The GMG is an inter-agency group aimed at

---

[9] Article 1, paragraph 2, of the IOM's constitution states that 'in carrying out its functions, the Organization shall cooperate closely with international organizations, governmental and non-governmental, concerned with migration, refugees and human resources in order, inter alia, to facilitate the coordination of international activities in these fields' (IOM 2017b, p. 6).

facilitating coordination and cooperation between twenty-two UN-related agencies involved in international migration governance (Koser, 2010; Pécoud, 2013) and constitutes a particularly important venue for the IOM in the emergence of new issues (IOM 9). Apart from these initiatives, even before joining the UN system as a related organization, there has been strong collaboration (as well as competition) with parts of the UN system and the UNHCR in particular (IOM 15; Elie, 2010), for instance through the IOM's having been part of the UN Country Teams for a long time. In past years, there has also been a tendency to cooperate more with non-traditional partners such as universities or the private sector (IOM 16; Michiels & den Boer, 2016), although not all newly established bodies for liaison with business and academia proved to be fruitful in the past (Georgi, 2010). In the IOM, there is no doubt among staffers that the organization simply 'needs partnerships' (IOM 4).

In the FAO, civil society relationships are constantly evolving, too. Because for years the FAO saw itself heavily challenged by various civil society groups as well as academia (McKeon, 2009), there is now a quite strict procedure for determining suitable partners for cooperation (FAO, 2013). Due to the need to uphold the public perception of impartiality, support mobilization happens mostly on the country level. Many FAO country representatives have a very good understanding of the policy landscape in their area of secondment. This embeddedness in the local context allows for and is sustained by close informal ties with the respective national governments, local actors such as NGOs, producer organizations, and academia. Officially, there are relations with as many as 200 NGOs – especially at the local level – which are utilized strategically by FAO country representatives to mobilize support for their work (FAO 7). On the broader global level, the FAO uses cooperation with civil-society campaigns, such as the Freedom from Hunger Campaign, and global fora, such as the Committee on World Food Security, to organize its allies (AusAID, 2012). Although cooperative efforts have been streamlined and somewhat reduced in recent years (Liese, 2010) and criticisms continue, especially about the FAO's cooperation with the private sector, we consider the FAO still to be highly active in acquiring both local and global support and a well-connected point of reference in the world of food security (Johnson, 2016).

Close informal relationships with relevant stakeholders also facilitate the FAO's pronounced efforts in *mapping* member states' key priorities. Alongside the country programming framework process to assess receiving countries' needs, the FAO operates an online platform called ADAM – Agricultural Development Assistance Mapping – where each donor is asked to name its primary funding priorities and policy interests. Thanks to good contacts with committee members (FAO 15, 17), as well as the aforementioned intimate relationships between FAO country representatives and respective government officials (Dionne, 2010, p. 217), such suggestions often succeed, thus opening up new areas for FAO involvement. Moreover, the IPA is very skilful in navigating the sometimes contentious political space, where the FAO has to maintain a delicate balance between the often seemingly irreconcilable interests of receiving and donor countries (FAO 7). IPA staffers do so by manipulating how they frame and communicate policy initiatives to their different stakeholders, as two officials succinctly describe:

Words are incredibly important. Sometimes new words just hide the old approach. And in this we are very [good]. (FAO 12)

You can slant an issue in a way that will pick the donors' interest. Using keywords is very important. Especially with cross-cutting issues, I think you can sell an idea better to a donor if you are aware of what are keywords they are looking for . . . you can frame issues that are not directly relevant to that in a way that is sellable and that makes sense. So it is not really selling something useless, it's rather making the case for something by accommodating the preferences and priorities of donors. (FAO 16)

The IPA regularly puts different spins on the same project to bring actors together. In addition to these rhetoric tools, staffers use their knowledge about member states' preferences and constellations to 'shop' for appropriate venues. Member states are not always monolithic or unitary actors, since they are often represented through various funding actors, like the Ministry of Agriculture and a national development aid agency. Knowing in advance what might resonate with whom is thus often considered to be key to securing support for the FAO's activities as it manages to strategically approach various funding partners, even in the same country (Dionne, 2010, p. 256).

Mapping the political space and anticipating the resonance of their work with their principals are equally vital parts of the IOM's work routine (IOM 16). Notwithstanding the specific topic or region, any IOM engagement is normally carefully pondered with respect to its possible consequences for the organization (IOM 4). In addition to formal mechanisms like council sessions and international fora, the IOM makes use of informal consultations to 'test the waters and see if there is an interest' (IOM 2, 7; Thouez & Channac, 2006). Not unlike the FAO, good personal relations on the country level are a definitive strength that helps the organization to 'have an ear to the ground' (IOM 5). Moreover, the IOM not only monitors member states' preferences but also actively tries to influence them rhetorically and by coalition building. Staff members stressed the importance of framing issues in a certain way in order to 'make it more interesting, or relevant or understandable to member states' (IOM 9) and to sell it as an IOM topic (IOM 13). Another official indicated the need to reach out to certain member states and build coalitions with them, especially at international conferences and negotiations: 'If you don't find governments willing to stand up during the negotiation and propose and highlight issues you are not going anywhere … You need to have countries speaking for you' (IOM 15). The IOM's pronounced mapping activities are in accordance with accounts depicting the IOM's relationship to its constituents as 'business-like', monitoring potential markets and 'customers' (Bradley, 2017). A 'consequence of this market logic is that, in order to sell its services, IOM must identify states' needs' (Pécoud, 2017, p. 9).

In the same vein, both the IOM and the FAO put considerable effort into *anticipating political sensitivities*, and they mediate them as much as possible later on during the drafting process. Throughout the process of IOM project development, there are regular consultations with the beneficiary countries, donors, and the host country or country of transit or origin (IOM 11). The IPA also stays in contact with all involved member states in order to keep them informed and to make sure that planning is going in the right direction (IOM 13). The degree of actual adaptation in the project documents then depends on the respective governments and their needs (IOM 3). Political anticipation with regard to policy development is a bit more complex, as it affects the entire body of members. IOM staff are well aware of possible sensitivities and avoid conflicts whenever possible. Officials stressed the importance of not going into sensitive issues if they are not too relevant (IOM 9, 16) or not using inappropriate terminology (IOM 6). Another staff member pointed out that 'there are ways of testing the waters with governments that might make things difficult' (IOM 4).

Overall, the IOM's IPA routinely detects potential conflicts and subsequently de-politicizes even the more controversial topics of migration governance by using technical frames or harmless 'feel good' terminology (Pécoud, 2017, p. 9).

At the FAO, we observe a similarly high level of anticipation and flexibility in accommodating member states' interests, which staffers deem essential to generate buy-in and more demand (FAO 7, 8, 14, 18): 'If you tread on a member state's toes, you will hear it loud and clear. But we know our clientele, and therefore we can anticipate what works and what not' (FAO 15). Or as another staffer added, 'Sometimes a project that is already fully planned has to be revised because the minister in country X changes and has new priorities' (FAO 14). Usually, the FAO IPA tries to accommodate such last-minute political changes, which often originate from developing countries with a less stable political environment. The IPA often pushes through more sensitive issues like gender or climate mitigation, which have to feature in project documents by rule (FAO 12), by watering down a given output by the simple rule of thumb: 'avoid labelling it, use other words' (FAO 13). Both the FAO and the IOM are hence very active in first anticipating political red lines and – if necessary – accommodating member states' changing sensitivities later on in the drafting process.

Last, with regard to the *use of implementation powers*, both organizations employ rather cautious approaches aimed at maintaining good future relationships with all member states instead of fervently pushing for implementation at all times. Critical scholars contended that 'IOM never criticizes its member-states and is unlikely to resist implementing projects that would be incompatible with its (non-existent) standards' (Pécoud, 2017, p. 9). Although many officials stressed that despite the IOM not being a normative organization, it still has 'principles' (IOM 2), and overall, the IOM is indeed rather passive in the actual strategic use of the organization's possibilities to call out member states' behaviour. As a non-treaty- or convention-based organization, the formal implementation powers of the IOM are quite limited. In cases where the IPA observes clear and stark implementation gaps or defective behaviour of certain member states, it rather relies on media work or information campaigns. To better identify such failure on the part of member states, the IOM has launched information on best practices, such as in the *Migration Governance Framework*, which provides guidance on how governments should manage migration

(IOM 11). 'IOM draws attention to failures to protect migrants ... but has not used overt shaming techniques more readily associated with compulsory power' (Bradley, 2017, p. 103). Most of the staff members depicted this modus operandi as 'diplomatic' (IOM 13), 'constructive' (IOM 3), 'pragmatic' (IOM 12), or 'problem solving' (IOM 1). To avoid too much attention, this is happening mostly behind the scenes: 'When something sensitive arises, the choice is always to discuss this behind closed doors, highlighting the problem but also coming up with a solution' (IOM 2). Staffers reported the conviction that over time, this careful approach would contribute to building trust with the respective member state, which in turn would allow them to slowly turn the screws and gradually change their language, ultimately resulting in positive changes (IOM 1).

> While UNHCR is the one that does advocacy, really pushes the rights of migrants and refugees and puts pressure on states, IOM is the one who maintains the communication and seeks the cooperation with the state. (IOM 12)

In that sense, the IPA's cautious approach is not just a result of the IOM's lack of a convention or treaty but seems to be a deliberate choice, because the staff feel that it is more effective and better suited for the IOM (IOM 1), especially in comparison to the UNHCR, which acts more as a normative 'counterweight' to its member states (Lavenex, 2016, p. 562; see also Elie, 2010).

We see similar behavioural patterns in the FAO bureaucracy. For example, the FAO-run secretariat of the International Treaty on Plant Genetic Resources for Food and Agriculture is mandated to increase the relevant knowledge of its signatory parties on plant genetic resources through offering knowledge tools and technical capacity building or awareness raising. In terms of implementation, the secretariat is mandated to remind deviant countries of their duties and plays an active advocacy role in promoting treaty implementation. However, as became clear during our interviews, some FAO officers interpret this part of their mandate rather conservatively:

> Probably some countries simply don't care about the treaty's implementation and then it is really up to them. Our treaty is, of course, not the only obligation they have to fulfil. There are millions of obligations and important issues to be addressed in this world. They have their own priorities and if the

treaty is not their priority, that is up to them. There is only so much we are allowed to do. (FAO 9)

Another example is the staff from the International Plant Protection Convention, which monitors various reporting and implementation obligations under the convention, for which 'FAO does have a [tracking] system' (FAO 16). In cases where these obligations are violated, the FAO would try to reach a solution by coaching:

It works to some extent, but we are not one hundred percent successful, because the political will has to be there. We will remind, we will try to coach, but we will respect the fact that they are sovereign entities. Of course, there can be disputes between contracting parties, but there is not a dispute with the secretariat. FAO would actually try to mediate conflicts between member states. (FAO 16)

The FAO thus pragmatically refrains from pushing more strongly for implementation at any cost, although it puts strong emphasis on monitoring and has a firm stance *internally* (OECD/FAO, 2016). In the FAO and in the IOM, the IPA clearly prioritizes avoiding conflict over flawless implementation, rendering its use of implementation powers rather cautious and highly strategic, which translates to a high score on this indictor.

In sum, both the IOM and FAO bureaucracies act strongly position orientated. First, constantly on the lookout for new fields of involvement to secure their own institutional survival or expand their activities, both IPAs are very active in mapping the political space and anticipating the interests of their principals. Such anticipation of political interests and sensitivities at an early stage is of immense importance to ensuring political alignment with the political interests of their principals and to subsequently achieve support for their position. Second, they strongly engaged in coalition building with external stakeholders in order to mobilize support among external partners such as NGOs, other IOs, private sector organizations, and academia. Such coalition building can further their institutional position vis-à-vis their principals and often helps to secure funding or the engagement in new areas of work. Third, during the drafting phase, staffers at the IOM and the FAO are keen to anticipate political sensitivities and seek to avoid touching upon sensitive issues as much as possible, framing policy problems and proposals in ways that do not interfere with the principals' preferences. Finally, both IPAs use their implementation powers strategically to avoid conflict that could jeopardize the IPAs' future engagement in the respective issue area or country.

5.2.2 Functional Orientation: Little Interest in Advocacy

The strength of their positional orientation stands in stark contrast to their functional passivity. Regarding *issue emergence*, both the FAO and the IOM are highly active in constantly taking up new issues, hence broadening their sphere of action over time. Taking a closer look at the role that the respective IPA plays in bringing up issues of and on its own, it becomes clear that the emergence of new policy ideas, proposals, and projects in both the FAO and the IOM is driven mostly by member states' needs and wants.

The IOM's IPA does not regularly bring up issues proactively. Due to IOM's project-based structure, topics are mostly set in accordance with donor priorities: 'Of course, what then gives impulse to these ideas, these suggestions, to these issues that emerge is also the funding that is attached, that enables any kind of follow-up activities' (IOM 2). In the same vein, another official described the IOM as being opportunistic and continued: 'We go where the money is ... Which is not to say that IOM doesn't bring up any concepts by itself, but it is clearly dominated by external impulses. We are a member-state organization' (IOM 6). Thus, in the end, the IOM 'can only do what states want (and pay)' (Pécoud, 2017, p. 14).

This does not mean that the IOM does not venture into new topics. Quite the contrary: the broadness of its mandate and the timeliness of its issue area enable the IO to take up a wide array of new issues and constantly broaden its scope (Georgi, 2010; Hall, 2015; Bradley, 2017). Due to the growing importance of migration-related topics, the IOM has lately had many requests from governments, which are then usually prioritized ad hoc (IOM 6). In conjunction with the IO's projectized nature, this further complicates long-term planning in setting the organizational agenda (IOM 12). One official described this situation and its consequence as follows: 'Everybody wants to work on migration, so we have to be less inventive in many ways, simply because there is so much to do, and people want IOM to do it' (IOM 4). Although the IOM has a very broad mandate and thus the possibility to actively cover a wide range of topics (IOM 12), it mostly sticks to issues and proposals that are brought to its attention by member states.

Policy initiation in the FAO is similarly driven by member countries' needs and interests but comes with slightly more proactivity on the part of the IPA. On the one hand, we see a similar pattern to that in the IOM, with the FAO's IPA being highly active in taking up new issues yet rarely any of its own. The use of country programming frameworks in cooperation with receiving countries is a good illustration of this. These frameworks are built around a dialogue with the respective government to single out its national aid priorities and identify its particular demand. This does not necessarily give the FAO much say regarding the choice of topics, but it offers sufficient possibilities for job creation.

On the other hand, the FAO's IPA does indeed occasionally bring up new issues on the global level in its thematic fora, such as the Committee on Forestry (COFO). COFO and similar venues offer member states the opportunity to delegate tasks of a more global nature (e.g. the development of guidelines on the restoration of drylands) to the secretariat. The COFO structures allow the secretariat to submit a secretarial note in which it can name topics the member states 'might ask FAO to work on or not' (FAO 17). These policy ideas are normally strongly linked to global or UN discourses and allow member states to pick and choose new projects and areas. While the IPA does not bring up new issues regularly in national programmes, it does so from time to time in thematic fora. Overall, however, the FAO bureaucracy, too, is rather member state driven in how the organizational agenda is set, yet less so than the IOM.

Turning to the actual policy drafting phase, both IPAs' sophistication in what we labelled '*solution search*' strongly depends on the type of output and donor at hand. Once the organizations have managed to secure a request for engagement, the actual policy or project drafting process mostly follows a rather 'rule of thumb' logic in order to save time and resources.

The FAO bureaucracy adheres to this satisficing logic in a significant majority of cases. Exceptions might be very large projects funded by big donors like the European Union or the Global Environment Facility. These donors come with very demanding project planning prerequisites, which put considerable emphasis on a consistent logical project framework, such as the evaluation of similar projects, preliminary field studies, and risk assessments (FAO 2). The bulk of smaller projects equipped with fewer resources and personnel, however, normally tend to a satisficing approach. Here, staff members rely mostly on their own expertise and experiences and follow a pragmatic 'what worked in country A, will also work in country B' method (FAO 1).

A similar thing can be said about the use of external expertise, which the IPA systematically relies on only under specific circumstances. One of the cases that usually includes a diverse set of actors from various backgrounds, such as academia, farmers' associations, NGOs, or other relevant actors, is the drafting process of voluntary guidelines (FAO 14, FAO 19). In the case of very technical guidelines, for example the voluntary guidelines on fire management, the FAO's role is usually limited to first facilitating technical discussion and then (based on these discussions) producing a draft that is further modified and amended several times by the expert bodies. This draws a picture of the FAO being more of a secretarial body to a group of experts than an expert itself.

When involved in more politically sensitive drafting processes, as in the case of the Voluntary Guidelines on the Responsible Governance of Tenure, the FAO adopts a primarily neutral stance, offering not the one solution they deem best but rather a draft with many brackets and tentative writing that essentially gets negotiated and torn apart by countries (FAO 2). Despite the fact that external expertise helps to bring all relevant knowledge to the table and ideally ensures local buy-in, it can thus also hamper consensus finding, prolong processes, or hamper the development of meaningful policies when opinions differ too much (FAO 2, 17). Overall, at the FAO, both the consultation of external experts and the optimizing of solution-search techniques are more occasional formal requirements than informal routines of the IPA in its day-to-day work.

Not unlike at the FAO, overall, the IOM bureaucracy's solution search can be characterized as rather satisficing. The IOM describes itself as rather 'hands-on' and 'projectized' (IOM 13; Pécoud, 2017). Therefore, project development constitutes the largest part of its drafting activities. However, in recent years, the IOM has increasingly engaged in the drafting of policies or policy papers, too. Here, the drafting process is not very standardized and can happen in any of the four departments. Therefore, solution-search strategies strongly depend not only on the specific outputs but also on the individuals involved in the process (IOM 12).

The IPA's core task – the drafting of projects – is more strongly formalized and laid out in the recently updated Project Development

Handbook, which provides the staff with very detailed and specific guidance on the complete process from the development to the evaluation of a project. The standardized system is meant to ensure that projects live up to a certain standard, and it seems that staff members largely adhere to it (IOM 14). This holds particularly true for large, complex projects for which additional research (IOM 3) or extensive needs assessments are done (IOM 15). However, more often than not, staff has to deal with severe time constraints, especially when it comes to humanitarian action and emergency response, often impeding a more thorough approach (IOM 2, 6). Accordingly, the interviewed staff members characterized the evaluation of alternatives as rather 'ad hoc' (IOM 12), 'practical' (IOM 14), or 'pragmatic' (IOM 6):

> There is constant time pressure. It has to go fast. And there are templates … sometimes, you see some 'copy-paste'. Which is not to say that the people do not put some thought into project proposals or reports, but seeing the enormous time pressure, people try to facilitate their work as much as possible. (IOM 6)

The rather satisficing drafting process is further complicated by a number of dysfunctions with regard to *internal coordination*. Although for somewhat different reasons, staffers in both organizations perceive coordination to be a quite challenging part of their daily work routine. At the IOM, we find a rather fragmented coordination structure, which is likely due to its very decentralized organizational structure and the cross-cutting nature of the very issue of migration. Until the structural review implementation starting in 2009, the field offices were supposed to be coordinated by a rather loose regional office structure with little authority and even fewer resources for coordination or communication within or between the different regions: 'There have [thus] been times when there was a less systematic approach, less control over chiefs of mission and a lot more cowboyish behaviour' (IOM 4).

In response to this problem, the IOM installed an elaborate coordination mechanism, which is based on regional thematic specialists (RTSs) who work in the different regional offices. As most of the project development is supposed to happen at the field level, it has to be coordinated with the responsible RTS: 'So any project that is developed and has implications on [e.g.] labour migration, that regional thematic expert has to approve and if there are any issues, refer to headquarters' (IOM 11). These RTSs meet on a regular basis at the headquarters, and there is a lot of formal and informal exchange (IOM 6). The coordination with regard to policy development seems to be less standardized, but it is still rather extensive:

We have meetings of the senior management and the extended senior management team every week. We have meetings of the policy coordination committee when we also have regional directors present ... There are often different stages at which we consult and then recheck ... So there is a lot of consultation, and the regional offices are very useful for that. (IOM 4)

According to many interviewed staff members, these mechanisms work quite well (see IOM 11, IOM 14). As one official stated:

I have never seen a paper at IOM which has not been coordinated amongst many different divisions, missions, regional offices ... I am not sure whether the result of the coordination is as efficient as it could be, but the active coordination is pretty much entrenched in the culture of IOM. It would be unacceptable, I think, to write something and not have it reviewed by the relevant colleagues. (IOM 16)

Although coordination is now more institutionalized, it is still more negative than positive. More often than not, documents are reviewed rather than coproduced by the relevant divisions or offices. While negative coordination is not a problem per se with regard to efficiency, in the case of the IOM, there are still some more hitches that complicate coordination. For instance, one official pointed out that often, the comments from the regional office or headquarters come at a time when the funding is already secured, which can make it hard to integrate them (IOM 2). Moreover, the IOM is still perceived as a 'franchise' (IOM 2, 4). This means that every mission has to be self-sustained by its projects and that some regional offices are basically independent because of their large number of projects and the size of their budgets (IOM 2). As a consequence, many of these offices dig in their heels (IOM 12), and there are many 'turf wars' (IOM 6) between the different offices and the headquarters. Accordingly, one official stated that 'it sometimes makes you question if this is really one organization' (IOM 12). As far as daily routines are concerned, IOM coordination thus appears to be to rather on the negative side and still exhibits some hiccups despite recent reform efforts.

Similarly, at the FAO, many staff members reported on severe silo thinking between the various departments, for which the FAO has long been infamous (FAO 1, 3, 11, 15). Again, this problem might stem, in part, from the nature of the issue at hand. Agriculture is certainly a contested area for many states, and ideological diversity seems only natural considering the FAO's vastly differentiated membership. Such a diversity in principals' views and beliefs often translates itself into a lack of policy coherence.

FAO is ... schizophrenic. It often preaches contrary things. It is not homogenous and has bad internal communications. For example, FAO has recently published a handbook on organic agriculture while promoting GMOs [genetically modified organisms]. (Interviewee in Dionne, 2010, p. 142)

In order to cope with these long-standing shortcomings, FAO management also undertook reforms to restructure internal working routines towards a more cross-departmental style. The recent installation of new horizontal strategic objective clusters (FAO 18) seems to have brought about some positive change (FAO 3, 12). However, sceptical observers fear that instead of igniting behavioural change, this effort will only replace the vertical silos with horizontal ones (FAO 2, 19). One expert found very frank words for his feelings on coordination:

If I had to score coordination on a scale of one to ten, it's a three to four. It is horrible. Well, it really depends on the teams ... But you have to be fair and admit that it is inherently difficult to coordinate and communicate with ten thousand people. Everyone is totally overworked and on tight deadlines. The best way to know what is going on is to hang out in the cafeteria at nine a.m. and to prick up one's ears. That, however, can give you a caffeine shock and is also very time consuming. Even stuff like our intranet; of course, like any other UN organization, we have such a tool. You get hundreds of articles and documents every day, and nobody has the time to read all that. It very drastically shows you the limits of your own capacities ... It is a nightmare if you want to coordinate a position paper in-house. In the end, when everyone has 'contributed', there is nothing substantial left and you produced one of these typical UN documents that makes everyone happy but has little content any more. (FAO 15)

Moreover, coordination is said to be strongly dependent on the individual willingness of the civil servants involved (FAO 11, FAO 3), and in the end, the review of proposals by senior staff of the department is essential (FAO 13). Although it remains to be seen how the new coordination system will become part of the bureaucratic routine, for now our evidence suggests that the FAO follows a modest model positive coordination by ambition yet regularly fails to achieve this aim.

Reforms at the FAO are not restricted to coordination and structure but also touch upon *evaluation*, which has been subject to repeated critiques (FAO 5; DFID, 2011). As a consequence, formally, the FAO has put considerable effort into improving its evaluation mechanisms in recent years. Many projects and programmes now feature built-in evaluation and monitoring mechanisms, which most staff adhere to regularly (DFID, 2016). However, the evaluation office is comparatively small and ill-equipped given the overall size of the organization, and the projects and programmes it evaluates are usually hand-picked by member states (FAO 5). In addition, the result of this institutional exercise is frequently strongly contested both by member states and within the IPA, which is also the result of difficulties in communicating the activities and results of the evaluation office (DFID, 2016; FAO, 2017).

While the formal requirements are thus fulfilled by the book where possible and when requested, an even more pressing problem seems to lie in the lack of systemic feedback loops and mechanisms for learning from these evaluations. In informal terms, not much has changed since the independent external evaluation in 2007, when inspectors raised doubts about the effective use of evaluation results in the FAO (FAO, 2007, p. 295). Staff reported that monitoring and evaluation is 'much more important and normalized in other organizations' (FAO 1). Even though former projects' end-of-assignment reports are collected in project databases (FAO 6), staff members held the belief that 'these feedback mechanisms are not very institutionalized or too widely used' (FAO 3). We thus consider the FAO's evaluation efforts to be low in both informal and formal terms, since learning is not part of the IPA's quotidian routine, and systemic evaluation still depends on member states' demands and remains contested.

Much like the FAO, in recent years, the IOM, in response to criticism by some of its big member states, has recognized its lack of systematic evaluation efforts and is attempting to tackle it in different ways (IOM 3). It has put stronger emphasis on evaluation and monitoring in the new and revised Project Development Handbook and has been trying to incorporate results-based management by using the objectives and principles laid down in the Migration Governance Framework, which should allow for a long-term survey of measurable impact beyond single activities. However, the organization is still at the beginning of this process, and it remains to be seen how it will play out in the future.

> We are still moving from theory to practice. In theory we should be able to aggregate all the outcomes into what happens at the regional level and how that translates at the global level. But it is still baby-steps we are taking in that direction. Still a lot of work to do. (IOM 1)

Still, evaluation efforts at the IOM are strongly influenced by its project-based structure. Although some sort of evaluation occurs in any project, the depth and quality of the evaluation strongly depend on the project and its specific donor requirements (IOM 12). As evaluation efforts are thus mostly linked to the donor, one staff member pointed out that this makes it very difficult to give a realistic assessment in these reports so as not to endanger future funding: 'This necessarily means that it won't be conducted openly and honestly. You don't look at the real existing problems. It is about presenting yourself in a good way' (IOM 12). Moreover, evaluation efforts are not streamlined as to their form, which could be external or internal and conducted either in multiple intervals or just at the end of a given project (IOM 5). This makes the IOM's evaluation efforts seem fragmentary and of very limited informative value for large parts of the organization. Even though the we see evaluation efforts gradually evolving, at present they appear to be rather low.

We see the IOM's *policy promotion* efforts as similarly evolving yet still comparatively low. The IOM is rather passive in the promotion of its policies and other outputs. Compared to other organizations of this size, the organization has relatively little visibility:

> We tend to be less visible and not as much known as other organizations, in terms of media outreach and for the international community and the world at large to know who we are and what we do. (IOM 11)

Follow-up and media outreach activities vary on the sort of output (IOM 5) and the individuals involved (IOM 16). There are several reasons for this. First, there is a lack of resources for these kinds of activities, especially in the more operational areas (IOM 15). Second, some of IOM's activities touch upon very sensitive issues, and it might endanger the projects and its beneficiaries if those issues were to be publicized (IOM 5). Third, with migration being such a broad topic and the IOM covering such a wide array of activities, it can be difficult to advertise them in a catchy, coherent fashion:

You don't advertise migration. When you talk about migration, you can talk about a number of different things, while UNICEF in that sense or WFP or UNHCR have a very specific target within their mandate and that makes it easy to communicate with very vast audiences or the public in general about refugees, or education and children, or about food … So it is natural that some of these organizations are much more geared to share in a very broad way thoughts or policies, while we are maybe meant to share and to discuss this in a much smaller audience. (IOM 8)

However, many of the interviewed staff members pointed out that the IOM is making a concerted effort to enhance its communication capacity to achieve greater visibility for itself and its work, as well as to improve the way migration is perceived by the wider public (IOM 1, 2, 3, 4). It remains to be seen how these efforts will further develop and how the IOM's currently low policy promotional efforts might gradually improve in the future.

In the case of the FAO, policy promotion takes place primarily through the usual media channels, flagship publications (e.g. the *State of Food Insecurity in the World* report), and at conferences of relevant epistemic networks (FAO 4). However, between the various departments and units, we found considerable differences with regard to both their available outreach resources such as trained personnel and the respective subject matter they are concerned with. As we have seen at the IOM, too, compared to broader narratives of future projects or clearly structured programmes with easily identifiable beneficiaries, very technical issues, for instance, are sometimes hard to phrase in a catchy public relations message.

In addition, effective policy promotion can be hindered simply by the project mandate given to the FAO. As one expert from the field of national policy support explained, often there is extensive capacity support to the requesting partner country only from the policy formulation phase to policy approval in the responsible national legislative organ:

[O]ur role stops at the moment of adoption. Obviously, it is important to look at implementation as well. And there may be other initiatives for FAO to look at it like spin-up or follow-ups from our programme. But not us. We have to stop somewhere. Even though for many developing countries, implementation is one of the main obstacles. For further engagement of FAO, you need a new request. (FAO 20)

This evidence suggests that there is a will to better and more intensively promote policies, but that the FAO needs to be mandated to do so (FAO 17).

   Summing up, we see few institutionalized bureaucratic routines in the FAO's and the IOM's IPAs when it comes to their functional orientation. While both IPAs are in principle interested in attracting new topics, they are rather reactive in the emergence of new issues. Instead of developing their own agendas according to their mandates, they happily engage in the issues brought up by their member states or external actors, without being too critical. In addition, the two IPAs also show much less ambition in the quality and coherence of their drafting of policies and other outputs. Where entrepreneurs and advocates extensively evaluate different alternatives in the search for the best possible solutions (see Chapters 4 and 6), both IPAs rather adopt a satisficing approach using simple heuristics to find solutions that meet the minimal demand. Also, since consolidators put less focus on policy consistency and a satisficing approach requires less horizontal coordination, overall, the two IPAs often refrain from extensive positive internal coordination activities. Finally, with regard to implementation, while they are very well aware of the political implications in that phase, they do not put too much additional informal effort into the evaluation of their policies, and they mostly refrain from extensive policy promotion activities. Taking into account the clear prevalence of positional bureaucratic routines in the IOM and the FAO, both IPAs come very close to what we proposed to constitute ideal-typical consolidators.

5.3 The IOM and the FAO: Struggling to Keep Up with Challenges from Within and Without

How can we account for the similar consolidator style in the FAO and the IOM? It seems that sustained struggle for organizational survival alone cannot explain the emergence of a functional orientation. Similarly, a normative focus does not automatically come with advocacy and a functional orientation on the IPA's part. Conversely, taken on their own, both decentralization and dependence on voluntary funding are insufficient to explain the IOM's and the FAO's consolidator style. In our theoretical framework, we proposed that the consolidator style emerges from a combination of internal and external challenges. Consolidators are thus the most intensively challenged type of international administration, since they are pressured from the inside and the outside simultaneously. In the following, we show how this is indeed the case for the IOM and the FAO.

5.3.1 Pressured by External Challenges

Consolidators consider themselves to be exposed to high external challenges, since they normally operate in an institutional environment that they perceive as highly competitive in securing their standing and resources. Moreover, staffers perceive their own actions to be under constant political scrutiny. These external challenges induce them to manoeuvre in a highly strategic way with regard to their positional orientation.

The FAO's perception of being politically challenged comes as no surprise, given the sheer number of controversies around the organization itself, its policies, and the effects of those policies over time (FAO, 2007; see also Shaw, 2009). In the 1970s, the FAO came under attack from the left especially for cooperating too closely with multinational, agribusiness firms at the expense of the poor (Johnson, 2016). Later, it was criticized heavily by environmental activists and scholars for promoting unsustainable agriculture to the detriment of both the environment and, ultimately, its own goal of eradicating hunger (Hildyard, 1991; McKeon, 2009). While both lines of criticism still reverberate in variations, the often highly political character of agriculture, especially in developing countries, continues to affect the IPA, which has to manoeuvre its course with utmost caution (FAO 20).

In addition, the FAO is still perceived to be under pressure from its member states. As a result of mounting discontent about the FAO's effectiveness and efficiency, the first comprehensive external evaluation report on the organization was published. The book-length document demanded no less than that the FAO completely reinvent itself in a process of 'transformational change' (FAO, 2007; Shaw, 2009, p. 173). Although much change has been achieved already through ambitious organizational reform (DFID, 2013a, 2016), the perception of a political challenge is still widespread among staffers (FAO 3).

IOM staffers perceive similar pressures from the civil society arena, with continuous criticism from leftist organizations, migrant activist groups, NGOs, and academia (Geiger & Pécoud, 2014; Georgi, 2010; Georgi & Schatral, 2012). In accordance with its motto 'managing migration for the benefit of all', the IOM is accused of employing an all too market-based, cost-benefit logic to the subject of migration. The main line of criticism is that instead of advocating on the behalf of migrants themselves, the organization was 'geared towards the needs of a global economy' (Pécoud, 2017, p. 10): that is, it saw its main role to be matching the labour demands of highly developed economies in the global North with the surplus labour force of less developed countries in the South (ibid.). Some especially fierce and normative critics go so far as to posit that this would contribute to a global North–South 'apartheid regime' (Georgi & Schatral, 2012, p. 213). In addition to this critique of over-representing the capitalist interests of rich nation-states at the expense of migrants and their human rights, the IOM is frequently attacked for assisting exclusionary border policies in its management of refugee camps and detention centres (Andrijasevic & Walters, 2010). The IOM is described as strategically glossing over the fact that it mainly serves its rich member states by employing an empty human-rights rhetoric, which is deemed incredible given that the organization is not bound by the UN human rights framework (Ashutosh & Mountz, 2011; Koch, 2014). Although certainly not agreeing with its fiercest critics, the IPA is very aware of these controversies and the fact that its work touches upon many sensitivities.

Political challenges originate not only from civil society outside the organization but also from member states within the IOM, as one staff member pointed out:

I see an area of conflict between IOM's mandate and the political reality that IOM is mostly bound to what member states want and fund. The most influential member states are normally those with the most restrictive migration policy ... That can be a very toxic environment. (IOM 6)

In addition to these political pressures from civil society and member states, the IOM and the FAO are faced with profound domain challenges that stem from their respective organizational environments. Food security and nutrition are complex issues, and just as there are numerous cooperative relationships, there is certainly intense inter-organizational rivalry in the organizational field (Margulis, 2017). In this domain, over thirty international organizations are competing over turf, expert authority, and funding. Ironically, one of the FAO's direct competitors in the UN system is the World Food Programme (WFP), which attracts nearly six times the funding (Lall, 2017). The WFP was originally established as embedded into the FAO structure as a subordinate. It became an official part of the UN family, independent of the FAO, after decades-long internal struggles, which are said to still instil distrust in the FAO–WFP relationship (McKeon, 2009; Ross, 2011). Moreover, as an executing agency of the Global Environment Facility (GEF), the FAO finds itself in permanent competition with other GEF-implementing or executing agencies like UNEP and, especially, the powerful United Nations Development Programme (Andler, 2009; Margulis, 2014). The GEF is an intergovernmental environmental organization that finances project benefiting the environment and the climate in developing countries as well as countries in economic transition, working closely together with a number of IOs, civil society organizations, and the private sector. Competition in the global food security regime is not restricted to struggles over budget and competencies. It also pertains to epistemic authority, because since the latest world food crisis of 2008, the FAO has been struggling to position itself vis-à-vis the World Bank to establish 'which institution is most expert' (Margulis, 2014, 2017, p. 517). Within this crowded field, given the past decades' budget cuts, the FAO is moreover competing for voluntary funding.

Staffers at the IOM also perceive severe domain challenges. Comparable to the FAO, the IOM works in a highly competitive, fragmented, and incoherent environment (Betts, 2011; Freitas, 2013; Koch, 2014). Although the bottom-up structure of the global *Migration Governance Framework*, which emerged in the absence of a hierarchically superior multilateral institution, has been reordered somewhat with the partial inclusion of the IOM into the UN family, the field remains crowded and contested. The organization must compete with a large range of inter-governmental agencies and NGOs for jobs and funding (Geiger & Pécoud, 2014). As migration flows become more and more visible and politicized in major Western donor countries, this trend is likely to continue. 'Migration is a sexy issue … so everybody wants to be in on it' (IOM 4).

Yet the competitiveness that the IOM's civil servants are experiencing is not solely grounded in their need to navigate a crowded field. It also stems from the organization's self-perception as a business-like actor (Bradley, 2017). The IPA sees itself as a service provider that has to maintain a comparative advantage over other organizations in the market by being more efficient and by offering the most convenient services to its 'clients', its member states (Geiger & Pécoud, 2010; Hall, 2016). Even though the IOM has been immensely successful in terms of growth and relevance in recent years, the perception of competitiveness is unlikely to change, since it is founded endogenously in the IOM's self-understanding rather than only imposed exogenously from the organizational environment.

5.3.2 Constrained by Internal Challenges

Internal pressures, which constrain the ability of an IPA to pursue and develop a consistent organizational goal, are determined by two elements: the degree to which staff share a common belief system, and the cognitive slack an IPA enjoys vis-à-vis its principals. Due to pronounced internal challenges, staffers in the IOM and the FAO see their hands tied by a functional, advocacy-orientated routine.

Both the FAO and the IOM have only limited cognitive slack; that is, the lack of resources, space, and time for the development of new organizational outputs. Although the IPA certainly continues to rely strongly on its research output, there are still some restrictions in resources needed to produce them. The FAO does have its Research and Extension Unit, which develops tools and methodologies for agricultural innovation systems, but this research capacity is not replicated throughout the entire organization (Unger, 2019). Although the unit puts much effort into the development of and data collection for the FAO's monitoring indicators, because of coordination issues and resource shortages, the other departments do not always benefit from this.

Moreover, there is a definitive lack of personnel resources. After the most recent budget crisis, many posts remain frozen, leaving an understaffed organization that is no longer able to 'attract the best' (FAO 2). The IPA is thus facing a decrease in expertise and personnel, which naturally has an impact on project design. Moreover, for years, politicized employment policies led to the hiring of staff that was either not up for to task or not familiar with the FAO's 'Western' ways of doing business in FAO (Dionne, 2010, p. 158). In conjunction with the FAO's projectized working style, the understaffing problem also puts the FAO's civil servants under a lot of time pressure, which especially hampers the development of longer-term strategies (CGD, 2013).

Finally, the FAO's staff have only limited space to pursue their own policy goals. The FAO has a rather hierarchical organizational structure established by the thematic committees that approve the various departmental working programmes and must also endorse normative outputs, like guidelines, before they can be passed on to the General Conference for final adoption. This has had profound consequences for how the IPA integrates research into policy making, as Nora McKeon, herself a former staffer, finds:

[T]he idea that a 'safe space' for independent scientific activity can be delimited and defended has proved to be illusory. The scope of the normative activity of institutions such as the FAO is affected by political decisions of the governing bodies that approve its programmes of work and budget. Even the content of normative efforts, or at least the way in which it is presented, is sometimes influenced by self-censorship influenced by what the secretariat feels the most powerful governments are, or are not, likely to find acceptable. (McKeon, 2009, pp. 92–3)

At the IOM, the space to produce the optimal output is less restricted by formal than by informal supervision by member states. Although major decisions have to pass the governing bodies by consensus of the member states, the IPA has a certain degree of procedural discretion, since it can decide not to pass specific policies through the council if those policies are mainly internal (IOM 4). Its overall high degree of autonomy in monitoring goes so far that some IOM member states even monitor the IPA remotely from their own capitals rather than onsite in Geneva (Hall, 2016, p. 90). This does not mean, however, that the IPA is operating unsupervised. Rather, member state procedural control is exerted through the back door of bilateralism (Graham, 2015). In this modus operandi, member governments do not govern through multilateral institutions, such as the governing council, but directly through voluntary contributions. In other words, with the IOM being so projectized, each individual donor can shape the projects, programmes, and processes it funds. Thus, big donors especially can frequently steer and control the IPA through the granting or denial of voluntary contributions (IOM 13). This in turn restricts the IOM in the development of own ideas:

At the end of the day, we are accountable to member states first and foremost and then to beneficiaries ... We are talking about working with states and for states first and foremost. (IOM 16)

In terms of resources, the IOM has invested in its internal research capacities in recent years. There is now a Migration Policy Research Division, based at the IOM's headquarters in Geneva, which conducts and supports research on salient migration topics. In addition, since 2015, the IOM runs a Migration Data Analysis Centre based in Berlin. Again, however, these resources are not put to work across the board. In addition to coordination issues and lack of personnel resources, one reason for this are the time constraints the IPA faces. As the IOM acts mostly in crisis-related contexts and on a project base, staffers operate under almost constant time pressure.

With regard to the prevailing cognitive frames, we find rather contested belief systems and staff heterogeneity in both IPAs. The FAO's staff exhibits remarkable ideological diversity covering a broad spectrum of ontological views vis-à-vis modern agriculture and food security. Agricultural policy is not yet united by a common paradigm but by a multitude of discourses: for example, organic versus conventional food production, matters of genetic engineering, and large- versus small-scale farming. All these contradictory strands of thought are running in parallel in the Rome headquarters (Pernet & Ribi Forclaz, 2019). In contrast to the UNHCR, at the FAO we do not see a strong identification with the normative core of the IO's mandate, which would result in a strong common ground (see Chapter 4). This is also fuelled by the fact that the FAO increasingly employs staff with professional backgrounds as social scientists or economists, which differs broadly from the traditional staff-background profile of agriculture, agronomy, and ecological sciences (FAO 10).

A similar situation can be observed at the IOM. Due to its broad mandate and membership, its staff is very heterogeneous in terms of professional background and nationality, comprising officials from both migrant-sending and migrant-receiving or transit countries, which provides for very diverse epistemic beliefs and representation of national interests. Given that the service provider mindset favours rather diverse projects, which are then carried out by staffers with equally diverse epistemic belief systems, this translates into a lack of policy consistency (Georgi, 2010).

Moreover, in both IPAs we see that epistemic contestedness is fuelled by field-headquarters divides and fixed-term contracting. At the IOM, almost the entire staff is financed through projects, which often means that staffers work on a three-month-contract basis (IOM 6). In addition to elevating the above time pressure, this also makes for high levels of personnel fluctuation. Similarly, short contracts have been reported to be the subject of recurring FAO staff union protests. The development of a unified belief system is further hampered by divides between field and headquarters, which are a function of the IOM's and the FAO's decentralized structures and add even more particularistic perspectives by their very design.

To sum up, both the IOM's and the FAO's IPA can be regarded as highly challenged administrations. They must compete for financial resources while navigating a difficult institutional field equipped with limited cognitive slack and hampered by rather pronounced epistemic contestedness. In light of this challenge constellation, both organizations exhibit a strong positional orientation and their functional engagement is clearly less pronounced.

5.4 Conclusion: Organizational Consolidation after Failure and Success?

The introduction to this chapter showed that the IOM has grown immensely over recent years, while the FAO has been reduced considerably in both size and budget in its struggle for organizational survival. However, as we have explored in detail in the previous section, it is not only the FAO that works to consolidate its standing; the thriving IOM must do so as well. We argued that this similarity in style cannot be attributed to single structural factors but should be seen as a result of the pronounced internal and external challenges that both IPAs need to cope with in their everyday work routines.

Facing pronounced domain challenges, the IOM and the FAO are both very active in mobilizing support and mapping the political space in order to secure new opportunities for involvement. In light of the political challenges they are confronted with, they are, however, still very member state and donor driven when it comes to the initiation of new topics. With regard to the drafting process, they are very sensitive when it comes to anticipating political difficulties, and their lack of cognitive slack often hampers the staff's ability to conduct a thorough search for the best solution when they draft new projects, programmes, or policies. Similarly, but to different degrees, the internal coordination of the two organizations can be described as deficient, even though they are constantly trying to cope with this problem. The same applies to evaluation efforts, which are constantly being reformed but still have a rather low impact compared to other organizations, which might be in part attributable to epistemic contestedness. In terms of implementation, both presented organizations display a very strategic approach in cautiously preventing conflict, instead preferring dialogue and tenacity over strong pressuring means. Mostly due to a lack of resources and the nature of their respective issues, both IPAs are relatively weak in the promotion of their outputs.

Three broader lessons can be drawn from this chapter. First, we see that single structural features of the respective organizations and their IPAs are of not much help to assess the highly informal phenomenon of administrative styles. Rather, this chapter underlines the importance of considering how external stimuli are filtered through the organization, as we suggested in Chapter 2. Although this approach certainly adds complexity at the expense of simplicity, the IOM constitutes a case in point. Though largely neglected by academia and the wider public, the IOM has shown an unanticipated evolution from its beginnings as a small organization outside the UN system to becoming one of the largest humanitarian players with almost global membership. The external challenges it perceives thus do not stem from objective struggles to secure the organization's livelihood but, as we have shown, result from staffers' self-perception of being part of a service-providing enterprise operating in a market setting. What happens around the IPA only becomes intelligible through the lens of this institutional logic.

Second, the IOM's consolidator style supports our theoretical conjecture that IPA administrative styles are not sector-specific. The UNHCR, similarly working in the field of migration and refugees exhibits entrepreneurial style. As opposed to the IOM, which does not feature a pronounced orientation towards advocacy on behalf of its cause, the UNHCR strongly engages in advocacy routines as their functional orientation would suggest. This finding is further corroborated by recent research on the BIS, which has been found to be an advocate in its administrative style, whereas the IMF – similarly working in global finance and economics – comes close to the entrepreneurial ideal type (Knill et al., 2019, see also Chapter 4). In this case too, two IPAs displayed different administrative styles despite working in the same wider issue area. Even though operating in the same broadly defined field could, for instance, theoretically lead to similar domain challenges, and hence similarities in style, these challenges still need to be perceived as such by the IPA. Given these two empirical examples, it is safe to say that it is indeed not the traits of a policy sector per se determining the administrative styles of the IPAs operating within it.

Third, the cases of the IOM and the FAO demonstrate the stickiness of administrative styles. Once administrative routines can be considered a 'style', they are deeply rooted in organizational culture and strongly institutionalized among staffers. They are so routinized in the organization that they are rarely questioned and are, indeed, 'the norm'. In the FAO, we can see how the 2007 evaluation report in the wake of the 2008 food crisis is still considered a relevant challenge. In the course of over ten years, while there has certainly been much formal change, the IPA's behaviour has inertly remained in crisis-mode. Similarly, the IOM has undergone immense changes associated with its rapid growth. Even though these changes are ongoing, it appears that it is systematically strengthening its organizational and policy capacities, which could induce it to become more entrepreneurial in the future. Keeping the FAO in mind, however, it could take decades to gradually undergo a change in style. While this book is decisively not about change, we point out the potential of this future research avenue in the Conclusion.

6 | *Advocacy at UNEP and the WHO: How Expertise and Common Beliefs Shape an Administrative Style*

There are few examples of international cooperation and action as impressive as the protection and recovery of the ozone layer and the eradication of smallpox (Barrett, 2007; Grundmann, 2001). In 1987, all countries collectively banned chlorofluorocarbons (CFC) in household items such as spray cans, freezers, and air conditioning systems by signing the Montreal Protocol. Thanks to the international agreement, the ozone layer of the Earth's atmosphere has stopped thinning and is now even recovering slowly. Scientific projections indicate that the ozone layer should be returned to its 1980 level by mid-century (WMO, 2011). The eradication of smallpox has been similarly successful. The global eradication effort combined mass vaccination campaigns in every country with so-called ring vaccination aimed at those suspected of having been in direct contact with persons suffering from smallpox. As a result of these concerted actions, the last known case of smallpox occurred in Somalia in 1977 (WHO, 1980).[1]

The tremendous success of the Montreal Protocol can hardly be understood without considering the entrepreneurial role of the United Nations Environment Programme (UNEP) in administering the agreement (Sandford, 1994; Andersen, Sarma, & Sinclair, 2002; Bauer, Andresen, & Biermann, 2012). As highlighted by Bauer (2007, p. 15) UNEP contributed to the performance of the ozone regime by its 'strong expertise vested in the bureaucracy and an organizational leadership that maintains a clever balance between keeping a low profile while consistently instigating parties to move ahead'. In a similar vein, the eradication of smallpox and the near eradication of polio is hardly conceivable without the strong engagement of the World Health

---

[1] The last known human victim of smallpox died in 1978 after being accidentally infected in a laboratory of a British medical school.

Organization (WHO). The WHO has been extremely successful in mobilizing people and raising funds. It managed to frame the issue of smallpox eradication as a matter of international concern – and this despite smallpox having been eliminated in most industrialized countries by the end of the 1950s. In particular, the final stages of the eradication campaign from 1975 onwards were financed almost entirely by voluntary contributions of the member states and private donors (Barrett, 2007). Moreover, the WHO provided a range of scientific expertise and advice to the endemic countries suffering from smallpox (Henderson, 2016).

Remarkably, and despite their apparent common capability of solving problems of global scale, the two organizations could hardly be more different when considering their structural features only. We thus argue in this chapter that a central commonality of both organizations is their administrative style. These common behavioural patterns have allowed both IPAs to establish themselves as 'advocates' in the area of environmental and global health matters. As discussed in Chapter 2, advocates are strongly driven by a functional orientation. They are hence not satisfied with merely asserting themselves in relation to other organizations but are spurred on by the goal of constantly improving their policy outputs and outcomes. Moreover, we demonstrate that the emergence of a similar administrative style can hardly be explained with reference to the IOs' structural peculiarities. While the WHO must be considered a central and fully fledged IO, UNEP is often portrayed as being rather small and marginal to the United Nations' system. Therefore, it is not very surprising that the WHO adopted an advocacy-orientated administrative style during all stages of the policy cycle. UNEP in turn suffers from several structural characteristics that, from a theoretical perspective, make it more difficult for the IPA to leave a real imprint on the IO's policy outputs. Given these structural differences between UNEP and the WHO, we explain the evolvement of a common advocacy-orientated administrative style by the existence of the same kind and extent of external and internal challenges.

In making our argument, we proceed in four steps. First, we describe UNEP and the WHO in more detail. Here, we point out that the WHO should be considered a most-likely case for the emergence of an advocacy-orientated style, while UNEP is a least-likely case. In the second step, we show that both IPAs do indeed have a very similar administrative style, and this despite their quite different structural starting conditions. Third, we elaborate on why the existence of only a few internal and some external challenges are the most promising factors to account for the emergence of an advocacy-orientated style in both UNEP and the WHO. At the end of this chapter, we sum up our main findings and discuss the most relevant results. We reflect in particular upon why UNEP and the WHO are overall not as archetypical as the other IPAs assessed in this book, and we consider what this might tell us about our concept, theory, and case-selection strategy.

6.1 The Structural Diversity of UNEP and the WHO

UNEP is the lead agency for environmental issues within the UN family. It was established in 1972 at the Stockholm Conference on Environment and Development with the formal purpose to 'promote international cooperation in the field of the environment and to recommend, as appropriate, policies to this end, [and] to provide general policy guidance for the direction and coordination of environmental programs'.[2] Moreover, UNEP – together with the World Bank and the UN Development Programme (UNDP) – is one of the three UN agencies in charge of administering the Global Environment Facility (GEF). All in all, UNEP is thus supposed to act as an 'environmental catalyst as well as environmental conscience of the UN system' (Haas, 2016, p. 131). The key decision-making body of UNEP is the UN Environment Assembly (UNEA), formerly called the Governing Council of UNEP. It meets every second year to make strategic decisions on global environmental issues. The Committee of Permanent Representatives (CPR) represents the UN Environment Assembly between these biannual meetings. Remarkably, the two decision-making bodies are not similarly composed. The UNEA has universal membership of all 193 UN member states, while the CPR is an open-ended body consisting of representatives from all member states willing to participate. Currently, the UNEA comprises all 193 UN member states, the CPR only 118 countries.[3]

The WHO was created in 1948 as a specialized agency of the UN. The IO's main mission and objective, as stated in its constitution, 'is the

---

[2] G.A. Res. 2997 (XXVII), U.N. Doc. A/8730 (Dec. 15, 1972).
[3] See 'UN Environment Assembly and Governing Council', retrieved 20 August 2018, from http://web.unep.org/environmentassembly/un-environment-assembly-and-governing-council.

attainment by all people of the highest possible level of health'.[4] The organization is thus responsible for directing and coordinating health issues within the UN system and beyond. Accordingly, it sets norms and standards, articulates policy options, and provides technical support to its member states (Burci & Vignes, 2004). Moreover, the WHO has gained substantial competencies in global disease surveillance and control over the last decades (Hanrieder & Kreuder-Sonnen, 2014). All 194 member states of the WHO meet annually at the World Health Assembly (WHA), which constitutes the organization's key decision-making body. The assembly's decisions, in turn, are implemented and supervised by the executive board. The board is made up of thirty-four members, each of whom is trained in the field of health, proposed by a member state, and elected by the WHA. The director general is the administrative and technical head of the WHO secretariat. He or she is elected by the WHA for a five-year term.

Although both organizations were created with the main objectives of establishing a 'focal point' and 'anchor' for international action within their respective policy area, UNEP and the WHO feature quite different structural parameters. In particular, there are four aspects that from a theoretical point of view might be relevant for the emergence of a particular administrative style. These are (1) the overall organizational polity, (2) the supervisory and decision-making structure, (3) the location of the IPAs' headquarters, and (4) its formal autonomy.

Theoretically, one might expect that a basic requirement for developing an advocacy-orientated administrative style is the easy access to trusted sources of information and advice (Weible, 2005). In this context, IOs are in a paradoxical situation: while they are supposed to develop, adopt, and promote 'rules for the world' (Barnett & Finnemore, 2004), they are often situated locally, within a member state, and lack a truly global presence. From this perspective, an IPA's overall polity might be a crucial factor determining the emergence of a certain administrative style; the more an IPA is decentralized, distributing its presence among several of its member states, the easier it will be for the IPA to gather information and make the case for its policy ideas. The WHO, with headquarters in Geneva, six more-or-less independent regional offices, about 150 country offices, and a workforce of some

---

[4] Off. Rec. World Health Organization, 2, 100.

7,000 people, is active and across the globe.[5] Each country representation, though different in size, is led by a trained physician whose role is to work with the national government to implement and promote the WHO's policies and programmes. The country offices are usually located with a country's ministry of health and thus form a crucial link between the international and national levels (Lee, 2009, p. 34). They thus help the WHO acquire relevant information from the local context and to advocate for its policy aspirations. In contrast to the WHO, UNEP is a relatively small IO, with some one thousand professional staff, one-third of whom are located in its headquarters in Nairobi. UNEP has six regional representations but little to no operational presence at the country level. It is thus formally much more difficult for UNEP to directly address and have exchanges with member states' administrative staff, gather information, and push for action in its area of concern.

The WHO's structure brings both advantages and disadvantages. Critics argued, for example, that the WHO's geographical dispersion and strongly federalized structure inter alia impeded an adequate reaction to the 2014 Ebola outbreak as a result of coordination problems between the headquarters, the regional representation in South Africa, and the country offices in the epidemic countries (Kamradt-Scott, 2016). We made this exact argument in the previous chapter with regard to the FAO and the IOM, and it became clear that staff decentralization in itself cannot be a convincing predictor for a lack of informal agency in functional orientations. In this chapter, we thus turn to the competing hypothesis that decentralization can strengthen functional orientations. In light of this argument, as discussed in more detail below, the Ebola crisis can be considered an exceptional situation 'characterized by pervasive uncertainty, mistruths, and obfuscation' (ibid., p. 409) and thus cannot tell us much about the WHO's underlying standard operating procedures. In sum, it seems reasonable to expect that the WHO's global presence benefits the emergence of an administrative style that aims at policy advocacy. For UNEP's narrow operating radius, we can expect the exact opposite scenario.

Also, the emergence of an administrative style might very well be related to the amount of effort administrators must invest when dealing

---

[5] See 'Who we are', retrieved 22 August 2018, from www.who.int/about/who-we-are/en/.

with their superiors and how clear and consistent the signals are that administrators receive from above. In this regard, another marked contrast can be found between UNEP and the WHO. In most cases, international organizations are governed by an assembly responsible for establishing broader policy priorities and a smaller group charged with more executive and operational responsibilities (Hooghe & Marks, 2015). This is exactly how the WHO is organized. Here, the WHA sets the broader policy priorities while the executive board, elected by the WHA, manages and supervises their implementation. At UNEP, by contrast, the CPR is not elected by the key decision-making body (the UNEA). Rather, the CPR includes all countries willing to attend and participate, as well as agencies of the European Union related to environmental matters. As a result, the IPA must essentially serve two masters and two constituencies. This situation is further aggravated by the fact that the person representing a country at the CPR is typically not the same one attending the UNEA (Ivanova, 2009). In other words, although a permanent representative might have worked and supported a particular project or policy proposal for months, under the existing decision-making arrangement, her recommendations can be easily contested by a political superior. For the IPA, this unnecessarily hampers effective communication and planning since it creates a duplication of efforts when facing conflicting policy priorities and preferences (ibid.).

One further aspect that might impede the emergence of an advocacy-orientated administrative style is the location of the IPAs' headquarters. UNEP's headquarters are located in Nairobi, Kenya. Based on a spatial analysis of all international organizations working on environment-related issues, Ivanova (2009) shows that Nairobi is 'located far outside any political "hot spot"' (p. 167). Given the strong geographical isolation and the resultant the lack of face-to-face interactions with administrators from other relevant UN or environmental operations, the IPA must invest extra effort to effectively coordinate and catalyse environmental policies and actions within the UN systems (ibid.). It is questionable whether the location of the Division of Technology, Industry, and Economics in Paris can effectively overcome these shortcomings for the entire organization. The WHO secretariat, by contrast, is located in Geneva, Switzerland. Geneva hosts more than twenty UN organizations, programmes, and funds and therefore can be regarded as one of the 'leading centres of international cooperation' (Hensler, 2005, p. 2).

While the above-presented structural features seem to benefit the emergence of an advocacy-orientated style at the WHO but not at UNEP, the picture is somewhat different when considering the organization's formal autonomy. According to Manulak (2017), UNEP 'emerged as an organization with weak institutional standing [but] a secretariat with a high degree of formal autonomy' (p. 498). This is primarily due to the fact that the developed countries wanted to avoid the interference of developing states in the IPA's work that could obstruct the organization's efforts to tackle mounting environmental problems (ibid.). Ironically, this very autonomy was perceived to be problematic by developed countries later on when UNEP committed itself strongly to the fight against climate change and greenhouse gas emissions (Haas, 2008). The WHO, by contrast, ranks among the organizations that have only a mediocre level of formal autonomy (Bauer & Ege, 2017; Ege, 2019). As discussed in more detail below, although the WHO has been granted substantial sanctioning competences when it comes to enforcing compliance with its international health regulations (IHR), it possesses quite restricted agenda-setting competencies (ibid.). This difference in the degree of formal autonomy, however, strengthens rather than weakens the overall argument made in this book; in line with the findings made in Chapters 4 and 7, it shows that formal autonomy alone cannot explain why some IPAs develop bureaucratic routines aiming at policy advocacy while others do not.

6.2 Administrative Styles in UNEP and the WHO: Common Advocacy-Orientated Bureaucratic Routines Despite Structural Differences

Taking only their structural features into account, UNEP and the WHO should thus actually *not* have much in common. As indicated in the previous Section, the WHO bureaucracy is overall in a position quite favourable to developing an administrative style that strongly emphasizes activities related to improving the quality and effectiveness of the IO's organizational outputs. UNEP, by contrast, must overcome several adverse structural conditions that might prevent the IPA from establishing itself as a viable advocate for environmental matters. Such duplicative decision and supervisory structures, along with the relatively peripheral location of its headquarters, function to spatially bar the IPA from most international affairs. Yet, remarkably, we find that the bureaucratic routines of *both* IPAs are very much advocacy-driven. In other words, both IPAs, although to varying extents, have developed profound day-to-day practices of promoting their own policy ideas and proposals, solution search, internal coordination, policy promotion, and policy evaluation. This, however, does not necessarily imply that IPAs can completely forego paying attention to the political implication of their actions or the overall standing of their organization.

6.2.1 Functional Orientations: Pushing for Changes

UNEP features a decidedly active and entrepreneurial style when it comes to the *identification of new policy issues*. By its very institutional DNA, UNEP is supposed to bring up new environmental issues and trends emerging on the global scene. These new issues and trends, in turn, feed back into the definition of the four-year mid-term strategy (MTS) and the biannual Programme of Work (PoW). Given that both the MTS and the PoW need to be approved by one of UNEP's key decision-making bodies, the UNEA or the CPR, it goes without saying that the set of policy objectives has to run through a process of intergovernmental approval and scrutiny in which member states have the ultimate say (UNEP 5). Yet the IPA seems to be quite confident about its own influence on the internal agenda-setting process. This is particularly the case with UNEP, which has a Division of Early Warning and Assessment (DEWA) that is exclusively responsible for collecting, collating, and analysing data on the state of the global environment and for identifying new and arising environmental issues that require international policy actions and attention:

Obviously we are donor driven. They do have a say in the end, but they also look at what we advocate … But because the field of the environmental policy dimension is so wide, UNEP has a very huge role to play in pushing an agenda for work. We know what is happening, what the emerging issues are, primarily from the DEWA. So we can clearly push certain issues on the agenda. (UNEP 3)

In contrast to the patterns observed for UNEP, most policy issues do *not* emerge from within the WHO bureaucracy:

Basically, we do what the member states tell us to do ... Most of our work comes from the countries that give us the marching orders to move into a certain direction. Sometimes I truly envy my colleagues of the European Commission, because they decide for themselves what they want to do next. We simply cannot do this. (WHO 9)

In extreme cases, the organization even has to deal with issues that are of only marginal importance for the IPA itself but of particular concern for influential individuals within the member states. For instance, the WHO addressed the issue of autism after Sheikh Hasina, Bangladesh's prime minister, publicly called upon the WHO to take action on this matter (WHO 7). A similar process was also reported regarding the issue of road safety:

Road safety would never have landed on our priority list – at least not from our side. In fact, it was a very small niche programme called avoidance of involuntary injuries. But suddenly, 100 million dollars came, then another 50 million, and so on. And then a whole policy programme was set up – and this was actually quite successful. (WHO 3)

Comparable cases can be found in the literature about the WHO's action on pharmaceuticals (Mingst, 1990) and breast-milk substitutes (Sikkink, 1986). This passive attitude towards the identification and promotion of new health issues is at clear odds with the otherwise highly functional orientation characterizing the WHO's bureaucratic routines. A possible explanation for this striking behavioural pattern that most interviewees referred to – apart from the restricted agenda-setting competencies – is the joint medicine doctrine dominating the organization. In this context, it has been highlighted that physicians are often simply not accustomed to taking action on their own, acting only when patients visit and in response to immediate requests (WHO 2, 7).

Yet the fact that the WHO is usually characterized by a functional orientation becomes quite evident when shifting the focus to how the IPA *searches for different solutions* in policy drafting. First, before any concrete measure is taken, the WHO usually engages in a comprehensive data-collection process, either by its own research units (WHO 9) or by commissioning reviews and reports from external providers (WHO 4, 6). Based on the information gathered, the IPA develops concrete measures based on feasibility and country- or context-specific factors:

Let us take again the example of our global road safety programme. First, we collected data from all countries – also variables on socio-cultural peculiarities such reckless driving, and so forth. And all this is then incorporated in the guidelines. It is a fascinating process. (WHO 3)

Second, when developing guidelines and norms, the WHO bureaucracy follows a holistic and systematic approach. The internal Guidelines Review Committee provides a handbook that offers step-by-step guidance on how to plan, develop, and publish guidelines meeting the WHO's internal standards. The intent of the handbook is to ensure that the WHO's policy recommendations are accurate and meet the best standards possible in terms of both content and method (WHO 3). Sinclair et al. (2013) found that the guideline manuals are widely accepted and applied across the administration and that they do indeed help improve the quality of the WHO's organizational outputs.

When thinking of developing a guideline, there are a number of issues to address … As for the assessment, and the question of which factors go into it, there is an internal handbook for developing guidelines that lays out the consideration you should take into account and take a look at. The evaluation criteria are primarily effectiveness and safety … Moreover, we focus on quality and the issue of equity … For sure, there is a trade-off between all these different considerations in practice, and you often have much more data available on the hard stuff rather than on which options patients prefer as well as on the aspects of equity … But there is a decision-making table, and we go through this one by one. (WHO 4)

Much like in the WHO, UNEP administrators also engage in quite sophisticated strategies of solution search when they are about to draft a proposal or to start a new project. They rely on planning methodologies such as the logical framework approach or risk and impact assessments (UNEP 20, 22). Simply put, the logical framework approach provides a 'convenient overview of project objectives and encourages attention to possible higher-level justifications, external conditions, and the information needs of monitoring and evaluation' (Gasper, 2000, p. 17). Moreover, the administrators find guidance in internal project manuals that foresee a long checklist of aspects that need to be considered during the drafting procedure (UNEP 20). Yet, in slight difference to the WHO, it appears that the respective practices are not fully established and integrated across the organization. Our interview partners stated that some of the organizational outputs are more of a normative nature and thus are in fact unfeasible to plan and assess by using more advanced, often quantitative, decision-making tools (UNEP 3). In other instances, advanced methods of solution search were simply deemed to be too expensive and resource intensive for such a relatively small IPA as UNEP (UNEP 17). Hence, we can stipulate that UNEP tries to be as optimizing as it can with regard to solution search in informal terms, yet sometimes it is limited structurally by both its available resources and the very nature of its outputs.

Internal coordination appears to be rather a challenging issue in the WHO bureaucracy in general. This is true for two reasons. First, the dependence on external funding has led to a vertical segmentation of the programmes. Although some global health issues and diseases are similar and thus could be easily and more effectively addressed by the same division or department, they are often addressed by distinct and separated programmes to be better suited for attracting earmarked funds from donors (WHO 1, 3, 6). Second, the highly decentralized structure of the WHO bars the way to better coordination.

We hope that the trinity we are composed of allows us the optimal implementation of our priorities across all level, namely the country, regional, and global level ... However, from all my experience, the UNHCR is definitely fitter. They have to respond much more quickly and directly to the political ups and downs. They are fitter and more capable – and this is due their internal structure. (WHO 3)

Yet it seems that most WHO administrators have developed behavioural patterns that allow them to deal with the adverse structural conditions they face. Several interview partners – in particular those at the more operational level – emphasized that they have built their own personal networks across the organization through which they coordinate and gather the information they need (WHO 6, 9).

Informal approaches are my main channel ... I always try to find out who does what first and my informal network helps me a lot with this. It is much easier to do that informally as the WHO is so large and because the regions are organized so differently. (WHO 9)

Following the same logic, another interview partner reported, 'I made a virtue out of necessity. So whenever I go somewhere, during holidays for instance, I just go to the WHO address, ring the bell, and introduce myself' (WHO 3). Such tight personal networks within the organization are not a necessarily a crucial feature of a functional orientation but the emphasis placed on this matter by WHO civil servants illustrates the substantial efforts they invest in overcoming the obstacles of the structures they are embedded in.

Similar occasional efforts to deviate from the default mode of negative coordination can also be identified in UNEP. Here, projects are formally coordinated by the responsible task managers within the respective subprogramme the project is aligned to. Yet as many interview partners claimed, it strongly depends on the different projects and their leaderships how rigorously this provision is adhered to in practice (UNEP 5, 9, 10, 19): 'In our internal PoWs, projects we are supposed to identify other divisions or regional offices you'll be working with. So where applicable we have dialogue. But typically, it will be structured more on a needs-basis' (UNEP 5). In neither the WHO nor UNEP do we thus find a clear pattern of bureaucratic routines when it comes to internal coordination, which is why we consider their regular efforts to be medium.

When it comes to *policy promotion*, UNEP follows a highly differentiated approach. On the one hand, much of its public outreach rests on the publication of scientific factsheets, best practice stories, and on presentations at academic conferences (UNEP 8; see also Cardesa-Salzmann, 2016). This allows the IPA to put pressure on individual countries by 'simply bringing [up] the evidence ... from a position of strength' (UNEP 8). On the other hand, the IPA uses its central position within the epistemic community of global environmentalist to raise awareness for environmental issues and what can be done about them (UNEP 13). Accordingly, the institutional assessment report of the Multilateral Organization Performance Assessment Network (MOPAN) (2017) summarized that UNEP strongly 'leverages [its] partnerships and catalyses resources to deliver results at the national level' (p. vii). In the same vein, Haas (2008) reports that the United States and other industrial nations deliberately excluded UNEP from becoming more deeply involved in the United Nations Framework Convention on Climate Change (UNFCCC), knowing that the IPA would aggressively campaign for complying with the climate goals (see also Haas & McCabe, 2001).

Not unlike UNEP, the WHO puts much effort into promoting its policies. It does so in several ways, including by consulting its own technical staff in the member states to identify bottlenecks and possible drawbacks that need to be overcome (WHO 6) and by providing local groups with the information and expertise necessary to enable them to demand action from their governments. For instance, one of the interview partners highlighted that the IPA deliberately arranges country rankings based on performance rather than on their alphabetic order – and this quite often even against the explicit will of the poorly performing member states (WHO 6). All in all, both UNEP and the WHO thus try to enhance the impact and effectiveness of their programmes through strategies of both capacity building and policy promotion.

The strong functional orientation of both IPAs also becomes apparent in the system of *policy evaluation*. The WHO has an independent evaluation unit that focusses primarily on the analysis of output data when assessing the influence of the WHO's policies. It regularly evaluates the accessibility and comprehensibility of its guidelines and other organizational outputs by determining whether member states and non-state actors apply them in practice and consider them as useful or not; it does *not* make statements about whether guidelines and norms eventually led to a reduction of the number of people suffering from a certain disease (WHO 7). This distinct focus can be attributed to the scientific and technical spirit characterizing the organization.

Our influence only goes to the outputs ... I know that the Global Fund says one hundred thousand cases of malaria have been prevented due to our work. But we are much stricter. We cannot say exactly how many people the WHO rescued. For us it is the key question how our policy transfer into practice ... This is an organization of physicians, and as part of the Hippocratic Oath, doctors are not allowed to advertise. You will rarely find a doctor who says, I have made twenty-five appendicitis operations last year, and it all went perfectly. (WHO 7)

In its latest report on the WHO, MOPAN (2013) attested that the IPA is doing quite 'well in using performance information to revise and adjust policies and manage poorly performing initiatives.'[6]

---

[6] Other reports are more critical (see for instance JIU 2012). However, more recent organizational reforms have moved the evaluation function from the responsibility of the Office of Internal Oversight Services to stand alone as part of a new unit called Evaluation and Organizational Learning.

At UNEP, there is a similarly elaborate evaluation system in place (UNEP 5, 11). Still, the evaluation office is rather small and hence has to prioritize which programmes and projects should be evaluated.

Everything in UNEP is subject to evaluation but there are hundreds of projects. So trying to evaluate everything is a challenge and does not necessarily add a lot of value. You have to look at what are the returns to UNEP from doing that evaluation in terms of accountability and learning. (UNEP 18)

Additionally, the evaluation often has to deal with very weak information that renders assessments, particularly those of more normative organizational outputs, inherently complicated (UNEP 18). The IPA thus has formal evaluation practices and standards in place, but because of resource constraints, they are not consistently applied across the entire organization and for all of its organizational outputs.

In sum, both bureaucracies have developed a range of behavioural routines that clearly reflect the IPAs' overall functional orientation. Nonetheless, there are also some differences between the UNEP and WHO bureaucracies. While we do not find pronounced patterns of idea generation within the WHO bureaucracy, UNEP's IPA acts as an influential agenda setter in the global discourse on environmental policy. This image of UNEP's bureaucracy as an agenda-setting power is widely shared in the existing literature – even among scholarly contributions that are otherwise quite reluctant to praise the organization's overall performance (see for instance Downie & Levy, 2000; Tarasofsky, 2002). With regard to the other activities assessed, the standard operating procedures guided by the desire to enhance the policy effectiveness of the organization are equally or even more pronounced within the WHO bureaucracy.

6.2.2 *Positional Orientation: Standing on Not So Solid Ground?*

In the previous Section, we showed that both IPAs feature a strong functional orientation in their administrative styles. This pattern, however, does not mean that the IPAs completely disregard the political consequences of their policy proposals, projects, and actions. Accordingly, the UNEP secretariat not only emphasizes the development of new policy ideas but also checks for their political feasibility during the initiation phase. The *mapping of the political space* is thus also a relevant activity for the bureaucracy:

It is important to know the needs and priorities of our main clients, only then we are policy relevant [so] we are continuously in dialogue with governments in our organizational processes. (UNEP 8)

By taking part in the consultation processes of other IOs and by engaging in so-called regional visioning exercises, the IPA tries to stay abreast of its constituents' needs and priorities (UNEP 1, 20). In essence, a visioning exercise is a participatory approach that is frequently used in the context of environmental planning and resource management during which national governments or local communities are asked to think about a desirable future and to reflect upon the different steps it takes to achieve this vision (Davies, Doyle, & Pape, 2012).

In slight difference to UNEP, at the WHO we cannot identify clear patterns of administrative behaviour directed at the mapping of the political space. On the one hand, because the WHO depends on the support of its member states, it tries to take account of their needs and demands wherever possible (WHO 2). This is particularly the case when issues touch upon deeply rooted cultural beliefs concerning the causes and treatment of health issues such as HIV or mental health problems (WHO 1, 4). On the other hand, the quite technical nature of the IPA's work seems to prevent a more sensitive approach towards policy initiation (WHO 3, 5). Moreover, it was highlighted that the biomedical approach that dominates and is followed by most expert committees hinders the administrators who are involved from being fully aware of the social and political implications of their work (WHO 5). These internal contradictions within the WHO bureaucracy are perhaps best summarized by the statement that it often seems as if the WHO has 'enough technical and medical experts but not enough managers' (WHO 6).

With respect to *support mobilization* and the engagement with external actors, UNEP can draw on a vast global network of people and institutions all concerned with protecting the environment (UNEP 8). UNEP is said to be in an ongoing and fruitful exchange with these actors. As discussed above, this network helps UNEP to acquire the information it needs when it is about to adopt and design new policies and to ensure that they are also properly promoted. However, UNEP's outreach to non-governmental organizations, the broader civil society, and academia does not always take the form of real coalition building (UNEP 5). Our interviewees highlighted that their partners often either support a certain issue or they do not; they do not have to be encouraged or convinced to do so (UNEP 5, UNEP 8).

A somewhat more active style was reported for the WHO. Here, it was said that the IPA often receives 'orders' from (some of) the member states to deal with particular topics *before* the process of political opinion formation has actually been completed. It is thus the job of the WHO to find and build coalitions to guarantee the support for the issues the IPA is dealing with (WHO 4). In the context of the WHO's work, this usually involves dialogue and exchange with experts and representatives from civil society:

Our main role is to bring people together ... You formulate a group of experts, these are not just clinicians, there are representatives from civil society, groups that are affected, somebody from an NGO promoting drug-users' rights for example. And you need geographical distribution. (WHO 4)

In the same vein, the WHO bureaucracy also puts some efforts into *anticipating political sensitivities*. It does so by framing issues in a way that they do not touch upon too many sensitivities or harm the legitimacy and financial health of the organization. In this context, one of our interview partners highlighted:

All IOs in the area have developed effective framing strategies ... And why? Because they managed to create striking images. And this allowed them to tap billions [in] financial support. The WHO noticed that too and worked on its communication. (WHO 1)

Accordingly, when the WHO required further resources to start its 'endgame' campaign against polio, it 'spun the issue in a way to ensure continued support for the programme us[ing] framing strategies to make sure that all donors know what is at stake' (WHO 4).

Such political sensitivity is even more pronounced at UNEP. Here, staffers repeatedly stressed the importance of being responsive to member states' needs and to managing the IPA's projects and activities in an adaptive manner:

You have to manage your projects adaptively and anticipate. We always incorporate [governments'] concerns if it makes sense for the project and there is no major deviation. (UNEP 15)

Another common view among the staffers is that UNEP has different roles to play. Sometimes, UNEP simply functions as a neutral producer of scientific information and evidence, leaving the discussion completely to the member states. In other instances, the IPA has to serve specific political ends:

[In these situations] . . . you have to think about how you get to the end result and when there are sticking points, you need a strategy for dealing with them. Then you have to be much more pragmatic and tactical because you have a specific outcome in mind. So, it depends on the role the organization is playing and there will be instances of both neutrality and more strategic ones. (UNEP 18)

In sum, these statements reflect an overall rather high degree of functional politicization, an awareness of various role identities, and a general understanding of the existence of political redlines and a need to pay attention to these.

The WHO possesses substantial *formal enforcement powers* when it comes to overseeing its international health regulations (IHR). The IHR are a legal instrument that is binding for all member states. Their aim is to prevent and respond to acute public health risks that have the potential to spread and thus to threaten people worldwide. In this context, the IPA can impose sanctions or embargoes to ensure that all countries collaborate in sustaining global health security. Accordingly, the WHO must be considered a true 'decisionist authority' (Hanrieder & Kreuder-Sonnen, 2014, p. 331) when it comes to emergency governance in global health and, at least formally and more generally, one of the 'world's most powerful international organizations' (Chan, 2010). Together with the IMF (see Chapter 4), the WHO is thus the only organization in our sample that possesses substantial formal powers to force members to comply with its policies. Yet the crucial question in the context of administrative styles is not if IPAs formally possess the respective formal power but whether they also tend to make full *use* of their formal power.

Over the last decade, the WHO declared public health emergencies of international concern in response to four cases. These are the H1N1 influenza pandemic (also known as swine flu), the setbacks in global polio eradication efforts, the Ebola outbreak in West Africa, and the Zika Virus in Brazil, which later spread to other parts of South and North America. Taking a closer look at those instances in which the

WHO declared a so-called public health emergency of international concern (PHEIC), it becomes apparent that the IPA generally did not refrain from open conflicts with its member states (Cortell & Peterson, 2006; Fidler, 2009; McNeil Jr, 2014). In this context, the WHO's management of the SARS (severe acute respiratory syndrome) outbreak can be considered the most outstanding example (Hanrieder & Kreuder-Sonnen, 2014). Here, the WHO publicly denounced countries that did not follow the recommendations suggested by the IPA (Loh, Galbraith, & Chiu, 2004) and published travel warnings for the pandemic states (Heymann & Rodier, 2004). This is particularly remarkable, since at that point in time, the IPA did not yet possess the formal power to take such actions (Fidler, 2004, p. 268). In fact, the WHO's members only ex post legitimized the measures taken by the IPA by reforming the codification of its emergency powers (Zacher & Keefe, 2008). As was pointedly highlighted by Cortell and Peterson (2006), '[t]he IO's professional staff of medical and public health advocates [thus] sought to do what was necessary to stem the epidemics of infectious disease, not to follow the political dictates of its principals' (p. 271). In other words, the IPA's actions preceded the extension of its formal mandate. Given these insights, the WHO's 'too little, too late' reaction to Ebola must be seen as the exception rather than the rule regarding the WHO's otherwise quite rigid use of its formal powers. Although some of the WHO's management dysfunction in the context of the Ebola outbreak can be directly attributed to the IPA's customary practices in dealing with its highly autonomous regional representations, budget cuts and efficiency savings in the immediate year prior to the Ebola outbreak had temporarily undermined much of WHO's emergency response capacities (Kamradt-Scott, 2016; WHO 2).

UNEP was initially established as a focal point for environmental action in the UN system. Accordingly, and in contrast to the WHO, UNEP does not have any form of formal power. As highlighted by Palmer (1995) 'UNEP can push states, probe their policies, and plead with them; it cannot coerce them. UNEP lacks teeth' (p. 48). The most 'authoritative' force that UNEP can thus use to enforce compliance with its policy visions is to release information on environmentally poorly performing countries. Here, however, the IPA seems to try to strike a balance between making its point of view count and not engaging in direct and open conflict with the member states:

[It would be] simply political suicide to go against something. But as a scientific organization we need to make sure that the science comes out. It's a question of how you present it. Some issues will always be controversial particularly with transboundary issues ... First it is what it is: it's the science ... But it is also a framing thing. But the assessments come out and they do not always have the best things to say about the MS. But it is also a kind of competition between MS ... it's all about framing. You cannot pull out a country and say, 'You have done bad'. You simply name the ones doing well. So we keep the basic message but try to present it in the right way. (UNEP 3)

All in all, it thus seems that UNEP tries to do what is possible to sanction non-complying member states but only to the extent that it does not threaten the IPA's legitimacy.

When drawing together our findings, a somewhat mixed picture emerges. Both IPAs under study have developed administrative routines that show a clear functional orientation towards policy advocacy. While this is not particularly surprising for the WHO, it is all the more so for UNEP in light of the structural peculiarities discussed in the previous Section. At the same time, both UNEP and the WHO also adopted some informal routines and practices that aim at stabilizing or enhancing the political support for their organization. This positional orientation, however, is not nearly as pronounced as it is for other IPAs discussed in this book that come close to either a consolidating style (the FAO and the IOM; see Chapter 5) or an entrepreneurial style (the UNHCR and the IMF; see Chapter 4). Viewed from this comparative perspective, two things become clear: first, UNEP and the WHO secretariats come closest to the notion of an 'advocate'; and second, both IPAs are not as archetypical as the other IPAs discussed in this book. But how can we make sense of these findings? How can we explain that the two IPAs have developed an advocacy-orientated style despite their structural differences? And why, in addition, do their informal routines still display a remarkable functional orientation?

In response to these questions, we argue in the following section that the two cases under scrutiny (1) face only low internal challenges and restrictions to their bureaucratic policy capabilities, allowing the IPAs to engage in policy advocacy; but (2) they also have to deal with a medium level of external challenges, since they do not fly sufficiently below the radar to avoid becoming subject of unwanted attention. It is this latter aspect that makes both IPAs also feature some characteristics of a consolidator style.

6.3 The Common Sources of an Advocacy-Orientated Style: No Internal Challenges but Some External Ones

We have seen in the second section of this chapter that the IPAs of UNEP and the WHO differ in a number of structural and formal regards. Yet notwithstanding these differences in the overall organizational polity, the supervisory and decision-making structure, the location of the IPAs' headquarters, and their respective formal autonomy, the two IPAs exhibit a similar advocate style. It appears that neither of the four factors suggested can convincingly account for this commonality. Instead, as discussed in the second chapter of this book, we expect the internal and external challenges that IPAs face to determine their administrative style and the underlying orientations behind these behavioural patterns. Key to our argument is that IPAs' perception of external challenges is much better suited to explaining the emergence of a certain administrative style than considering the mere structural features of their organizational environment. If we turn to UNEP and the WHO, we find that both IPAs have to deal with rather few internal challenges. This implies that they have enough cognitive slack – time, space, and resources to work on and optimize the policy solutions they deem best.

When it comes to external challenges, the WHO especially has been frequently portrayed in both scholarly contributions and newspaper articles as being highly challenged. This is best illustrated by the titles of papers predicting that the WHO's 'end is nigh' (Bennett, 2017) and calling upon the organization to either 'change or die' (Smith, 1995) or to 'change at last' (Godlee, 1998; see also Chow, 2010). Unlike such works, however, our analysis suggests that the staff members actually do not perceive the apparent external threat as being so pronounced. The same can be said about their counterparts at UNEP. While the perceived external challenges of the pair of IPAs under scrutiny are far from being absent, they are perceived as being far less dire. In combination with the knowledge gained in the previous section, this finding supports our approach of relying on the perception of external challenges when trying to theorize why positional orientations emerge.

6.3.1 Expertise and Common Beliefs at UNEP and the WHO

In the case of the WHO, the level of cognitive slack is very high. The IPA is widely regarded as an 'expert house of scientists and physicians' (Das, 2010). Its success in achieving and sustaining this reputation mainly stems from the production of guidelines and policy recommendations that are based on scientific evidence and are widely cited and utilized among both researchers and practitioners (Freeman & Sturdy, 2014). According to Bauer and Ege (2017), the WHO ranks among the IPAs with the highest 'administrative differentiation', implying a high capacity to collect and process independent data and information and a strong degree of independence in the administrative leadership (see also Ege, 2017). Both aspects have been confirmed by our interview partners, who decisively highlighted the IPA's strong expertise on scientific health matters:

We are the only UN organization that has super experts. UNICEF, for instance, has to hire consultants. In contrast to us, they do not have the technical knowledge. You need decades and decades to gain this knowledge as an organization. And we have all this in-house. (WHO 9)

Similarly, interviewees reported that the IPA possesses substantial procedural discretion in its daily work:

For the most time, there was not much interest in our daily work. Nobody came to Geneva. Then suddenly a country representative showed up, then a German state secretary. Nobody here can remember the names, because in the next year there was another face again. On this basis, of course, one cannot exert long-term influence. (WHO 3)

In this context, procedural discretion does not imply that the IPA can more or less do what it wants; as discussed above, most of the issues that the WHO is dealing with do not emerge from within the bureaucracy but are being brought to the IPA from the outside. Rather, procedural discretion means that as soon as the agenda is set, the IPA possesses substantial leeway in how it intends to address and deal with a certain health issue (Eccleston-Turner & McArdle, 2017; Johnson & Urpelainen, 2014).

Moreover, the WHO staff is largely composed of physicians, epidemiologists, and other health specialists (WHO 3). This shared educational background – and the homogenous epistemic belief system that grows from it – not only facilitates policy advocacy by fostering the development of the IO's own policy preferences, but also makes it more difficult for the member states to directly intervene in the IPA's daily work. The shared values manifested by the Hippocratic Oath encourage WHO staff members to identify themselves much more strongly with the IO's overall objectives than with their country of origin (Cortell & Peterson, 2006; Lee, 2009). This epistemic spirit is further strengthened and extended by the fact that key managerial positions within the WHO are traditionally held by medical doctors (WHO 3, 9). In sum, it becomes apparent that the overall internal working conditions within the WHO bureaucracy facilitate the emergence of an administrative style aiming at policy advocacy. More precisely, the administration possesses enough bureaucratic capacities and scope of action to be able to come up with its own policy solution. The internal homogeneity of the staff, in turn, helps the IPA to act concertedly and to produce outputs that are endorsed by the entire organization.

Just as in the WHO, the internal working conditions at UNEP also seem to be quite favourable for the emergence of an advocacy-orientated administrative style. This manifests in a relatively high level of cognitive slack for and a strong normative homogeneity of the administrators. UNEP possesses, for instance, relatively high procedural discretion with respect to one of its major mandated tasks: the surveillance of the environment. Here, the IPA can freely choose the issues it wants to feature in its thematic assessments (UNEP 8). This is particularly remarkable, since the environmental indicators assessed essentially determine how a country is ranked and thus how its government's environmental performance is perceived and assessed by the public (Ivanova, 2005). This high procedural discretion actually holds true for all projects that are funded by its unearmarked resources (UNEP 15).

Oversight, however, becomes somewhat stronger when single or multilateral donors are involved or when outputs become very high level. GEF-funded projects, for example, have to be aligned with previously set priorities (Ivanova, 2005). According to Van der Lugt and Dingwerth (2015), this is the result of UNEP's mission creep into other policy areas, such as socially responsible investment (SRI), where direct oversight and control is low and the IPA can enjoy a much greater freedom of action (see also Andonova, 2017). With regard to its in-house expertise and research capacities, UNEP's staff have been repeatedly lauded for their environmental spirit, and staffers usually possess an impressive academic record (Bauer, 2009). Unlike the WHO, in its policy field, UNEP does not engage in direct monitoring and surveillance activities. Rather, it must be considered 'a central hub for all matters related to the environment' (Chen, 2011, p. 313). It acts as an 'information clearinghouse' (Ivanova, 2005, p. 29) that integrates and analyses all data coming in from universities, research institutes, and other UN agencies. Accordingly, UNEP's flagship publication, the *Global Environment Outlook*, is widely recognized as one of the most authoritative sources concerning the global state of the environment (Littoz-Monnet, 2017).

When considering the areas in which UNEP staff members obtained their academic degrees, it becomes apparent that their educational backgrounds are rather diverse, ranging from finance- or management-related studies to the natural sciences to humanities (Herz, Schattenmann, Dortants, Linke, & Steuber, 2008). At first sight, this might imply that processes of solution search and idea generation within the bureaucracy suffer from contesting epistemic stances. Yet as all our interview partners highlighted, the strong esprit de corps of being the 'guardian of the environment', as well as the strong leadership and facilitation skills of the administrative management, creates an atmosphere of mutual recognition, confidence-building, and inspiration (UNEP 3, 6). This is strongly in line with the existing scholarship that uniformly portrays UNEP as an institutionalized epistemic community rather than as an ordinary bureaucracy (Haas, 2008, 2016).

In sum, both IPAs can rely on central in-house research facilities and are not subject to strong procedural oversight: that is, they possess sufficient cognitive slack. Moreover, given their strong common belief system, they do not have to engage in epistemic battles between rival groups of experts over how policy issues are best addressed. Similar to their counterparts in the IMF and the UNHCR discussed in Chapter 4, these features facilitate the emergence of bureaucratic routines geared towards increasing the IO's policy performance.

6.3.2 The Perception of External Challenges in UNEP and the WHO: Challenged but Not Threatened

The extent to which the IPA perceives itself as vulnerable to and challenged by the outside determines whether, and if so, to what extent, it develops adequate administrative routines that safeguard its position. It is not enough that there is a challenge to the organization per se. The threat must also be seen as such through the eyes of the IPA.

Ever since its creation in 1948, the WHO has had to deal with political controversies, largely resulting from a divergent understanding in the rich North and the poor South of the concept of health and thus of the proper scope of the WHO's mission and responsibilities (Chorev, 2012; Yamey, 2002). Yet since the turn of millennium, the critique has substantially increased, both in tone and in frequency. This has several reasons. First, while the WHO's management of the 2009 H1N1 pandemic was perceived by its member states to have been nervous and overreactive (Dumiak, 2012; Carney & Bennett, 2014), its management of the 2014 Ebola outbreak in West Africa was deemed too slow and ineffective (Kamradt-Scott, 2016). Second, the WHO stands accused of spreading fear by politically campaigning on issues such as sugar use and obesity and by that turning itself into a 'lifestyle nanny' (Bennett, 2017). Third, many observers of global health matters claimed that the WHO is overcommitted and overextended as a result of its dual role as norm setter for all countries and technical adviser to specific member states. As argued by Gostin et al. (2015), it seems that the WHO's resources are 'entirely incommensurate with the scope and scale of global health needs' (p. 855). This is made particularly apparent by the fact that the WHO is largely financed by voluntary contributions that are mostly conditional and thus cannot be directed to where the organizations' needs are greatest. In the biannual 2014–15 and 2016–17 budgets, more than 80 per cent of the funds received were specified (earmarked) as extra budgetary contributions donated by member states, philanthropic foundations, and private individuals (Clinton & Sridhar, 2017).

Remarkably, and despite these political attacks against the WHO, the IPA does not really perceive itself to be challenged in its domain of global health policy.

Actually, I do not feel that somebody points a gun at us. There is a clear frustration of the donor countries and you can easily recognize this when reading some statements that were made at the WHA – despite all the diplomacy. But it is not the same pressure I felt in the other international organizations I worked before. Expressed in a negative way, the WHO is a monolith of public health administration. But in positive terms, it is also a true heavyweight. (WHO 3)

The statement shows that the IPA is fully aware of the fact that it is politically contested from the outside. Yet it also reveals that the IPA is quite confident when it comes to its own advantages and benefits. This is primarily because the IPA conceives of itself as central to the domain of global public health matters and thus hard to attack and dismantle.

Over the past twenty years, global health infrastructure became much more complex with the Global Fund, with GAVI [the Global Alliance for Vaccines and Immunization], with UNAIDS [the Joint United Nations Programme on HIV and AIDS], and so forth – with all these partnerships and initiatives. They have done a lot of good for the world because they were able to attract resources. But for sure, there is some level of competition. In the end, we need to do our job well and the funding that we need will materialize. And I think we are not really suffering from this plurality of agencies. There are some tensions, and some individuals might feel it when it is about getting money, but in the end, money always flows in the right direction and that is what is most important. (WHO 10)

Following a very similar reasoning, another interview partner high-lighted that the WHO is (by now) indeed only one among many actors in the area of global health, but due to its standing and reputation, it is still the most important one:

If anything comes out with the logo of the WHO on it then it clearly has a better status than those without it. And that is still the case. They come to us and ask whether we want to join a project since having the WHO on board just gives everything a certain blessing (WHO 6).

In fact, current political trends seem to support the administrators' perception that the WHO is difficult if not impossible to 'get around' or bypass in the domain of global health policy (WHO 2, 3, 6). Despite all the political criticism that the WHO's crisis management faced in the context of the Ebola outbreak, donors have pledged about USD 70 million to WHO's newly established 'Contingency Fund for Emergencies' to be better prepared for future epidemics.[7] This money can be used to fund initial responses to global health emergencies and to be spent at the full discretion of the IPA. In a similar vein, the WHO's alleged 'overreaction' to SARS did not de facto lead to cuts in the IPA's

---

[7] See 'Contingency Fund for Emergencies (CFE) Contributions and Allocations', retrieved 22 August 2018, from www.who.int/emergencies/funding/contingency-fund/allocations/en/.

competencies but to a re-regulation of the IHR that actually strengthened rather than weakened the WHO's authority (Hanrieder & Kreuder-Sonnen, 2014).

UNEP, in exact contrast to the WHO, must deal with strong challenges in its policy domain but is largely unchallenged by its principals. The field of global environmental governance has become an increasingly complex policy domain, with overlapping responsibilities and competing organizations and interests (Young, 2002). On the one hand, there a number of 'senior' UN agencies, such as the FAO, the WMO, and the UNDP, that had already had responsibilities in environmental matters long before UNEP was established. On the other hand, the number of new international organizations dealing with environmental issues has exploded over the last three decades. As observed by Imber (1994), 'UNEP could [thus] no more be expected to "coordinate" the system-wide activities of the UN than could a medieval monarch "coordinate" his feudal barons' (p. 83). These domain challenges are further aggravated by UNEP's very limited financial resources. UNEP's biannual core budget is about USD 40 million and represents only 6 percent of the organization's total income. In our sample of organizations, UNEP is hence the IPA with the second lowest share of flexible and unearmarked funding; only the IOM has a core administrative budget whose share of the organization's total budget is smaller (see Chapter 5). This unreliable and discretionary financial structure forces the IPA to compete with other organizations offering similar policy programmes or services.

Despite these domain challenges, however, UNEP is hardly politically challenged. Quite the contrary: member states of the European Union and the African Union have even sought to upgrade UNEP's constitutional status and to create a United Nations Environment Organization or a World Environment Organization (Biermann, 2007). In this model, member states would be inclined to shift more of their environmental competencies to the organization and to provide for a much more sustainable funding structure (ibid.). Although these political plans have not yet been substantiated and have gained only minor support at the latest United Nations Conference on Sustainable Development in Rio (Rio+20), all states 'reaffirmed UNEP's role as the leading global environmental authority' (Inomata, 2016, p. 79). Moreover, as a result of Rio+20, UNEP became the only UN subsidiary organ granted universal membership (Ivanova, 2013). In essence, this decision implies that individual countries no longer have to opt to be part of UNEP: they become so automatically as part of their member-ship of the UN family. Among the IPA's administrators, these develop-ments were perceived as political signals indicating the principals' wish for a stronger rather than a weaker role of the organization in the field of environmental policy (UNEP 3, 6).

In sum, the discussion shows that both IPAs under study have to deal with certain external challenges. While the WHO is primarily chal-lenged politically but can rely on its good reputation in the area of global health matters, UNEP faces stiff competition in its policy domain but enjoys great political support and approval among devel-oped and developing countries alike. Taken together, the perceived external challenges are thus of a medium level. They are not as pro-nounced as is the case for the IMF and the UNHCR, which reveal informal routines that come close to an entrepreneurial style (Chapter 4), or the FAO and the IOM, which come closest to the consolidator ideal type (Chapter 5). However, external challenges perceived by UNEP and the WHO secretariats are considerably higher, as is the case for their counterparts at NATO and the ILO, which display a servant administrative style (Chapter 7).

6.4 Conclusion: Advocates, Yet Not Unchallenged from the Outside

We have seen in this chapter that a mere focus on the structural features of organizations is not sufficient to explain the emergence of an advo-cacy-orientated style. Despite very different structural peculiarities in the overall organizational polity, the supervisory and decision-making structure, and the location of the IPAs' headquarters, both the WHO and UNEP adopted a range of behavioural routines that reflect the IPAs' overall functional orientation. Yet we also find that the two IPAs under scrutiny also adopted some informal routines and practices that aim at stabilizing or enhancing the political support for their organiza-tion. While these practices are not as pronounced as in IPAs reflecting style patterns coming close to the entrepreneurial or consolidating ideal type (see Chapters 4 and 5), they still render UNEP and the WHO not as archetypical as the other IPAs assessed in this book.

We explained this finding by the fact that both IPAs face low internal challenges but must also deal with a medium level of external challenges. More specifically, we demonstrated that the administrators in both IPAs can rely on central in-house expertise and research capacities and are not subject to strong procedural oversight mechanisms. Another common trait of both organizations is a shared epistemic belief system among the administrators that allows them to act in concerted manner. These aspects clearly favour the emergence of administrative routines aiming at the constant improvement of the IOs' substantive policy performance.

At the same time, however, neither organization is sufficiently unchallenged as to not have to position itself vis-à-vis other actors or present itself positively to its principals. While the WHO can draw on its central position within its policy domain, it is far from being undisputed or unrecognized by its principals. UNEP, by contrast, enjoys the general support of its member states but must assert itself in an increasingly crowded policy domain.

The answer to the question of whether more archetypical advocates exist empirically strongly depends on whether there are IPAs that do not face external challenges but still have substantial policy influence. The relatively small amount of research on, for instance, the Bank for International Settlements indicates that the organization might be a strong candidate for the emergence of a 'pure' advocacy-orientated administrative style given the secretariat's 'secured long-term funding through its banking activities and unique position within the international architecture of financial governance, in which it does not have any real direct competitors' (Knill et al., 2019, p. 16). We can have similar expectations of other organizations whose subject matter is of such a highly technical nature that they attract fewer political controversies and less competition in their policy domains. Other possible aspirants for the emergence of a true advocacy-orientated administrative style include the International Civil Aviation Organization and the World Meteorological Organization.

7 | NATO and the ILO as Servants: the Dedicated Steward and the Saturated Dinosaur

Compared to the other three types of administrative styles we dealt with so far, the servant style presumes a relatively passive and instrumental role for IOs' bureaucratic apparatus. Servant administrations work according to the established rules and follow a routine pattern of strictly adhering to the formal procedural and legal arrangements that define their tasks and functions. They appear to possess little agency of their own to influence the policy process but solely implement and act according to their principals' political will. For IR scholars, especially those of the realist variety, this style is certainly not surprising. From that perspective, the assumption that servant-style IPAs were the least challenging type in theoretical and analytical terms suggests itself. Their passivity and limited agency then constitute a rather uninteresting case, as they do not deviate from the rules. Here, IO politics and policy would indeed be little more than the sum of member states' interests.

However, as we have repeatedly claimed elsewhere in this book, this assessment is premature and clearly falls short when seen through the eyes of scholars in public administration and organizational theory. Quite to the contrary, a pattern of bureaucratic passivity in the international sphere constitutes a rather curious case. On the one hand, one would expect IO staffers, as exceptionally well-trained experts in their fields, to have a strong commitment to advancing substantial policies. On the other hand, theories of organizational ecology and survival would predict that organizations *must* constantly expand and evolve. In this chapter, we therefore seek to address why exactly it is that the IPAs of the International Labour Organization (ILO) and the North Atlantic Treaty Organization (NATO) do not try to act more entrepreneurially in defending and pushing their own interests and political will.

In several regards, the two IOs we are concerned with in this chapter are very dissimilar. For NATO, a servant style comes as less of a surprise. NATO operates in the field of high politics, which is reflected in NATO's rather low authority, especially in terms of delegation (Hooghe et al., 2017, p. 123), and accounts of its limited formal institutional autonomy (Mayer, 2014a, p. 9). NATO's IPA could thus indeed be expected to work in the spirit of a servant style, as it is navigating a particularly sensitive field in which states retain the upper hand more than in most others. Its associated low formal authority and rather narrow portfolio could be seen to translate directly into a servant style if one were to assume that 'doing more' was impeded by the IO's design and field.

The ILO could hardly be more different. In sharp contrast to NATO, the ILO clearly operates in what has been described as low politics (Cox, 1973). The organization, which is about to celebrate the centenary of its establishment, has a strong normative mandate (Helfer, 2008), high legitimacy (Senghaas-Knobloch, 2004), a 'substantial degree of autonomy' (Maupain, 2013, p, 118) and encompassing delegated authority (Hooghe et al., 2017, p. 123; Reinalda, 1998). Judging by formal characteristics only, the ILO thus constitutes a quite unlikely candidate for exhibiting a servant style. Nevertheless, just as does NATO's IPA, the ILO's IPA comes close to our ideal type.

How can we explain this similarity in styles? Why are both IPAs not trying to more actively influence IO policies and their institutional standing? Turning to the conditions under which IPAs display a servant-style behavioural pattern, we argue that despite the IPAs' structural and organizational dissimilarity and consistent with previous chapters, two conditions jointly explain why an IPA qualifies as a servant rather than an entrepreneur: high internal challenges and few external challenges. We find that it is a mixture of 'tied hands' from internal challenges and a lack of urgency in terms of perceived external challenges in their daily business that renders the IPAs in both the ILO and NATO servant-like. The cases of the ILO and NATO underline the necessity of taking the *conjunction* of internal and external challenges into account. A servant style does not emerge from being constrained internally only, but the lack of perceived outside pressures is equally important. Throughout our interviews, we found that whereas NATO's IPA emphasizes its role as a loyal steward and literal 'servant', the ILO's IPA narrated the conviction that the organization does not really need to exceed minimal requirements. It is hence not only that an IPA *cannot* behave more entrepreneurially, but also, and in conjunction, that it subjectively does not *need* to do so.

In the remainder of this chapter, we proceed in four steps. First, we describe NATO and the ILO and point out similarities and differences in formal terms, focusing on their issue area, service function, and mandates. Second, we show the extent to which NATO's International Staff and the ILO's IPA are both real types of a servant style administration and demonstrate how this specific style translates into concrete processes of policy making in the respective organizations. Third, we show that despite their differences, the two show similarly high levels of internal challenges and find themselves subject to comparably low levels of external challenges, which can explain their similar styles. At the end of this chapter, we sum up our findings and point out what we can learn from them in empirical and conceptual terms.

7.1 NATO and the ILO: an Odd Couple

Prima facie, NATO and the ILO do not share many commonalities except their servant style. The ILO was established in the aftermath of World War I (1919), and incorporated a number of pre-war non-governmental organizations (Cox, 1973). NATO's organizational machinery was set up according to the 1949 North Atlantic Treaty's provisions (Megens, 1998). The ILO later became part of the UN system (in 1946), while NATO is not embedded in any comparable institutional context. The ILO's membership is inclusive and almost global, with 187 countries to date, whereas NATO has 30 exclusively Northern American or European member states. Both organizations are unusual in terms of their structure, yet in very different ways. The ILO is one of the very few – and certainly the most significant – IOs to formally allow for non-governmental actors in its governance structure (Hurd, 2013, p. 163). The ILO's unique tripartism includes representatives of trade unions and employers' associations, each of which has a quarter of the votes in both the International Labour Conference (ILC; the ILO's discussion forum) and the Governing Body (the ILO's executive organ).[1] Each country

---

[1] The Governing Body consists of fifty-six members with fourteen seats for workers and fourteen for employers. Ten seats are permanently reserved for countries of chief economic importance (Hooghe et al., 2017, p. 711).

delegation accordingly consists of two government officials and one workers' and employers' representative (in ILO jargon) respectively (La Hovary, 2015). The ILO's bureaucracy (the 'office'[2]) employs 'some 2,700 officials … at its headquarters in Geneva and in around forty field offices worldwide. Among these officials, nine hundred work in technical co-operation programmes and projects' (ILO, 2016).

The security alliance's administrative body and organization, on the other hand, is unique in that it is divided into a civilian (the International Staff, IS) and a military structure (the International Military Staff, IMS).[3] Headed by the secretary general, the IS employs around 1,100 civilians in NATO's Brussels headquarters (NATO, 2017a). NATO's principal decision-making body is the North Atlantic Council (NAC), which deals with all areas of alliance policy except defence planning and nuclear policy. The NAC consists of representatives of all member states and meets at different levels and with varying frequencies (Dembinski, 2012; Lindley-French, 2006).[4] Although this dual structure of NATO and the tripartism of the ILO are similarly unique, they certainly do not make for a true similarity in structure. Rather they further emphasize differences of the two IOs and their IPAs.

In addition to profound dissimilarities in these very general features, the two organizations differ in certain more theoretically relevant ways, namely in their policy fields, mandates, and functions. Security and defence issues continue to touch upon the very core of state sovereignty. In this realm of high politics and in matters as delicate as counterterrorism and warfare, states, wanting to retain as much control as possible, should be reluctant to loosen the reins on IOs (Lipson, 1984). IOs in this field have hence been theorized as tending to be less independent than those working in fields of low politics (Jachtenfuchs, 2005; Snidal, 1990). Indeed, in NATO, the IPA's servant-style passivity seems to support this contention. The ILO, however, should, according to this reasoning, be more independent, and as a consequence, more

---

[2] As in the previous chapters, the ILO's IPA comes to mean the 'office' (i.e. its headquarters administrative staff).

[3] In line with scholars such as Mayer (2014b), our focus with NATO lies on the IS, not the IMS, to ensure comparability across all IPAs examined in this book.

[4] At the ambassador level, meetings take place at least once a week, often more frequently. Ministers of defence meet three times a year, while ministers of foreign affairs convene twice a year. Heads of state and governments gather occasionally at NATO summits.

active and influential than we find it to be. The organization is first and foremost concerned with the 'world of work', and national stakes in social policy are certainly lower than in defence matters. The policy field an IPA works in thus seems to be a weak predictor of its agency, influence, and style. This becomes even clearer when taking into account previous work that found the IPA of the OSCE, similarly in the field of security and high politics, to be highly entrepreneurial in its daily routines (Eckhard & Kern, 2017).

Moreover, NATO and the ILO differ strongly in the scope and normativity of their mandates, which further substantiates the conjecture we made in Chapter 5 that mandates alone appear to be ill-suited to explain administrative styles. 'NATO's administrative elements were designed as (and still chiefly are) supporting bodies, to a high degree constrained and dominated by member states' (Mayer, 2014a, p. 5). Above all, NATO is a system of collective security, but there is certainly more to the IO than just Article 5 of the treaty, which was evoked only once, in the aftermath of 9/11.[5] In addition to its forum role, it also provides technical military advice and political counsel to support national decision-making processes. Its mandate is thus not normative but rather aimed at technical and administrative support, which is theoretically well in line with its IPA's servant style.

The ILO, in contrast, has a strong normative mandate to promote social justice and labour rights, which in theory should contribute to an advocacy-orientated style rather than a servant style (Barnett & Finnemore, 2004; Hall, 2016; Hughes & Haworth, 2011). Its main instruments are recommendations and conventions. Whereas the recommendations are not ratified by member states and serve as general guidance for good conduct in the world of work, conventions are legally binding once ratified by a country. Conventions must be discussed in every member state, but ratification is voluntary. Signatory member states are obliged to submit an annual report on the state of the convention's implementation. In terms of enforcement, the Governing Body, after an extensive review and complaint process, can recommend sanctions against signatory member states that fail to fulfil their obligations (Helfer, 2008). While not binding to non-signatory states, these formal powers lend further credibility to the ILO's normative authority

---

[5] Article 5 contains NATO's central principle of collective defence that 'an attack against one Ally is considered as an attack against all Allies'.

(Van Daele, 2008). Again, whether an IO's mandate is strictly technical does not appear to be a decisive factor in explaining a servant style.

The same holds true for related arguments on the function of IOs or the services they provide. The functional perspective on IOs holds that states establish IOs (and thereby IPAs) because co-operating in IOs allows for carrying out certain tasks more efficiently than if they were to not collaborate (Keohane, 2005; Pollack, 2003). IOs then could have any combination of one or more of three broad service functions: assisting in bargaining, policy analysis and expertise, and operational enforcement and execution (Eckhard & Kern, 2017; Koremenos et al., 2001; Moravcsik, 1999). The assumption here is that those IPAs that were designed chiefly to assist in bargaining should be servant-like, while those concerned with policy expertise and operational enforcement should be more entrepreneurial. Considering the differing functions of the ILO and NATO as described above, it becomes clear that service functions are of limited use in explaining the IPAs' servant style. Administrative styles are neither fully determined by IOs' purposes nor written into IOs' and IPAs' design by rational member states.

In sum, NATO and ILO differ in a number of formal characteristics. The two organizations make for an odd couple because besides their similarity in style, they could hardly be more different. In contrast to NATO, the ILO is embedded in the wider institutional structure of the UN and is older and larger in both membership and staff size. Its membership is almost global and inclusive, whereas NATO has a primarily regional scope and is made up exclusively of a small number of Western nations. As opposed to the ILO, whose focus on low politics and its high formal autonomy should give the organization enough leeway to entrepreneurially act on its own terms, NATO is more confined, both in its autonomy and in the nature of its field of high politics. The ILO's service function as experts and operational-support providers, as well as its normative mandate, stand in stark contrast to NATO's technical mandate and core function of assisting in bargaining. Taking these differences into account, it becomes clear that the similarity in style of the IPAs of the ILO and NATO cannot be consistently and satisfactorily explained by their policy field (Lipson, 1984; S. Mayer, 2014b; Snidal, 1990), their mandate (Hall, 2013, 2016), or their rational design and service functions (Koremenos et al., 2001). Instead, we contend that the combination of overall low external challenges to the IPAs and the pronounced internal challenges they deal with are better suited to explaining their servant patterns of behaviour. Before returning to this argument in the next Section, we will show exactly how NATO's and the ILO's IPAs both follow routine patterns of behaviour that come close to the servant ideal type.

7.2 Administrative Styles: the ILO and NATO as Servant Administrations

Servants are ideal-typically characterized by the absence of both positional and functional orientations in their bureaucratic routines. In the following, we show how that style manifests itself empirically and the extent to which NATO's and the ILO's IPAs actually do not exert independent influence on the policy process. As in previous chapters, our discussion is structured along the differentiation of the two orientations, with the respective bureaucratic tasks loosely stretching along the policy cycle (policy initiation, policy drafting, and policy implementation). Starting with their functional orientations, we explore the IPAs' administrative styles in more detail. In assessing the ILO's and NATO's IPAs' standard operating procedures over our nine indictors, we see that both indeed come close to the servant ideal type.

7.2.1 Functional Orientations Are Marginal

In *policy initiation*, servant-style bureaucracies typically do not generate new policy proposals from the inside. Rather, they respond to impulses and carry out those tasks that have been explicitly assigned to them. Novel ideas are hence brought into the IPA from the outside.

In NATO, 'it's first and foremost nations that bring forward requests' (NATO 1). Due to NATO's identity as a security and defence organization, security challenges or events of instability often determine the issues on the organization's agenda (NATO 1). Thus, it is frequently the general security environment that shapes requests from member states and the IPA's agenda.

[W]e are driven by our security environment. So we react. And we are more a reactive alliance than a proactive alliance ... So as an organization, I think we are pretty adaptive to our environment. (NATO 8)

There are, however, certain occasions when the IPA itself actively generates policy proposals. As is common in other IOs, the secretary general can influence the organization's course, depending on his style and personality (Hendrickson, 2006, 2014).[6] In addition to the possibility of integrating new ideas into their speeches, the secretary general has a number of informal channels to lobby the member states directly when travelling to their capitals (NATO 2, 8) or in lunch meetings with ambassadors (NATO 11). The same cannot always be said about the International Staff more generally. Although there are a number of informal fora meant to stimulate dialogue and creativity (Mayer & Theiler, 2014), active bureaucratic agenda setting is the exception rather than the rule. This is, in part, a result of NATO bureaucrats always needing a political sponsor – that is, nations to support their ideas (NATO 2, 8). '[T]o provoke a reform process, you do need the member nations to take lead. Because leadership lies with the member nations' (NATO 12). Thereby, member states can, for political reasons, prevent issues developed by the IPA from being discussed further. One official summarized this situation in a rather vivid picture: 'So you see, the idea is, you can have your own ideas, but then the nations will chop your head off if you go too far' (NATO 1).

Similarly, the ILO bureaucracy 'reacts to things' (ILO 4). Partly, this is due to the processes of issue selection and agenda setting being very formalized (ILO 14). The biannual Governing Body meetings and the ILC are the main venues for constituents to express their needs and demands towards ILO staff. In the course of these events, the administration has only limited means to influence which issues are prioritized or what shape the discussion will take (ILO 2, 5, 10, 13). One senior interviewee summarized the IPA's role in issue emergence as follows:

It is a love–hate relationship when it comes to that. Our constituents very much insist on their sovereignty and we are the clerks who do as they are told – not the other way around. (ILO 10).

In addition to member states ultimately setting the agenda, the workers' and employees' offices also participate in the selection of issues to be addressed, further limiting the IPA from holding its ground in this phase of IO policy making.

---

[6] As of 2020, all NATO secretary generals have been men.

Of course, the secretariat tries to think about how to give shape to those discussions, but we have some very involved constituents, too . . . So it wasn't as though the office were the only experts in the game. (ILO 13)

This lack of engagement in issue emergence is reflected in the bureaucracy's self-description as the 'guardians of the standards' (ILO 4) and staffers' constant emphasis on the 'demand driven-ness' (ILO 5) of their mandate. Both NATO and the ILO thus do not routinely attempt to influence which policies enter the agenda and do not regularly take informal measures to increase the odds of policy ideas to be realized. Rather, issues are taken into the IPA from the outside, be it from current events, the member states, or – in the case of the ILO – the constituents.

In the drafting phase, that is during the actual preparation of documents and the writing-up of policies, the ideal-typical servant does not play a very active role. Whereas more entrepreneurial IPAs put special emphasis on finding the best possible *policy solution* to a given problem by carefully evaluating as many alternative options as possible, a servant style administration sticks to solutions that satisfice the principals' demand.

The process of policy formulation in NATO is heavily influenced by the necessity of placing considerable emphasis on consensus. All policies decided upon in the NAC are an expression of the collective will of all member states, and decisions are to be made on the basis of unanimity (Deni, 2014). The IPA's approach to solution search is shaped by member states' interest and the question of which drafts they would most likely approve (NATO 8, 9). This leads to a situation where 'information is secondary in this organization' (NATO 1):

In an organization that is based on consensus, there is no objective information. If the only way to agree in a summit community is to say the earth is flat, we would say the earth is flat, even though we know it's not. Because the consensus is what ultimately counts, and so there is no objective information out there. (NATO 1)

In routines that can be described as the polar opposite of optimizing, the consensus requirement can thus lead to situations where ideas and decisions would be 'completely . . . stupid if really done. But the fact is that is the price we have to pay for consensus' (NATO 9). Moreover, many staffers expressed that in their self-understanding as loyal stewards, more entrepreneurial activities would simply be inappropriate. If they were to act more aggressively with less consideration, they could not adequately fulfil their self-proclaimed role as 'facilitators':

What makes NATO unique is this consensus thing, because that gives you so much trouble. And such a lot of work, which is not seen in the results. Just to keep alliance's unity ... I mean, before I came here, I used to laugh about that definition of NATO – 'No Action, Talk Only'. But hey – twenty-eight countries.[7] Even if that's all they do, they are not at war with each other. (NATO 11)

As a rule, then, NATO's bureaucrats rarely attempt to optimize policy drafts but merely work to find solutions that satisfy the lowest common denominator of member states' interests.

For the ILO, on the other hand, consensus is not a primary concern. Because every convention is subject to voluntary ratification, they only require two-thirds of the constituents' votes to be adopted and many other less sensible decisions only require a majority vote. Generally, the administration's influence in the drafting process depends on the type of document that is being drafted by the ILO. With conventions, the process is very formalized in three steps. First, a survey is distributed to all constituents to assess their needs, opinions, and existing practices on the subject. Second, a group of law specialists drafts the so-called 'state of law and practice', which is then, third, discussed in two readings at the ILC. During this process, there is almost no independent role of the bureaucracy. When processes are less codified, as for instance for recommendations, the secretariat is ordered to write up a report of the ILC discussions and suggest and draft a proposal. In principle, the administration could therefore influence the drafting process.

Still, it is only in a few units – most of which deal with issues of budgeting and planning and consist predominantly of economists – that the solution search could be described as somewhat optimizing (ILO 10, 14). The major share of the ILO's bureaucracy rather adheres to a 'rule of thumb' logic without excessively evaluating alternatives. Optimizing solution search is considered to be too expensive and to require too much effort (ILO 3). Technically, requirements are rather high, 'a little bit heavy but certainly safe' (ILO 7), but normally – and especially in smaller projects – the de facto routines are more informal (ILO 6).

---

[7] As of the summer of 2016, when this interview was conducted, Montenegro and North Macedonia were not yet part of NATO.

Implementing high standards of solution assessment is further hampered by member country's demands and the tripartite involvement in the solution-search process. The principals' political will is considered more important than the objective 'best' solution (ILO 4, 5, 11). The politically viable way is often preferred over the technically sound solution because the bureaucracy is very aware of its weak position vis-à-vis its principals (ILO 9, 10). In addition, the knowledge of how to really 'optimize' is distributed unevenly across the heterogeneous epistemic backgrounds – hence the slightly different approach some economists employ. One statement indicates this epistemic divide and the low overall significance of techniques like log frames within the ILO:

Often, I would be discussing how to write a log frame with a colleague in, say, our norms unit and he has actually no interest in actually learning how to do this. They quickly need it for this specific pot of money that we want to have access to but long-term in their career it doesn't affect them. (ILO 14)

In sum, in neither NATO nor the ILO does the bureaucracy regularly take up an optimizing strategy when it comes to the identification of policy-problem solutions.

Since satisficing routines require fewer *horizontal coordination* mechanisms, a servant-style administration is typically characterized by negative (as opposed to positive) internal coordination. In NATO's bureaucracy, coordination is impeded by conflicts of interest and mutual disregard of its military and civilian structure (NATO 7, 9). '[T]he International Staff and International Military Staff traditionally hardly interact' (Dijkstra, 2015, p. 136). This situation prevails, although measures have been taken to strengthen cooperation through co-location of similar divisions of the International Staff and the International Military Staff (NATO 7, 9; Mouritzen, 2013). Yet generally, NATO's IPA makes many informal efforts to improve internal coordination. Apart from a number of problems caused by NATO's organizational structure, many interviewees described coordination in NATO as rather functional. Administrative coordination within NATO's IPA seems to function quite well, since there is a pronounced effort to overcome structural difficulties in informal, often personal interactions between different divisions (NATO 1, 2, 3, 6, 11; Mayer & Theiler, 2014).

However, while certainly functional overall, the default mode of coordination in the IS is more negative than positive. As a general rule, there is always a leading division for policy drafts, and although other divisions are certainly involved in the circulation of drafts, we do not see regular patterns of truly positive coordination. At times, the advantages arising from being the leading division entail a certain potential for conflicts, as one interviewee put it:

We had this several times that our inputs were completely ignored by the other leading division. And we get the second draft, and nothing is in it. That is a classical way of keeping sure that you are really in control. (NATO 1)

The interaction between different divisions of the International Staff hence does suffer from turf wars (NATO 4). In addition, there are challenges to internal coordination that seem to be of a structural origin, caused, for example, by time constraints and lack of resources:

As the staff gets cut back, and as the workload increases, coordination for me is more of a mechanical problem than a philosophical or a structural problem … We also have less and less time for coordination, because the Private Office wants this, it wants that. So the deadlines are shorter, the numbers of documents are greater, and the number of staff is smaller … So overall, I find the biggest problem is simply just getting time to do it. But that's not a small issue, that's a real issue … That's becoming a bigger and bigger problem. (NATO 3)

In sum, coordination in NATO can be considered a mixed type. We do observe informal efforts to promote positive coordination, but the default mode of negative coordination and turf wars often render them unsuccessful.

In the ILO, on the other hand, at times, the lack of coordination goes so far that country offices might not know that a mission is being launched in their country or that the International Training Centre of the ILO can be unaware that HQ has been working on an issue for years, as some interviewees reported anecdotally (ILO 10, 12). Certainly there are formal requirement guidelines on how to coordinate, and there seems to be some improvement lately, but these guidelines are still not always implemented effectively (ILO 9; MOPAN, 2016, p. 34).

Coordination is sometimes not only problematic, it is also clearly negative. Departments have been reported to intervene themselves when something affected them negatively and the department leading on the issue had 'forgotten' to inform them that it was even working on the issue (ILO 13). This lack of positive coordination favours silo thinking. The different educational backgrounds of different bureaucrats in different departments and the spatial distance from HQ to the field offices aggravate this situation:

There is like a ridiculous amount of silo thinking, because each of our colleagues is very, very specialized ... to the extent that our social protection department has, I would say, about six, seven different silos of people who don't necessarily talk to each other or are feeling quite competitive about each other ... and that is very difficult to overcome ... [I]t then becomes very difficult for colleagues in the field to talk to, say, a specialist in social protection because they don't know who to talk to. (ILO 12)

One factor that further complicates positive coordination should be mentioned, since it can be traced to a specificity of the ILO. Unlike in NATO, because in the ILO there is no such thing as a strong 'work-in-progress' culture, staffers rarely circulate unfinished drafts, as one bureaucrat explains:

[I]t can be very difficult to get information out of people because no one in the ILO likes to produce the document that is [half-baked] even when it would be ideal. I mean you don't necessarily need a whole concept or idea when you need to send it around to the specialists, but that will rarely happen. It will always be ... they will produce a full document and then it will go through the period of ... reviews, because that's just a cultural thing to the ILO that people do not like to admit they don't know anything. I don't, but generally speaking, everybody thinks they are an expert on their thing, you know ... So it can be quite difficult. (ILO 14)

Whereas we see a mixed pattern with regard to coordination in NATO, where some informal efforts are undertaken to get everybody to the table in the early stage of the policy-making process, in the ILO we cannot detect such behaviour on a routine basis. Rather, administrative coordination in the ILO appears to be decisively negative and, still, is often highly dysfunctional.

When it comes to the implementation of policies, the ideal-typical servant, again, plays a rather passive role. As a consequence, a typical servant administration will not put much emphasis on promoting or monitoring the implementation of policies adopted by its member states.

In *policy promotion*, the ILO's IPA does indeed not really deem much effort to be necessary. Promotional activities play a minor role in the day-to-day routines of the majority of staffers. The ILO 'play[s] it safe' (ILO 3). Measures such as reminders to update the website for external visibility are rare, since they happen only every three months or so and are perceived rather to be an annoyance than a helpful tool (ILO 3; ILO, 2018, p. 66). In the ILO, there is widespread belief that the constituents themselves are the major platform for promotion (ILO 13; ILO 12). Although some member states would like the ILO to communicate its activities more clearly (MOPAN, 2016, p. 19), ILO administrators rely mostly on the workers and employees to promote the ILO both in their respective country and internationally. However, this lack of external visibility is not necessarily conceived of as a problem, at least among staffers. It seems that a major role in explaining this very passive behaviour can be attributed to a notion of exceptionalism, which reverberates throughout the organization.

The problem is, institutionally we are not seen. If [you ask] most of my colleagues, 'How do we sell ourselves?' they won't know. Like they have no reason or objective to sell ILO to anybody. They are just like, 'Oh, we are the ILO, we are the gold standard. They need to adhere to us not the other way around'. (ILO 14)

In contrast, one main narrative for NATO's similarly passive role at the policy implementation stage is that the core task of its administrative body is still to support nations' decision-making processes (Mayer, 2014a). Once decisions about operations and the required capabilities are finally made, other (mostly military) actors carry out their implementation automatically (see, for example, NATO 3). As a consequence, NATO's IPA does not have much leverage, or indeed does not see the necessity of monitoring or enforcing implementation or promoting particular policies.

[I]f they ask us to do it, it is because they want to do it. We don't impose it on them. They want to reform; they want to take advantage of the expertise, because NATO is in many ways the highest standard for many of these things. So, we don't have a problem with take up. (NATO 3)

Accordingly, with the exception of the newly set up Public Diplomacy Division, whose main interest is to bolster the alliance's legitimacy, there are not many promotional efforts in NATO's IPA. Initially fraught with problems, this division has been evolving, but its relevance and priority status were in jeopardy after the end of the Afghanistan mission (Tomescu-Hatto, 2014; Dijkstra, 2015). Overall, routinely emphasizing promotional activities across the whole organization is not part of NATO's pattern of administrative behaviour.

Finally, ideal-typical servants do not make a particular informal effort to *evaluate* their impact and procedures. This can certainly be said about the ILO's evaluation system and the IPA's routines in this regard. Although the evaluation system in the ILO is undergoing revision after several malfunctions and has been reformed over the last couple of years (ILO 13; AusAID, 2012; DFID, 2011), the overall picture of evaluation efforts here continues to be quite mixed. High commitment to reform and a clear ILO-wide strategy in this regard have not yet be able to fully overcome the policy-practice gap in policy and programme evaluation (MOPAN, 2016, p. 21). Despite a number of measures taken from 2012 onwards and the setup of an independent evaluation office more than ten years ago, at HQ, systematic evaluation still plays only a minor role in day-to-day practice. The technical co-operation (TC) units place a stronger emphasis on evaluation, but they too do not exceed what is formally required (ILO 7). Those requirements vary with the size and cost of the respective projects (ILO 13), and as a rule account for only 1.5 per cent of the overall project budget (MOPAN, 2016, p. 23). Evaluation practices hence do not always live up to the IO's ambitious goals and differ considerably across the core staff and in the TC portfolio, where evaluation also does not really work systematically (ILO 14). Knowledge management constitutes a problem in both formal and informal terms, since a 'generational gap' exits in organizational learning (ILO 10). The IPA's evaluation efforts in the ILO are therefore low to medium at best.

However, they still do exceed the ones present at NATO. There, assessments are conducted in a very limited manner, in only a few policy areas or with regard to specific reforms or operations (see NATO 5, 12). However, there is no institutionalized or formalized evaluation mechanism to be applied on a regular basis. Moreover, knowledge management has been perceived to be problematic or even largely absent since at least 2012, when a staff reform re-established fixed-term tenure for policy officers (Dijkstra, 2015). For that reason, while the ILO's IPA scores low to medium in its evaluation practices, the alliance's evaluation efforts can be considered rather low.

To sum up this section on functional orientations, neither NATO's nor the ILO's IPA puts much emphasis on a functional orientation in their bureaucratic routines. With the exception of coordination in NATO and evaluation and solution search in the ILO, where the picture is somewhat more mixed, both IPAs exhibit behavioural patterns that correspond closely to what the servant ideal type predicts. Interestingly, in many interviews, this passive behaviour was mirrored in some recurring pattern of self-descriptions. NATO's IPA takes its role as a facilitator of compromise very seriously. At the ILO, many are convinced that going beyond what is formally required would contradict their role as 'the guardians of the standards'. However, at the ILO, a second motif comes into play: representing the 'gold standard' themselves. In many regards and as opposed to NATO's IPA, ILO staffers often did not justify their instrumental role with their *duty* to stick to their role, but the *lack of necessity* to change their routine and become more active. We will revisit this argument briefly in the conclusion of this chapter.

7.2.2 *Only Little Indication of Positional Orientations*

Turning to the positional orientation underlying administrative styles, we described ideal-typical servant administrations as acting much less strategically than entrepreneurial IPAs. This should become visible in their not emphasizing the set of activities we associate with positional goals.

In the initiation stage, this means that servants do not actively *mobilize support* from their broader organizational environment, and they engage in comparatively little collaboration with outside partners. Even though NATO does not work in total isolation, there is very little collaboration with external partners. While this is often for political reasons – as in, for example, the tensions between Turkey and Greece, which are a potential strain on the relationship between NATO and the European Union (see NATO 7) – there is also a more general pattern of non cooperation in NATO. 'NATO keeps organized civil society at a distance, providing NGOs with no opportunities for meaningful and regularized participation in its policy-making' (Mayer, 2008, p. 110; Tallberg et al., 2014). There is not an accreditation system for civil society actors to enter the organization and use NATO as a forum for lobbying their cause, nor do we see much outreach towards NGOs on NATO's part (Mayer, 2008; Tallberg et al., 2014). Except for a very small number of officially recognized organizations, as far as civil society is concerned, we find a pattern of mutual disregard for cooperation and the building of support networks. Similarly, NATO cooperates with only a very small number of other IOs, and with them, only to a limited degree. Although NATO maintains relationships with the EU, the OSCE, and the UN, these ties do not go so far as to really classify NATO as building a network to support the IPA's cause in policy initiation (Franke, 2018; Koschut, 2018). Even though cooperation efforts have been increased modestly. NATO remains a 'comparatively self-contained organization' whose 'organization-set is quite limited due to its character as a single-purpose organization, classification requirements, little discretion for its headquarters, and NATO's adverse image among potential partners' (Biermann, 2014).

We find a similarly distinct disregard for civil society cooperation in the ILO, as long as support mobilization other than for implementation on the ground is concerned (Thomann, 2008). Because the ILO already subjectively includes a relevant share of civil society – the very segment its IPA deems most relevant – additional coalitions are almost obsolete in their eyes (ILO 7, 9, 11, 14, 13). Regarding its representativeness, the IPA is even somewhat suspicious of other organizations:

We *are* representing society. Greenpeace or Oxfam – by what right [do] they speak for society? Who elected them? . . . Well, thou shalt have no gods before us. (ILO 10)

Another reason for the ILO's IPA not to reach out to civil society too much is that the constituents are quite wary when it comes to these relations. When the tripartite plus programme that was meant to strengthen the ILO's ties to civil society (with regard to promotion) was launched, both workers and employers advocated strongly against it because they feared that it would diminish their own influence. Opposition was especially strong in countries such as India, where trade unions are politically weak and have fierce domain struggles with various NGOs (Baccaro, 2015). In practice, this fear of losing significance hinders IPA staff from really interacting with NGOs other than for implementation purposes on the national level. One intervie-wee puts this ongoing problem mildly: 'Certainly, some constituents within the ILO are not happy with it – mainly the workers group' (ILO 3; see also Thomann, 2008). In sum, neither the ILO nor NATO really build strategic coalitions with civil society actors to promote certain issues to their member states.

Second, in the administration stage, servant-style administrations will invest only a small amount of capacity in *mapping political dynamics* among their principals, since their main objective lies in executing the tasks delegated to them. As a consequence, for the ideal type, continuous mapping of opportunities for new policy proposals should not be deemed necessary.

The ILO's bureaucracy does have an idea about what might or might not resonate with its constituents: 'Well, we know roughly what could interest whom. Also, we sort of know what would be a non-starter because there is resistance somewhere' (ILO 11). However, these rare efforts are 'rather decentred' (ILO 2) and do not follow any clear strategy or routinized pattern. More accurately, 'mapping of the political space' – if happening at all – is a by-product of meeting by chance or of random side talks at formal events. The bureaucracy appears not to think of mapping as particularly important, or alternatively, it considers it too time consuming to seriously engage in such practices on a regular basis (ILO 3, 4).

NATO's approach in this regard is somewhat different. When it comes to the mapping of political space, NATO's behaviour deviates slightly from what the ideal type would predict. Due to the aforementioned consensus requirement in the NAC, NATO's bureaucratic apparatus is often very sensitive in continuously mapping its principals' political positions. Those routines, however, are more pronounced with the higher echelons of the organization. Higher ranks in the bureaucracy especially play an important role during the policy initiation phase in figuring out nations' positions and trying to find solutions that are acceptable for all thirty member states (NATO 2, 11). There are various formats – both formal and informal – for discussing issues and policy projects in advance with different member states' representatives; these include the Visegrad format and the two well-established groups of NATO's biggest budget holders, the so-called QUART (consisting of the United States, the United Kingdom, France, and Germany) and the QUINT (the QUART plus Italy) (NATO 1). Naturally, these high-level meetings pertain mostly to the upper echelons and the secretary general in particular. It is worth noting, though, that sometimes the secretary general's techniques to get an impression of current member state positions are highly creative – if not almost experimental.

[Y]ou may team up unlikely countries, if [the secretary general] thinks some-thing should be addressed, but he knows that this is highly controversial between nations. He would for example choose the French, the Polish, and the Germans to test out a thought he has on something we could do with Russia. Because if these three can agree, then it is highly likely that everybody else will find themselves somehow in the whole mix. (NATO 11)

Mapping of political space is indeed very important to NATO's bureaucracy. However, we did not find mapping activities to be equally and informally important across the board. As opposed to political anticipation (discussed below), which runs as a clear pattern through-out NATO, the picture is not entirely clear cut. The ILO, on the other hand, seems not to see too much value in this political exercise and therefore undertakes only very few mapping endeavours.

Once a topic enters the organizational agenda, servant IPAs should similarly not engage in *anticipating* potential 'red lines' of individual member states when it comes to negotiating and formulating specific proposals. Whereas entrepreneurial IPAs move strategically in depoli-ticizing contentious issues, servants refrain from such behaviour and stay as far outside member-state conflicts as possible.

At NATO, member states' red lines are crucial not only during the policy initiation phase, but also at the drafting stage. In NATO's bureaucracy, it is considered vital to know and understand these red lines, which are either common knowledge or detected with the help of consultations (NATO 1, 3, 7, 8). International Staff hence spends a lot of time and effort on identifying interests and depoliticizing topics. Detecting common grounds requires sound knowledge of nations' interests and also 'an element of tactics' on the side of bureaucrats drafting the respective policy:

[I]t will polarize around common ideas. So de facto, you are in a situation where you are facing groupings. So you have to assess them. Who thinks what, etc.? Within those groupings, and within the nations, the national views, what is actually a red line, a hard point? (NATO 6)

In the ILO, political anticipation constitutes an equally crucial part of the drafting stage. Strategies of functional politicization, however, are almost absent. This is because anticipation in the ILO is to a lesser extent a strategic move but more of a pure requirement. The 'organiza-tion's corporatist structure ... gives employer associations and trade unions veto power over policy developments at a time in which these actors are increasingly unable to agree on concrete policy measures' (Baccaro & Mele, 2012, p. 195). The bureaucracy does not act to gain a strategic advantage. Rather, like NATO, they are forced to detect political red lines because of the complex governance structure of the ILO and its limited implementation powers (ILO 7, 8; La Hovary, 2015):

We have to anticipate where the consensus is likely to be because we have to get buy-in from all three groups really for something to be implemented. (ILO 13)

We have a lot of pressure ... We would get a lot of criticism in our governing body if we don't have our constituents involved in that process. (ILO 6)

If you forget, you are going to get slapped on the wrist very hard ... They insist to be consulted. (ILO 4)

Both in NATO and the ILO, the IPA displays routine patterns of political anticipation. In the ILO, however, while the awareness of political red lines is high, on the staff level, this does not necessarily mean that functional depoliticization plays an equally important role. Rather, instead of spinning the issue differently, thorny issues would be omitted altogether. Because the picture is therefore mixed to a certain extent, we label their behaviour in this regard as medium.

Last, and consistent with their generally passive role in policy initiation and formulation, servant-style administrations should avoid provoking conflict with member states in the implementation stage. In case of non-compliance, ideal-typical servants do not make overt informal efforts of enforcement or persuasion beyond their *formal powers* or what has been explicitly ordered. Because NATO's mandate is designed to facilitate decision making among its member states and implementation is usually carried out automatically, NATO's IPA usually does not encounter noncompliance issues. Once all member states have agreed on a decision, its implementation is usually carried out by other (mostly military) actors (see, e.g., NATO 1, 3, 6). As a consequence, NATO's IPA neither has much leverage to enforce implementation nor does it need such regulatory instruments: '[W]e don't have a problem with take-up. Where we do have it ... [we] just cut off the programs. So then we are done' (NATO 3). The few things there are to monitor or implement are hence not pondered strategically.

In the context of the ILO, issues of implementation have been debated heatedly – not least in the ongoing academic and political discussion about the ILO not having 'teeth' (Douglas, Ferguson, & Klett, 2004; Weisband, 2000). The ILO's formal implementation power is even called a 'paper exercise [that] doesn't really have any practical implication' (ILO 6; see also Elliott & Freeman, 2003). Especially in non-binding recommendations, the ILO's room for man-oeuvre is very narrow and 'compliance with ILO norms depends on a combination of public identification, embarrassment and shaming (a mild stick), and technical assistance to promote compliance (a mild carrot)' (Trebilcock & Howse, 2004: note 132). The IPA, however, does not really perceive this as a major problem. Rather, it often refrains from employing its formal powers so as not to jeopardize relationships with member states (ILO 12; Hartlapp, 2007). Whereas some do report 'finger pointing … on a constructive basis' (ILO 11), a number of interviewees emphasize persuasion instead of putting pressure on governments because 'this is the one thing [the ILO] can do' (ILO 4). The ILO has in the course of its history been quite successful in establishing labour standards globally (Helfer, 2008; MOPAN, 2016). Public dissent with member states remains an occa-sional but rather rare occurrence. We therefore see a mixed picture at the ILO, both in the academic discourse surrounding its implementa-tion powers and in its actual bureaucratic routines in dealing with potential conflict.

In sum, regarding their positional orientation, both the ILO and NATO deviate slightly from the ideal type, especially in their high/ medium level of political anticipation and in the NATO IPA's mapping efforts. Both IPAs do place some emphasis on the anticipation of their member states' sensibilities and interests. NATO's bureaucrats con-ceive of political anticipation as a vital strategic tool to fulfil their role to their member states' satisfaction. It is also for this reason that the NATO administration deviates from theoretical expectations with regard to the mapping of political space. For the ILO bureaucracy, engaging in political anticipation is not an active decision but a requirement that is inscribed into the organization's very structure. The bureaucracy is very aware and self-conscious of how tied its hands are in that regard (ILO 8): 'Very sensitive; probably too sensitive. Unfortunately, at times … the discussion success criterion is only what receives the least criticism' (ILO 7).

7.3 Constrained Inside, Unchallenged Outside

We have seen in the beginning of this chapter that the ILO and NATO differ in key formal regards, such as autonomy, size, scope, mandate, function, and policy fields. Although they are hence dissimilar in many organizational features that have frequently been employed as defining characteristics of IOs overall (Bauer & Ege, 2017; Biermann & Siebenhüner, 2009; Hooghe & Marks, 2015) and determinants of administrative behaviour and influence in particular (Barnett & Finnemore, 2004; Koremenos et al., 2001; Simon, 1997; Snidal, 1990), they do exhibit a similar servant administrative style, as we demonstrated in the previous section. The theoretical advantage of our conceptualization is therefore exemplified by these two organizations: instead of relying solely on those almost canonical indicators for explaining their similarities in styles, we focus on two key explanatory umbrella variables, namely the internal and external challenges to an organization (see Chapter 2). Again, we argue that the behaviour of the two IPAs can be explained in light of two factors in conjunction: their high internal challenges and rare or absent perception of external challenges.

7.3.1 Internal Challenges: Neither the Means nor the Voice to Formulate their Own Ideas

Internal challenges in the sense of our overall theoretical framework (see Chapter 2) are defined by epistemic heterogeneity and a low level of cognitive slack, previously defined as the resources, time, and space to come up with an IPA's own ideas and proposals. High internal challenges constrain the IPA from developing a routine functional orientation. When an IPA's cognitive slack is limited because of staff characteristics or lack of procedural discretion, it does not command the means to actively and substantially influence IO politics and policies. Where epistemic heterogeneity is very pronounced, the IPA has less of a chance of speaking with one voice in pushing its own ideas.

Regarding cognitive slack, NATO is fairly challenged. First and foremost, its lack of slack can be traced back to strong restrictions on cognitive space. It is a well-supported finding that the IS continues to be 'to a high degree constrained and dominated by member states' (Mayer, 2014a, p. 5). NATO's member states are notorious for micro-managing the IPA at all stages of the policy-making process (Mouritzen, 2013): '[A]llies in NATO are control freaks. They want full political control on any more significant issue' (NATO 8; also NATO 11). This tendency pertains not only to those decisions and proposals of chief relevance to a given member state; indeed, no issue is too insignificant for principal interference (Mayer & Theiler, 2014). NATO's heavy consensus rule aggravates the IPA's situation in this regard. Often, staffers not only find themselves micro-managed by a single member state on a given issue, they also must balance a number of highly involved principals at very early stages in the process. Strong inclinations towards exerting strict procedural oversight early on thus narrow the IPA's possible scope of autonomous action considerably.

In terms of resources and time, NATO's IPA is less constrained yet still far from truly having slack. Although NATO's policy functions and divisions have increasingly gained heft over the last years, overall personnel resources for the IS have been kept flat (Dijkstra, 2015). In other words, while there are now more staffers concerned with a substantial focus, in essence, they do not necessarily also have the means to come up with innovations of their own (NATO 3). To this end, NATO does have a few explicitly research-orientated pro-grammes, such as the Science for Peace and Security Programme, a wide-scope tool that is meant to bring about 'scientific research, innovation, and knowledge exchange' (NATO, 2017b). However, the lack of space, competing interests, and the heavy consensus require-ments regularly overlay the focus on research on the political stage (NATO 8). In addition, time constraints frequently impede the devel-opment of optimal solutions (NATO 3). After the 2012 wave of inter-nal reforms in particular, staff have been reported to fight the quite severe increases in workload (Dijkstra, 2015). Taken together, the NATO IPA's restrictions on space, resources, and time make up for a pronounced lack of cognitive slack.

Much like NATO's staff, the ILO's staff are challenged in terms of cognitive slack. Technically, the IPA does command plenty of research resources. The ILO has traditionally produced a number of high-quality flagship research outputs, and many studies emphasize the centrality of research bodies in the organization. Although the organi-zation has both a research and a training centre, only some of the information generated there finds its way into the administration's daily workings (ILO 12). This is because the ILO International

Training Centre and Research Department often seem to work in isolation from the rest of the organization. Similarly, the technical co operation departments have been found to operate quite detached from the standard setting (Standing, 2008). These divisions hamper the diffusion of ideas generated by the research department. In a sense, research and innovation appear to be outsourced to the relevant departments. Some observers go so far as to state that the ILO 'suffers from an institutional "anti-intellectualism" in that its senior administrative staff … distrust innovative thinking' (Standing, 2008, p. 374).

With a view to time constraints, the ILO's slow, heavy, and bureaucratic recruitment procedures have led to a shortage of personnel, which diminishes the time individual staffers can spend on thinking through potential IPA issues and ideas (ILO, 2018). With their hands full, IPA staff are often restricted to providing rather ad hoc inputs (MOPAN, 2016, pp. 15, 17). In terms of space, the ILO's organizational architecture provides many avenues for the constituents to influence the office's work informally throughout the policy process. Despite the above-mentioned problems with circulating documents in the ILO, whenever drafts are actually sent around, the constituents will receive a copy to comment on. The permanent offices of the employers and workers are formally part of the office, are highly engaged in the process, and participate 'on equal footing' (Dahan, Lerner, & Milman-Sivan, 2012, p. 695; La Hovary, 2015). This applies for almost all project proposals, recommendations, and, of course, conventions (ILO 3). All policy products are therefore developed jointly with a high degree of exchange between bureaucrats and social partners. In addition to the constituents, even in its day-to-day doings, member states are on the IPA's toes. Especially the heavyweights among the donors like the EU or the United States exert considerable (informal) influence on the ILO's policies (Haas, 1964; Patz & Goetz, 2019). The ILO's IPA, therefore, does exhibit a clear lack of cognitive slack in that it does not regularly and consistently command sufficient time, space, and resources to behave more entrepreneurially on a routine basis.

Turning to the IPAs' epistemic composition, we find that although the rather narrow mandate of both organizations naturally renders the level of specialist expertise in NATO and the ILO quite high, their epistemic beliefs are indeed heterogeneous. In NATO, we see that even beyond the structural differences and communication issues between civilian and military staff, NATO's personnel are highly diverse in epistemic backgrounds. NATO International Staff employees are recruited competitively from a number of fields and professions, such as journalism, political science, law, engineering, and the military. This lack of internal cohesion and esprit de corps has long characterized the IS and does not appear to have changed significantly (De Wijk, 1997). Moreover, despite the formally only weak country quotas, there is a noticeable diversity of nationality, which is further enhanced by the fixed-contract basis that many employees work on (Mouritzen, 2013). Staffers who have been trained in their home countries often retain their national allegiances because they need to plan for their future employment. As one interviewee points out:

So the other people rotate in and out . . . And while they're here, they still have their national frameworks, their national loyalties. That doesn't mean they are not loyal to NATO, but that also means that they are looking to a career that will continue outside of NATO. (NATO 11)

The ILO's staff, too, have highly heterogeneous epistemic and social backgrounds, which stand in the way of a truly collective mindset. While national divides are less of a problem, the tripartite structure of the ILO is reflected in the professional backgrounds of its employees, who have often worked with either workers' or employers' organizations prior to joining the ILO. The spectrum of staff's educational backgrounds ranges from social scientists, lawyers, and economists to experts in very specific areas, such as forestry. Because the social sciences are especially disparate and contested with regard to normative preferences and attitudes, there is much epistemic heterogeneity even within this group. Not unlike the situation in NATO, short-term contracting further contributes to the IPA's pronounced heterogeneity and lack of continuity (MOPAN, 2016, p. 13). In sum, IPAs in both the ILO and NATO are highly challenged internally in the sense of our theoretical framework, since they are composed of epistemologically heterogeneous staffs with only limited cognitive slack.

7.3.2 External Challenges: A Rather Comfortable Niche

Furthermore, and in conjunction, the absence of credible external challenges renders any effort to consolidate the IPAs' institutional standing unnecessary. In assessing external challenges, we take into account pressures stemming from the IPAs' organizational domains and the political headwind they consider themselves confronted with from member states and civil society.

On the political challenges side, NATO's IPA deems itself to be not entirely unchallenged. NATO's member states are dependent on the alliance, since carrying out military manoeuvres without international support generally raises concerns of legitimacy. Moreover, most member states do not command sufficient military capabilities to individually carry out major missions without additional support from partners. Given NATO's limited membership of twenty-nine European and Western states with comparable values, interests, and objectives, the principals' political interests tend to be quite homogenous most of the time, that is, in peaceful periods. Although NATO's enlargement has been predicted to involve an increase in discord among the member states, this has not necessarily resulted in greater opportunities for the bureaucracy to influence decision making (Mayer, 2014b; Noetzel & Schreer, 2009). Certainly, there is a long-standing history of divides among NATO's member states, both before and after enlargement, over relations with Russia and missions in Bosnia, Afghanistan, and – above all – Iraq, to name just a few (Kaplan, 2004, pp. 10–12; Webber, Sperling, & Smith, 2012). These unanimities, however, do not regularly factor into the IPA's day-to-day routines. In the bureaucracy, there is widespread belief that NATO as an organization itself seems not to be an issue of major concern for its principals – at least in peaceful times – as one interviewee recalls anecdotally:

I worked for the Secretary General Jaap de Hoop Scheffer, and he said, 'When I was the foreign minister of the Netherlands, I only thought of NATO twice every year – when I came to NATO, and I had to give a speech. Rest of the time NATO – I left that to my ambassador.' It's not that they don't like NATO … But you're doing a million things, and NATO comes across this more as some sort of specialized, niche organization. And, you know, unless there is a major issue, like the Russians attack us, I leave that to my ambassador. (NATO 2)

An important facet of this self-understanding is that staffers report that since security policy is naturally a hot-button issue in general, many of the political challenges in terms of salience and civil society are not really attacks on NATO per se but what it stands for more generally. Although the number of annual protest events against the IO has increased, this number is comparable to the number of protests held against other IOs (Tallberg, Sommerer, Squatrito, & Jönsson, 2015). Civil society protests have been ongoing and have often focused on warfare specifically and Western dominance more generally (Suri, 2006). For the staffers at NATO, this continuous stream of criticism, often from the left side of the political spectrum, is perceived as a source of 'white noise', because as the IS, they do not really feel that they themselves are the target of protest and because protest has been NATO's constant companion for decades. Put differently, many staffers believe that there is little that can be done differently to appease critics, since by definition, they are a security organization and a Western alliance and can hardly act otherwise. In sum, even though security policy in general is a hot-button issue especially when conflict breaks out, the IS usually works in peacetime and does not perceive civil society protest as a major threat to its legitimacy and standing. On the perception level, political challenges to NATO can thus be described as intermediate at most.

Turning to the ILO, we find a perception of even fewer political challenges. This is, however, not due to homogenous interests among the member states. The ILO's principals are very heterogeneous since its membership is almost global and the tripartite structure adds further complexity (Baccaro & Mele, 2012; La Hovary, 2015). In the case of the ILO, however, this situation is perceived to be more of a natural obstacle for independent influence than a comparative advantage for the bureaucracy. Because the principals' involvement in the policy-making process is so remarkably strong and every document needs their approval, the IPA has to be very careful to navigate this structure (Patz & Goetz, 2019). It always runs risk of stepping on some constituent's toes and thereby slowing down if not stopping the policy-making process. In that sense, the very heterogeneity that is inscribed to the ILO's polity hinders the bureaucracy (see Section 7.3. on anticipation). This, however, does not make for a perception of political challenge in our sense because it is perceived not as pressuring but as a traditional part of the ILO's DNA.

The ILO's record of having navigated its course through political crises, such as the US withdrawal over Palestine's observer status and its historical standing as a Nobel prize-winning core institution of the UN system, contribute to an overall feeling of security among staffers (Maupain, 2013). The world of work is set comparatively low on the global agenda. Labour rights are far from being a hot-button issue, at least for major donors. Protest and criticism on the part of civil society revolve, if at all, around the aforementioned weak implementation powers of the organization. Usually, civil protests in the world of work happen on the domestic level, geared towards member states' governments, unions, or employers, but they do not target the ILO as an IO. However, despite this low international salience, the issue is not as irrelevant as to make the ILO fear for its status. Keeping up labour standards has come to be normatively related so closely with being a developed (Western) country that pulling out of the organization would now be considered an affront (ILO 5, 14). On the political challenges side, the ILO's IPA deems itself safe.

A very similar cognitive frame seems to be at work when looking at the perception of domain challenges in the ILO. From a historic perspective, too, the ILO was not without objective domain challenges, most prominently in the 1990s, when the World Trade Organization considered adding labour standards to its mandate, which could have led to an eclipse of the ILO's relevance (Helfer, 2006, 2008; Reinalda, 1998). While the resulting 1998 Declaration on Fundamental Principles and Rights at Work certainly marked a turning point in how ILO conventions apply, overall, the crisis was overcome without much change to the IPA's conception of itself (Dahan et al., 2012, p. 692). Today, like many specialized UN agencies, the ILO does objectively face some domain challenges, albeit to a lesser extent than other members of the UN family. The ILO is increasingly facing competition, mostly with regard to funding (ILO 6, 8, 12). Then as now, the administration's subjective perception of those threats is strongly mitigated by its self-understanding. This is true for two reasons. First, a comparatively high share of the ILO's budget is core funding (ILO 4, 11). Furthermore, widespread confidence prevails that this comfortable position is unlikely to change in the future.

We are really the last ones. And I think it is because, for one, we predate the UN – totally – and we are almost seen as a separate animal, a very specialized organization. We have the tripartite structure, so we have member states who are giving us money on three different levels. So we got money from employers, we've got money from the governments, from trade unions – mainly from member states. They can't be seen to not be investing in us. (ILO 14)

Second, when it comes to the ILO's core task and mandate, it is indeed in a unique position as the go-to organization with an exclusive mandate (Baccaro, 2015). The ILO's focal position within the domain and its high level of legitimacy render the IPA's perceived domain challenges rather low (Abbott et al., 2015; Senghaas-Knobloch, 2004, p. 142; Thomann, 2008). One staffer put it succinctly: 'They need you. They cannot decide not to work with you …They can't afford to do that alone. They need the ILO, they need the expertise' (ILO 5). Therefore, and despite the moderate level of actual competition, the ILO thinks itself safe.

Domain challenges in NATO are not reckoned to be very pronounced among staffers. As the leading European and North American security institution, the alliance does not suffer from considerable domain challenges (Flockhart, 2014, p. 71). Although the field of defence and security policy in general may be labelled as a 'crowded labour market' (Landman, 2002, p. 86), NATO can be considered as the predominant player, with the competency and capability to drive its smaller competitors out of the market (Landman, 2002, p. 86). On the whole, NATO's closest competitors in the field are the OSCE, the UN, and the EU. While the IPA does collaborate with all of them to a certain degree, it retains its own stance and position within the field (Koschut, 2018). Although there is still some competition over prestige, especially with the UN, in recent years, the NATO-UN relationship has changed for the better (Franke, 2018, p. 33). After decades of increasing partnership, often ad hoc, now they are even described as a having an almost symbiotic relationship (Kaplan, 2010). Furthermore, because of the principle of common funding, all twenty-nine member states contribute to NATO's budget according to a cost-share formula that is firmly based on gross national income. Although at times heatedly discussed among member states, contestation for funding is not *perceived* by NATO staffers as being a major issue: 'The cost share is not the challenge anymore. The challenge is what you spend it on' (NATO 4). While the common funding is used only to finance NATO's core budget, including maintenance and personnel costs, actual military operations are paid for by member states. This points to the importance of national interests and preferences, but again, it does not impose a greater burden of competing for money upon the organization, since for most of the member states, spending for NATO constitutes an integral part of their defence budgets.

To sum up this section, we conclude that both IPAs under study are substantially challenged internally as a result of their lack of cognitive slack and epistemic contestation. In light of these internal constraints, the IPAs' hands are tied in pursuing more advocacy-orientated routines. Their only very weakly developed functional orientation reflects these constraints. On the external challenges side, staffers in the ILO and NATO consider themselves rather safe. In NATO, the perception of little if any domain challenges is coupled with a medium degree of subjective political pressure. While overall they thus score low on external challenges, it is this political pressure that might – however intermediate – bring about NATO's routine emphasis on practices of political anticipation. Although staffers reported not feeling too affected by principal complexity in peacetime, it is quite conceivable in an environment of increasingly heterogeneous principals (Dijkstra, 2015), and with the emergence of new security challenges as a constant theme (Webber et al., 2012, p. 10) that the IPA needs to navigate its course carefully, especially given the consensus rule. NATO's behaviour in anticipating red lines and mapping the political space as empirical 'deviations' from the ideal-typical positional orientation of a servant style can thus be understood against the backdrop of its political challenges.

In the ILO, staffers reported exceptional levels of subjective security from external threats, both on the political level and in the organizational domain. The notion of ILO exceptionalism in its standing and relevance permeates staffers' view on external challenges on every level. To speak in rather strong terms, it is this subjective invulnerability that explains the IPA's passivity in positional orientation, which becomes visible in routines of rarely ever mobilizing support, its non-conflictual approach towards implementation, and the absence of patterns of regularly mapping the political space.

7.4 NATO, the ILO, and the Servant Revisited

This chapter was guided by the question of how it is that two IPAs as different as NATO's and the ILO's do not become more active on their own in advocating their cause and consolidating their institutional standing in the organizational domain. The servant-style nature of NATO's IPA appears to be quite intuitive considering that its lack of agency fits the organization's low formal autonomy, technical mandate, operation in high politics, and main function of providing a forum for bargaining. For the ILO, at least at face value, the servant style comes as more of a surprise given the ILO's moderate to high formal autonomy, normative mandate, realm of low politics, and main function of supplying expertise and operational support. Yet we have shown that indeed the ILO and NATO exhibit similar administrative styles, despite these pronounced differences in key structural characteristics. They assume a rather instrumental and passive role in both functional and positional regards. Notwithstanding certain minor deviations from what the ideal type would predict, especially when it comes to the anticipation of red lines and mapping the political space, both IPAs act as servants to their principals. While this similarity could not be explained by the organizations' mandates, policy fields, or functional design and services, we saw that the two IPAs find themselves in a similar situation as far as internal and external challenges are concerned. Pronounced internal challenges stand in the way of more active advocacy in the spirit of a functional orientation. At the same time, low to medium perceived external challenges do not render positional routines necessary.

We contend that there are at least two major points to take away from this chapter. Discarding the servant as the least attractive type would be premature both in empirical and conceptual terms. For one thing, the case of NATO especially shows that we must not understand a servant style to be inferior in a normative sense. Servant behaviour should not necessarily be equated with either suboptimal performance or the absence of intentional action per se (Boyne & Walker, 2004; Davis, Schoorman, & Donaldson, 1997; Van Slyke, 2007). In NATO, for instance, it might be precisely the servant style of its bureaucracy that constitutes the major source of the alliance's success. In the context of NATO's persistence after the Cold War, some argued that NATO developed 'general assets for political consultation and decision making' (Wallander, 2000). These 'assets', which here come to mean the neutrality and servant nature of the administrative body, helped, moreover, in dealing with new challenges after the dissolution of the Soviet Union. The IPA's passive stance lent NATO credibility in constituting a negotiation forum for its member states, which contributed to assuring its continued existence and relevance (McCalla, 1996). Although anecdotal, these points emphasize that servants are not automatically ineffective or subordinate to others but rather simply represent a different way of carrying out an IPAs' day-to-day business.

Further, the ILO and NATO administrations narrated distinctly different motifs. NATO's bureaucracy seems to be driven by a deeply held understanding of duty and dedication to its mandate in the spirit of true stewardship. The ILO's administrators, while certainly dedicated as well, pointed towards saturation as a justification for their servant style. The servant style is echoed by a self-perception as a saturated 'dinosaur' (ILO 14) in the case of the ILO, and a 'servant of the nations' (NATO 2) narrative of dedication at NATO. Although this could be merely a way of justifying their limited policy influence ex post or from reporting bias, the understanding of how staffers themselves explain their passivity reveals interesting insights. These different emphases certainly do not constitute the sole reasons for the respective IPA's servant style. Yet they underline the importance of considering both internal and external challenges in explaining administrative styles. Simply contending that IPAs are servants because that is the only alternative in a statist environment short-changes the investigation. It is true that the ILO and NATO are heavily constrained internally, which renders advocacy difficult and rather unlikely. At the same time we see that, given their respective positions and their understanding of them, there is simply no real need to put more effort into gaining or defending ground in the organizational domain. IPAs are servants in style not only because they *cannot* do more but also because they *need not* do more.

8 | Conclusion

Real Dwarfs, Illusory Dwarfs, or Even Giants? International Public Administrations as Actors in Global Governance

The rationale for this book emerged from several observations. First, there is no doubt that over the last decades there has been a steep rise in the establishment of IOs. This trend reflects the evolution of an increasingly relevant additional level of international governance that complements and interacts with subnational, national, and supranational governance levels in highly complex and multifaceted ways.

Second, the institutionalization of international policy-making structures, mostly in the form of IOs, has been accompanied by the creation of differentiated bureaucratic substructures within these organizations. The rise of IOs is hence also a rise of international bureaucracies. In many ways, these IPAs fulfil functions comparable to those of national ministerial bureaucracies and agencies. Similar to their national counterparts, IPAs play important roles in the initiation, preparation, and implementation of public policies (Eckhard & Ege, 2016; Knill & Bauer, 2016).

Third, we are left with a rather ambiguous picture when we turn our focus from the empirical observation of this phenomenon to the question of its analytical relevance. Based on our discussion in Chapter 1, we can attribute this deficit to two basic problems characterising IPA research. The former problem can be labelled as the 'illusory dwarf' problem. The analytical relevance of IPAs and even IOs has been overlooked because of a highly remote research perspective, and scholarship has neglected IPAs a relevant factor in understanding patterns of policy making beyond the nation-state. IPAs have had a shadowy analytical existence. Research concentrated on national interests and, later on, on the role of private actors in global governance (Cutler, Haufler, & Porter, 1999; Czempiel & Rosenau, 1992; Knill & Lehmkuhl, 2002); IOs were often conceived of as mere platforms of international negotiations rather than independent sources of political influence. In this world, IPAs were at best distant dwarfs whose examination was unnecessary to understand international policy making. Until a decade ago, little scholarship acknowledged the specific impact of public administration in the context of international relations and global governance (e.g. Armingeon & Beyeler, 2004; Diehl, 2005; Mahon & McBride, 2008; Strang & Chang, 1993).

The latter problem, by contrast, can be characterized as the 'illusory giant problem'. Rather than taking a perspective on IPAs that was too remote, scholars plunged deeply into the world of IPAs, often taking a perspective that was too close to draw general conclusions on IPA agency beyond case-specific accounts. Because of potentially biased case selection (with a focus on those cases in which IPAs were influential), there is a considerable risk that IPA agency might have been overestimated. Along these lines, a new field of academic literature has emerged that cuts across the disciplinary boundaries of international relations, public administration, comparative politics, and policy analysis. Although different disciplines still apply a variety of conceptual perspectives when addressing IPAs, the literature is united in finding that IPAs matter for policy making beyond the nation-state – hardly surprisingly in view of the predominant close-up perspective (Busch, 2014; Eckhard & Ege, 2016). In sum, IPA research has been somewhat stuck between approaching the phenomenon with either too much distance or too much proximity, implying that IPA agency has potentially been either systematically under- or overestimated.

Fourth, despite a growing interest in IPAs, we still have no systematic answer to the question of if and to what extent IPAs can be considered an independent source of influence in international policy making. Is there an analytical need to study IPAs in order to explain policy making beyond the nation-state, or can IPAs be considered merely agents of their political principals, implying that it is primarily the latter's interests and strategic interactions that matter? In short, is there a role for IPAs beyond the space of formally granted autonomy, and if so, how do IPAs fill this space?

Departing from the above considerations, this book sought to provide a systematic answer to these questions which goes beyond evidence from singular case studies and mere formal features. In so doing, the focus has been on three central questions. First, our goal was to assess the presence or absence of IPA agency in international policy making. Do IPAs have the potential to influence the initiation, formulation, and implementation of their IOs? In answering this first question, we had a special interest in the specific ways the potential influence of IPAs matters, or – put differently – the identification of dominant orientations guiding IPAs' behaviour in this regard. Second, our objective was to shed light on the causal factors that underlie the presence and direction of IPAs' influence.

To investigate variation in IPA influence, we set out to capture IPAs from a meso-level perspective, striking a balance between a sufficiently detailed assessment of IPA behaviour and the need for systematic comparison. In doing so, we developed the concept of administrative styles, understood as informal routines guiding administrative behaviour. The concept of administrative styles provides us with a measure for assessing administrative influence potentials. We can assess how IPAs typically behave in policy making. To what extent are they routinely only following formal rules or deviating from or bypassing these rules? While this measure does not allow us to precisely determine the manifestation of administrative influence on specific policy decisions, we are able to identify dominant bureaucratic orientations that might be more or less directed at exerting such influence beyond the discretion formally granted by the political principals.

Our comparative study of administrative styles and their determinants yields a range of empirical and theoretical findings, which will be summarized in Section 8.1. In Section 8.2, we discuss several theoretical implications emerging from these findings before turning to discuss a number of limitations of our study and potential avenues for future research (Section 8.3).

8.1 Empirical and Theoretical Findings

A first key finding of our empirical analysis is that IPAs indeed develop quite different behavioural routines when it comes to their activities along the policy cycle. We find significant variation in 'how things are usually done' across organizations. The empirical analysis revealed that, for instance, the FAO and IOM bureaucracies have developed routines and standard operating procedures that are primarily directed towards influencing the institutional conditions under which the IPAs need to operate and thus towards enhancing the standing and reputation of their organization. This positional orientation is reflected in a strong focus on activities related to the mapping of the political space, the mobilization of support, the political anticipation, and the strategic use of formal powers. In other IPAs, by contrast, administrators put a much stronger focus on the substantial aspects of their daily work, trying to leave a real imprint on their IO's policy outputs and to develop the most well designed and effective polices. As our comparison of UNEP and the WHO has revealed, this functional orientation manifests itself in day-to-day practices that strongly favour the development of the IO's own policy ideas and proposals, solution search, internal coordination, policy promotion, and policy evaluation. Moreover, we also find IPAs, such as those of the IMF and the UNHCR, that have developed routines combining a strong positional and functional orientation, that is, they optimize their work to achieve substantial policy influence and safeguard their position vis-à-vis their principals and organization in their direct organizational environment. In the secretariats of NATO and the ILO, by contrast, these ambitions were found to be largely absent.

Based on these findings, a second key insight of this book is that an administrative style should be considered a configurative function of whether IPAs seek to exert influence and if so, how. IPAs that primarily act as servants (as do those of the ILO and NATO) refrain from attempts to routinely develop their own ideas and stances and to slip them into the policy-making process. Similarly, they do not actively try to shape or change their institutional environment. These IPAs thus play an instrumental and passive role in both political and managerial regards. The IPAs of the FAO and the IOM, in turn, were found to channel their energies to the positional aspects of their day-to-day work but to neglect actions that aim at enhancing the quality and effectiveness of their policies. They can hence be described as consolidators, since they combine administrative routines directed towards institutional consolidation with only weak policy advocacy. In contrast to the IPAs following a consolidator style, more advocacy-orientated ones, such as those of the WHO and UNEP, are not satisfied with merely protecting their organizational standing but are driven by the goal of improving their policy output and outcomes. An entrepreneur, in turn, is the combination of advocate and consolidator administrative styles and thus comes with both intensive bureaucratic advocacy in substantial policy making and activities aimed at strengthening the administration's position. We identified such an advanced stage of entrepreneurship in the cases of the IMF and the UNHCR.

The third major theoretical insight gained in this book is that the emergence of a particular administrative style can essentially be explained by the extent to which IPAs are facing internal and external challenges. As shown in our analysis of the IMF and the UNHCR, the combination of few internal challenges (in terms of cognitive slack and homogenous epistemic belief systems) and high perceived institutional constraints (i.e. subjective pressures in an IPA's policy domain and a political contestation through its principals) brings about strong and pronounced entrepreneurial activities. Exactly the opposite scenario was found in the comparison of NATO and the ILO. Here, the perception of only minor external challenges and the absence of bureaucratic capacities to develop and formulate their own organizational policy ideas have led to a more servant-style pattern of administrative behaviour. The cases of the IOM and the FAO revealed that a consolidator style emerges from a combination of high internal challenges and the administrators' self-perception of being highly challenged from the outside. Our chapter on UNEP and the WHO, in turn, showed that strong expertise in the bureaucracy and a common belief system contribute to the formation of an advocacy-orientated administrative style, while, at the same time, a medium level of perceived external challenges prompts both IPAs to also feature at least some characteristics of a consolidator.

An important empirical limitation to this study is certainly that none of the IPAs in this book do *not* perceive any external challenges while at the same time possessing the bureaucratic capacities to exert substantial policy influence. In other words, we did not find one conjunction of determinants, namely low internal pressures and high external challenges in our sample. Based on this alone, one could ask the question of whether or not a 'true' or 'pure' advocacy-orientated IPA actually exists on the global scene or if any IPA willing and capable of exerting policy influence inevitably also has to work towards consolidation. We consider this question, however, to be of an empirical rather than a theoretical nature. As discussed in Chapter 6, it is certainly worthwhile to apply the concept of administrative styles to a wider range of organizations. Here, the most promising way ahead could be to consider organizations that, because of the very technical nature of the subject matter they are dealing with, attract fewer political controversies or competition in their policy domain. Previous research has shown that, for instance, the Bank for International Settlement might constitute such a case (Knill et al., 2019).

Throughout this book, reference to the perception of the internal and external challenges of an IPA could consistently explain the emergence of particular administrative styles and their underlying orientations. At the same time, the influence of a number of other factors, especially those of a more formal and structural nature, could be effectively ruled out. Our sample included organizations with very different structural features and peculiarities. This allowed us to control for other influences, either through the pairwise comparison of IPAs with the same administrative style or by cross comparing IPAs that share the same structural features but are largely different in their bureaucratic routines. Despite comparable high levels of formal autonomy, it is only the IMF bureaucracy that developed an entrepreneurial administrative style, while the IPAs of the IOM and the ILO did not. Likewise, although both the WHO and the FAO bureaucracies are very decentralized organizations with strong field presence, they have adopted very different internal working procedures and behavioural patterns. The comparison between the IOM and the FAO, in turn, revealed that the total size and developments in terms of both staff and budget could not per se explain why different IPAs follow the same bureaucratic routines and practices. The case of UNEP highlighted that an IPA might establish itself as an advocate even if its headquarters' location (in Nairobi, Kenya) is situated far away from those of other IPAs and thus spatially bars the organization from most global affairs. Finally, the chapter on the ILO and NATO showed that none of the essential features of the IOs – the policy field, mandate and function, size and membership, or geographical scope – could convincingly account for the two IPAs' servant style.

Recent scholarship (inter alia: Graham, 2017; Patz & Goetz, 2019) has taken an interest in which role budgets, and particular the extent to which an IPA needs to secure voluntary contributions, play in explaining IPA practices. The UN and its entities are especially heavily dependent on so-called earmarked funding, being resources exclusively provided for 'specific themes, sectors, regions or countries' (Tortora & Steensen, 2014, p. 4). At first sight, the IPAs under study in this book seem to support the idea that a strong dependence on voluntary contributions could be a predictor for how active an IPA is in coming up with new project and policy ideas. Of the eight IPAs we looked at, all but the ILO, IMF, and NATO are heavily dependent on such funding, which comes as no surprise given that they belong to the UN family, which received 70 per cent of its funding as already-designated monies in 2012 (Tortora & Steensen, 2014, p. 8). The fact that the two servant-style IPAs in this book do not (or not as heavily) depend on such contributions could lead to the conclusion that it is indeed money that makes the IPA world go around. However, the case of the IMF stands in stark contrast to this assumption, as it comes close to the entrepreneur ideal type, despite its comparatively low pressure to secure funding. In addition, among the IPAs that do need to compete for funding there is still variation in the extent to which they display a functional or positional orientation, respectively. In other words, while there is a definite need to further empirically investigate the effect of funding arrangements on IPA routines, on their own, they seem to conclusively explain neither the presence or absence of IPA agency, nor its underlying orientations.

We began this book with the tale of Michael Ende's Mr Tur Tur. This character is an illusory giant. When seen from a distance, he appears to be colossal. The closer one approaches him, however, the smaller he becomes, finally revealing himself to be a perfectly normal-sized man. Given the key research interest of this book and the resulting case selection strategy, we cannot definitively answer the question of whether IPAs generally tend towards being dwarfs or giants. We can, however, safely conclude that there is variance in IPAs' informal agency. In reality, it seems that some IPAs are indeed dwarfs that do not regularly work towards leaving their own mark on international policy making, while others strive to be giants making a difference beyond the sum of their member states' interests. Moreover, it has become clear that focusing merely on the formal autonomy granted to an IPA provides no entirely reliable proxy for the IPA's actual agency and influence. Rather, we need to understand informal behavioural routines of IPAs that affect the ways IPAs work with and use their formal powers. What might seem a dwarf from a formal autonomy perspective might turn out to be a giant when taking account of administrative styles, and vice versa.

8.2 Theoretical Implications

Our findings indicate two central aspects that have broader theoretical implications for our view on IPAs and their agency. First, we have shown that IPAs can develop informal routines that come along with different potentials for influencing the policies of their IOs in varying directions and that there is thus variation in IPA informal agency. Second, we have seen that these potentials are not fully determined by the formal autonomy delegated to IPAs. The study of these informal behavioural patterns is hence of crucial analytical relevance to fully understanding policy making beyond the nation-state.

This claim, however, stands in marked contrast to some theoretical accounts in the fields of International Relations and Public Administration. Similar to the research interest underlying this book, the central objective in these strands of literature is to study the conditions under which bureaucratic influence emerges autonomously from an IO's political superiors. Departing from this question, the theoretical debate has primarily focused on the question of how to best conceptualize the relationship between IPAs and their political masters. Some prominent research strands in this context, however, still put little analytical leverage on IPAs. This neglect results not only from the fact that, especially in the IR literature, the focus has been on IOs rather than on their administrative corpus, but also – and more importantly – from the theoretical perspective applied.

This becomes particularly apparent when focusing on the analytical frameworks that are more or less loosely based upon principal–agent theory (e.g. McCubbins, 1985; Bendor, Glazer, & Hammond, 2001; Hawkins et al., 2006; Pollack, 2003; Miller, 2005). The focus is on constellations of delegation, in which a group of political principals mandate an agent (the IPA) to fulfil certain tasks. As self-serving behaviour by the agent is assumed, the situation – from the perspective of the principals – can essentially be viewed as a control problem. Agency autonomy is thus seen as a discretion, that is, the product of delegated powers minus control mechanisms (Hawkins & Jacoby, 2006, p. 8). Basically, two sources of administrative autonomy are emphasized: the substance of the competences or statutory powers delegated to the agent (Cox & Jacobsen, 1973; Pollack, 1997; Tallberg, 2000; Johnson & Urpelainen, 2014) and operational resources (Brown, 2010; Ege & Bauer, 2017; Graham, 2017). To systematically capture delegation, Hooghe and colleagues (2017), for instance, collected data on seventy-two IOs in order to explain variation in the delegation (and pooling) of authority. With regard to the autonomy of the IPAs under study, they focused on indicators such as the degree to which the secretariat can exercise executive powers, set the agenda, draft the budget, or monitor member states.

Yet according to principal–agent accounts, administrative agency above all constitutes a problem that might undermine the efficacy of political leaders. It is deemed to be primarily a problem of effective control; to overcome information asymmetries, the principal must impose sufficient incentives (or sanctions) on the agent to align its self-interest with the principal's goals (Arrow, 1984; Laffont & Martimort, 2002; Miller, 2005, pp. 204–5). Once the principal imposes appropriate incentives, it can draw fully on the agent's competencies with little risk of control loss. In short, in principal–agent accounts, IPAs are analytical dwarfs. The analytical leverage is on the principals of IPAs (i.e. the political leadership of an IO and its member states), and there is thus no particular need to study IPAs as agents of their own right.[1]

The idea that this conception of IPAs as analytical dwarfs might be an illusion has been challenged, moreover, by more recent theoretical complements to principal–agent frameworks, such as the governor's dilemma (Abbott, Genschel, Snidal, & Zangl, 2018). At the heart of this dilemma lies the observation that principals generally face a trade-off between competence and control. Contrary to the assumptions of principal–agent accounts, control might undermine the agent's competence to effectively fulfil its delegated tasks. For instance, freedom from principal control might be essential for agents to serve as commitment devices, preventing policy reversals (by the current principal or its successors) in the face of time inconsistency (Kydland & Prescott, 1977) or political uncertainty (Moe, 1990). Governments establish constitutional (Levinson, 2011) and international courts (Simmons & Danner, 2010) to demonstrate their commitment to constitutional or human rights (Stone Sweet & Palmer, 2017). From these considerations follows that – depending on the concrete configuration of how the trade-off between competence and control is settled politically – there might be considerable leeway for independent agency beyond existing

---

[1] The most notable exception to this is certainly the work of Hawkins and colleagues (2006), who depart from a similar critique.

control options on the side of the principal. However, while acknowledging dilemmas in agency control, in this framework, it is also true that IPAs are analytically subordinate to principals. The focus is on the factors that determine the choice of the principals' control arrangements. Apart from political and budgetary constraints of the principal, these factors also include the competence of the agent potentially being undermined by hard political controls. While the choices of principals remain centre stage, the governor's dilemma hence acknowledges that certain characteristics of IPAs might reduce the control options for principals. Despite this acknowledgement, however, the dominant analytical focus remains on formal control arrangements. Informal behavioural routines of IPAs unaffected by formal controls are not explicitly taken into account.

In sum, overall, principal–agent approaches (including recent modifications) continue to be 'blind' to sources of IPA influence that might emerge outside of and independent from formal autonomy and principal controls. These theories are based on two assumptions that can be challenged on the basis of our research findings. First, they assume that if agents are granted formal autonomy, they will make full use of this discretion. Second, they assume that agents will not extend their activities beyond the limits of formal controls if controlled appropriately. In contrast to these assumptions, our findings indicate that IPAs might develop informal routines that deviate from formal autonomy. Different administrative styles might entail that IPAs typically remain below their formally granted space for action or that they systematically try to go beyond this space. Administrative styles matter in the way IPAs deal with their formal settings. As we have shown, they might be driven by different orientations and ambitions in this regard. Consequently, merely assessing the formal delegation and control relationship between principals and agents might not be sufficient to fully capture policy dynamics beyond the nation-state. While we do not question that formal autonomy matters, administrative styles constitute an explanatory factor that could greatly add to our understanding in this context.

Our emphasis on the analytical relevance of administrative styles furthermore more broadly resonates with claims to study 'international organizations as organizations', a perspective (Brechin & Ness, 2013) that assigns bureaucratic structures as well as the skills and attitudes of administrative personnel a greater role in explanations of organizational behaviour (Barnett & Finnemore, 2004). In essence, 'bureaucratization' is conceived of as a pathological form of organizational 'autonomiza-tion' – in other words, the tendency towards a growing insulation of the bureaucracy from political control (Bauer & Ege, 2016). That the orga-nization, once established, is likely to gain in autonomy is seen as a natural trend fuelled by organizational size, division of labour, and accumulation of task-specific expertise related to but not entirely deter-mined by formal competence endowment (Biermann & Siebenhüner, 2009; Ellinas & Suleiman, 2011; Marcussen & Trondal, 2011; Xu & Weller, 2008). While we share with these approaches the view that IPAs might develop dynamics beyond the radar of formally granted auton-omy, our argument goes beyond these claims that continue to concen-trate on formal or structural characteristics of IPAs, endogenous developments, and bureaucratization as an automatism written into IO structures.

Moreover, it remains unclear if and to what extent such features as bureaucratization might translate into observable behavioural patterns of IPAs. As we have argued in the theoretical part of this book, certain structural features can affect the extent to which IPAs perceive internal challenges to their policy-making capacities. Such structural features relate, in particular, to factors such as staff homogeneity and organiza-tional slack for research and the development of expertise. Our findings hence provide a complementary perspective to this research tradition insofar as we provide more specific accounts of the loose coupling of structural features and observable informal administrative routines. In addition, we offer a systematic perspective on how the tendency to 'autonomize' might vary. It becomes clear that, in fact, not all IPAs seem to have gained informal autonomy over time. Autonomization and bureaucratization are not automatisms. To the contrary, informal agency varies greatly and is not an entirely endogenous process, but influence potentials are clearly affected by external dynamics and challenges.

Lastly, our study adds the analytical meso-level and a comparative element to the scholarship on IO organizational culture (inter alia: Weaver, 2008; Weaver & Leiteritz, 2005; Broome & Seabrooke, 2007; Broome & Seabrooke, 2012; Vetterlein 2012). The more abstract macro dimensions of IO culture, such as ideology, language, and norms, manifest themselves in meso-level routines, which theo-retically puts administrative styles right in the heart of organizational culture scholarship (Weaver, 2008). Yet, the concept has the advantage of allowing for comparatively assessing IO culture beyond single cases and the very small-N. The 'loftier' macro-dimensions, e.g., norms and ideology, are almost by definition too strongly tied to specific issues to be compared cross-sectorally. Routines, on the other hand, are more or less a given in every IO, as all public organizations produce policy output of some sort. Their style does not depend on what is being done (the individual policies), but how it is done on an informal, regular basis, which gives the researcher an analytical angle for comparisons of vastly different IPAs.

In conclusion, our study suggests several avenues for how existing theoretical accounts of the nexus between politics and public administration at the level of IOs might be modified and complemented. First, dominant principal–agent perspectives could mitigate potential blind spots emerging from a merely formal focus on delegated administrative autonomy by explicitly acknowledging informal routines and agents' coping patterns with formal constraints. Second, studies emphasizing bureaucratic structures as sources of administrative autonomy must be complemented by more specific arguments of how structural features are translated into behavioural patterns and by going beyond purely endogenous explanations. Third, both of these aspects underline the need to take IPAs seriously when it comes to explaining public policy beyond the nation-state. Their analytical and empirical relevance can be reduced neither to their structural features nor to the formal spaces of autonomy granted to them by their political masters. Lastly, while the IO culture literature certainly takes IPAs' role in policy-making seriously, in our view, the literature could benefit from taking a meso-perspective, especially with regard to its comparative element.

8.3 Perspectives for Future Research

The major purpose of this study has been to shed light on the extent to which IPAs vary in their administrative styles, the factors affecting this variation, and the extent to which this variation is associated with different potentials of IPAs to influence policy making beyond the nation-state. In addressing these questions, we have offered a range of empirical, conceptual, and theoretical insights. At the same time, any specification of analytical focus entails certain limitations. Some of these limitations point towards particularly promising avenues for future research, which we will discuss in more detail in this section.

8.3.1 The Travel Potential of Administrative Styles

This book has analysed the concept of administrative styles for eight IOs. Given our research interest, we focused on rather prominent IOs, mostly from the global North. Moreover, we concentrated on formal public intergovernmental organizations. A remaining question is thus to what extent the concept of administrative styles can travel *horizontally* to other IOs and *vertically* to the nation state context.

With regard to the first aspect, there is actually nothing specific to the concept of administrative styles which would restrict an application to organizations with a less encompassing membership or to more regional organizations located in South America, Asia, Africa, or the Middle East. The strive for legitimacy and effectiveness is a key concern of modern bureaucracies that has been found in all kinds of different contexts (Evans, Haggard, & Kaufman, 1992). While we would thus argue that the concept can be quite easily transferred to formal public intergovernmental organizations in different contexts and with varying characteristics, we are more reluctant when it comes to extending the concept's application to more informal and experimental forms of global governance (Vabulas & Snidal, 2013). It is an integral part of the concept proposed that the bureaucracy tries to position itself vis-à-vis its political principals. This requires that principals exist in the first place and – if so – are identifiable. In the context of multi-stakeholder and global public-private partnerships, such identification is complex, if not impossible, given that the roles of principals and agents are strongly intermingled and do constantly switch. This suggests that scholars must proceed with caution when applying the concept of administrative styles to more informal forms of international cooperation.

These restrictions, however, do not imply that the proposed concept is of no relevance in the respective context. The style of an IPA might, for instance, tell us whether an organization is more or less likely to build up global public–private partnership. Following this reasoning, it is not by chance that Andonova (2017) finds the UNEP and the WHO especially – the two advocates in our sample – to heavily engage in collaboration with global NGOs, foundations, and multinational corporations. In sum, the concept's scope is limited to public intergovernmental organizations but the insights gained might still be of interest for students of other kinds of organizations.

Second, can the concept of administrative styles also be used to capture and explain bureaucratic influence at the national level? In our view, it is generally possible to transfer our concept to national bureaucracies. Yet, substantial modifications are necessary. First and foremost, the different indicators for measuring administrative styles need to be reviewed and, if necessary, replaced. Most importantly, this is because the different spheres of the policy process are far more separated and organized in distinct administrative entities at the national level. Oftentimes, once a law is passed, the responsible ministry has little to no possibility of influencing the implementation process. Likewise, the agencies in charge of implementation only rarely have the opportunity to shape the formulation of policies from the bottom up. As a result, depending on what kind of bureaucratic body the researcher is interested in, some of the stages of the policy cycle simply do not apply. As a consequence, there might be fewer indicators available for the individual bureaucracies and hence more problems distinguishing between their organizational routines.

There might be further complications regarding the factors explaining the variation in administrative styles. National bureaucracies should overall face fewer internal challenges given the common cultural background of the administrators. In countries with a strong *Rechtsstaat* tradition, we even cannot find substantial variation in the staff's professional background given the strong training in legal matters, that, for a long time, has been a prerequisite for accessing higher administrative positions (Rothgang & Schneider, 2015). Similarly, external challenges might not be as pronounced as on the international level. Although national bureaucracies clearly compete for budget (Peters, 2010), there is little reason to perceive threats comparable to the international level. It is, for instance, rather unlikely, that an entire ministry no longer receives money in the case of low performance. In sum, analyses directly transferring the concept of administrative style to the national context might only yield limited variation on both the key dependent and the independent variables. Accordingly, if at all, for the concept to be applied to the national level, the empirical assessment strategy would require major revisions.

8.3.2 *Administrative Styles and Policy Portfolio Change: Growing in Policy Breadth or Depth?*

Throughout this book, we have shown that IPAs have different potentials to influence the policies of their organizations. This, however, does not necessarily imply that IPAs can always flourish, realize their full potential, or leave a real imprint on their IOs' policies. Future research should thus delve more deeply into the question of whether and how the administrative style of an IPA affects 'its' IO's policies. There are many ways an IPA might exert such influence. IPAs might shape the broader policy paradigm dominant in their area of action, the goals pursued by the IO, and the means used to achieve those goals (Tallberg, Sommerer, Squatrito, & Lundgren, 2016). An IPA might thus influence not only *what* an IO does but also *how* it intends to achieve its objectives.

Given the extreme diversity in IO functions, however, it would be inappropriate to rely on a static analysis of IOs' actions and policy outputs. Rather, it seems necessary to analyse dynamics and change patterns in IOs' policy portfolios over time. In this context, we suggest a focus on two analytical dimensions to be especially promising. These are changes in policy breadth and policy depth.

Policy breadth refers to the number of policy targets addressed by an IO with regard to a given policy field and thus to the question of what an IO actually does. In the existing literature, the policy targets of IOs are often considered as ex ante determined by the IOs' statutes. Yet in reality, IOs do constantly engage in reinterpreting and broadening their mandates (Tallberg, Lundgren, Sommerer, & Squatrito, 2017). For instance, the WHO's scope of action expanded from crisis and emergency management to sanitary regulations, the control of malaria, tuberculosis, and sexually transmitted diseases, and ultimately to the promotion of primary health care (Hanrieder, 2015; Lee, 2009). Similarly, the IOM and the FAO have greatly expanded their responsibilities over the course of the last decades (Bradley, 2017; Pécoud, 2017; Shaw, 2007). In the case of the FAO, this went so far that one of the key reform proposals was to reduce the number of issues addressed and to put a halt to the IPA's tendency to arbitrarily expand its portfolio (FAO, 2007). Policy depth, by contrast, covers the number of policy means that are adopted to achieve a given policy target. The term thus captures how ambitiously IOs try to achieve their policy targets or how strongly an IO is committed to achieving a certain goal. For instance, the IMF's policy target of addressing balance of payment crises can be addressed by a range of different policy means, such as stand-by arrangements, flexible credit lines, or precautionary and liquidity lines (Chwieroth, 2010; Moschella, 2010).

But what effects might administrative styles of an IPA have on the development of policy breadth and depth of their respective IOs? In general, a servant style should simply imply less dynamic IO policy portfolios than those of entrepreneurial IPAs. Servants will pursue a highly instrumental role, as far as possible trying to avoid interference with the positions of their political leaders and member states. According to our classification, servants engage strongly in neither institutional consolidation nor policy advocacy. From this, it follows that changes in policy portfolios will be driven less by administrative activism than by political initiatives of IO leaders or individual member states. As a consequence, portfolio dynamics, in terms of both policy breadth and depth, can be expected to be relatively low. Where we still see pronounced dynamics, this should be easily explainable with a view to current events or outspoken demands of the principals.

In contrast, portfolios should develop much more dynamically if either a functional orientation or a positional orientation or both shape an IPA's administrative style. In this context, we can expect pronounced variation, depending on the extent to which IPAs can be classified as advocate, consolidator, or entrepreneur. In the first case, the strong policy capability shaping administrative routines should favour growth patterns that are primarily based on policy learning and continuous improvement of policy design and implementation for existing policy targets rather than a constant search of opening up new policy areas and policy targets. The primary motivation of an advocate is to increase its policy effectiveness rather than its institutional autonomy and legitimacy. As a consequence, portfolio growth for advocates should be based primarily on increases in policy depth rather than policy breadth.

By contrast, exactly the opposite pattern can be expected for consolidators. Here, the main motivation driving administrative routines lies in positional interests of the bureaucracy. Gaining new competences, political autonomy, and resources are typically prioritized over the development of effective policies. As a result, increases in policy breadth should exceed increases in policy depth. Consolidators seek more but not necessarily better policies: accordingly, the fine tuning of existing policies is less important than opening up new policy targets, even if such developments might be accompanied by decreases in policy consistency. Based on these considerations, we can expect that for consolidators, policy targets should grow faster than the use of different means over time. Finally, due to its combined functional and positional orientation, an entrepreneurial style should come along with simultaneous growth dynamics in policy breadth and depth.

Following such an approach could also allow testing for the *relative* explanatory power of the concept of administrative styles with regard to organizational outputs. The WHO, for instance, is said to have been dragged into all kinds of policy issues primarily because of its federal design, which grants the regional representation near autonomy from the headquarters with regard to their programming authority (see Chapter 6). An advocacy-orientated style per se thus does not necessarily mean that an IO's policy portfolio cannot become overstretched with regard to the range of subjects covered. However, following our theoretical considerations, we should expect that organizations such as the FAO or the IOM (see Chapter 5) that are decentralized *and* driven by a positional orientation should grow faster in policy breadth than in policy depth when compared to the WHO.

8.3.3 Administrative Styles and Formal Autonomy: Mutual Reinforcement or Mutual Weakening?

A third potential research avenue pertains to the interplay of administrative styles and formal autonomy. While we have shown that administrative styles constitute a potentially important explanation of administrative influence, they are undoubtedly not the only one. The most important additional factor that plays a role in this regard is the formal autonomy granted to IPAs by their political masters. The two sources of administrative influence differ in their degree of independence. Whereas administrative styles can be considered a more independent source of bureaucratic influence since they remain outside the radar of political control, formal autonomy is a direct result of the degree of political delegation and control. Yet despite these differences, (potential) administrative influence on policy making can be conceived of as the aggregate of two different sources: administrative styles and formal discretion.

We consider formal autonomy and administrative styles as sources of influence that do not determine each other. As argued in Chapter 2, this view emerges from the fact that the literature emphasizes rather different factors that influence variation in terms of formal and informal arrangements. While formal autonomy is primarily explained against the background of principals' preferences, institutional path dependencies, and functionalist reasoning (Pierson, 2000; Koremenos et al., 2001; Hawkins et al., 2006), informal routines, like administrative styles, have their roots in factors such as socialization, esprit de corps, and administrative perceptions of external challenges regarding the competition in organizational fields or political threat (Knill, 2001; Knill et al., 2019). As a consequence, a highly autonomous IPA does not necessarily need to adopt an entrepreneurial style, while an IPA with low autonomy may not automatically adopt a servant style. For the IMF bureaucracy, high autonomy coincides with an entrepreneurial style, while in the ILO case, a similar autonomy level is accompanied by a servant style (see Chapters 4 and 7). If we accept the argument that administrative styles are not determined by formal autonomy, the central question that arises is how these two sources interact. We suggest that one can distinguish four ideal-typical configurations of bureaucratic influence potentials (Table 8.1). We see no reason to assume a priori that any of these four constellations (as well as any patterns lying between the different extreme poles) should be more or less likely to emerge empirically.

The first scenario (tame dog on a short leash) combines low formal autonomy with a servant style. In this case, the potential for

Table 8.1 *Formal and informal sources of administrative influence*

		Administrative style	
		Servant	*Entrepreneur/Advocate/ Consolidator*
Formal autonomy	*High*	Medium influence (Tame dog on a long leash)	High influence (Wild dog on a long leash)
	Low	Low influence (Tame dog on a short leash)	Medium influence (Wild dog on a short leash)

administrative influence on IO outputs can be considered very low, with formal arrangements and informal routines mutually reinforcing each other. From the IPAs studied in this book, the NATO bureaucracy comes very close to this scenario. The mutual reinforcement of both factors can also be expected for the second scenario (wild dog on a long leash). Here, high formal autonomy is accompanied by an administrative style characterized by strong functional and/or positional orientations. In this case, we would expect the policy influence of the bureaucracy to be very high. The IMF secretariat provides a good illustration for this scenario.

By contrast, a mutual weakening of formal autonomy and styles can be expected for the two remaining scenarios, in which administrative influence will remain at a medium level. The third scenario (wild dog on a short leash) refers to the combination of low autonomy and a pronounced functional and/or positional style orientation. This is the typical case, in which IPAs seek to overcome their formal constraints by strong routines of advocacy, consolidation, or entrepreneurialism. In this constellation, administrative influence hence primarily emerges from administrative styles rather than formal autonomy. Exactly the opposite holds for the fourth scenario (tame dog on a long leash). Although IPAs can be highly influential in view of their formal discretion, their servant style induces behavioural patterns in which they typically remain below their formal influence potentials. As shown in Chapter 7, this pattern applies to the ILO secretariat's high formal autonomy, and a unique position made the ILO's administration 'lethargic' in the sense that the IPA does not use the full potential it has been granted through its mandate.

Of course, these considerations are only theoretical. In our view, a more thorough empirical assessment of interactions between formal and informal sources of administrative influence provides a highly promising area for future research. In theoretical terms, such endeavours would help greatly to achieve synergies between approaches linked to the principal–agent framework and those emphasizing informal bureaucratic dynamics. Moreover, it would be of analytical interest to study long-term sequences in the development of IPAs. For instance, do entrepreneurial IPAs gain more formal autonomy over time or can we observe the exactly opposite scenario, with the principals trying to 'leash their headstrong agents'? And can we observe similar long-term dynamics for servant IPAs?

8.3.4 *Stability and Change of Administrative Styles*

Finally, this book is not about change. Rather, its major purpose is to identify administrative styles and account for their variation across different IOs. Our analytical interest was thus clearly on a static comparison of administrative styles rather than assessing their stability and change over time. Our focus on variation rather than change was based on the assumption that administrative styles, as a matter of fact, display high stability over time. We conceived of administrative styles as organizational routines related to the initiation, formulation, and implementation of public policies, and we have shown in this book that the formation of administrative styles of IOs is strongly affected by specific constellations of endogenous (internal) and exogenous (external) challenges perceived by the IPA in question.

Evidence from our case studies indeed provides empirical support for this stickiness assumption. Although from a merely factual view, internal and external challenges to an IPA might have changed over time, such changes are often not perceived as such by the IPA itself. Obviously, organizational routines, once established, are not only constantly reproduced, but also affect the way staffers perceive external and internal challenges. The IPAs of the FAO and the IOM are cases in point. Even ten years after the 2008 food crisis, the FAO secretariat continued to reproduce administrative routines directed at consolidation. In a similar vein, the IOM bureaucracy sticks to a consolidator pattern despite its continuous and rapid growth over the last decades. Administrative styles reflect deeply institutionalized organizational routines that display high stability towards endogenous and exogenous change.

However, our research design provides anecdotal rather than systematic evidence for this finding. Although our evidence resonates well with the literature on organizational routines, it is by no means unchallenged. There are various studies emphasizing that certain organizational routines might display different levels of stability (Howard-Grenville, 2005; Pentland, Hærem, & Hillison, 2011; Turner & Fern, 2012). On the one hand, the observation of such variation might emerge from different levels of analysis. The longer our observation period and the more fine grained our measurement scale, the higher the likelihood of detecting changes in organizational routines (Knill & Lenschow, 2001; Pentland, Hærem, & Hillison, 2010). On the other hand, variation in the stability of routines might be affected by the effort required to accomplish them and the extent to which they are embedded in the organizational context. The more that organizational routines entail demanding and mindful activities and the more that any change of these routines would affect also other parts of an organization, the higher is their stability, and vice versa. Examples of the former constellation that are emphasized in the literature refer to the adoption of specific patterns of interaction (Lazaric & Denis, 2005), avoiding political confrontation and striving for legitimacy (Feldman, 2003), maintaining an established truce (Nelson & Winter, 1982; Zbaracki & Bergen, 2010), and avoiding variations that could upset other routines (Howard-Grenville, 2005).

In general, these findings lend strong support to our conception of administrative styles as organizational routines that display high stability over time. Administrative styles, as specified in this book, refer to demanding rather than effortless or mindless activities. Moreover, these patterns are broadly embedded in the organizational context. Although there is much to suggest that administrative styles display inertia over time, more knowledge is needed to shed light on the conditions under which even highly stable administrative styles may undergo adaptation. As we have seen in the case of the IMF, for instance, administrative styles may indeed undergo considerable change, along with fundamental changes in the internal and external challenges an IPA is facing. In further investigating changes in styles, potential factors of analytical interest might include the degree of factual changes in internal and external challenges, the time period during which different internal and/or external conditions prevail, and the structural and formal features of an organization. It is only on the basis of such systematic assessments that we are able to make reliable statements on the extent to which IPAs, as dwarfs or giants, will maintain this status over time or whether their role and relevance as actors in global governance is likely to change.

Appendix 1

Administrative Style	Organization	Positional Orientation				Functional Orientation				
		Support Mobilization	Mapping of the Political Space	Political Anticipation	Strategic Use of Formal Powers	Issue Emergence	Solution Search	Internal Coordination	Policy Promotion	Evaluation
Servant	ILO	low	low	medium	medium	low	low	low	low	medium
	NATO	low	medium	high	low	low	low	medium	low	low
Consolidator	IOM	high	high	high	high	low	low	low	low	medium
	FAO	high	high	high	high	medium	low	low	medium	medium
Advocate	WHO	medium	medium	high	low	low	high	medium	high	high
	UNEP	medium	high	high	medium	high	high	medium	high	medium
Entrepreneur	UNHCR	high	high	high	high	high	medium	medium	high	high
	IMF	medium	high	high	high	high	high	high	high	high
Percentage (%)	low	25	12.5	0	25	50	50	37.5	37.5	12.5
	medium	37.5	25	12.5	25	12.5	12.5	62.5	12.5	37.5
	high	37.5	62.5	87.5	50	37.5	37.5	0	50	37.5

Note: Appendix 1 summarizes our findings horizontally, that is, across each of the eight indicators. When comparing the different indicators with each other, there are in particular two aspects that stand out: First, it seems that IPAs are generally quite active in anticipating political red lines. Furthermore, it becomes clear that overcoming the default mode of negative coordination presents a substantial challenge for most bureaucracies under scrutiny. This lack of variation implies that – within the scope of the organizations analysed – not all of the indicators are equally powerful in capturing differences in the IPA's internal working routines. At the same time, the values we found for these two indicators are hardly surprising. Properly following a routine of positive coordination is highly demanding and should thus be the exception rather than the rule. Conversely, not anticipating principals' preferences could end up being costly for an IPA, which is dependent on its relationship to its principals. We hence acknowledge the low empirical variance we observe on these two indicators but note that this is strongly in line with the general expectations towards bureaucracies. For this reason, we would furthermore argue that it is important to retain those two indicators in the overall measurement because their presence/absence can be viewed as particularly telling.

Appendix 2

Orientation	Indicator	Servant		Consolidator		Advocate			Entrepreneur		Share
		ILO	NATO	IOM	FAO	WHO	UNEP	UNHCR	IMF		
Positional Orientation	Support Mobilization	5/8 (0.625)	5/8 (0.625)	3/8 (0.375)	3/8 (0.375)	2/8 (0.25)	3/8 (0.375)	6/8 (0.75)	0/8 (0.000)		0.42
	Mapping of the Political Space	5/8 (0.625)	1/8 (0.125)	3/8 (0.375)	3/8 (0.375)	2/8 (0.25)	4/8 (0.50)	6/8 (0.75)	7/8 (0.875)		0.48
	Political Anticipation	2/8 (0.25)	0/8 (0.000)	3/8 (0.375)	3/8 (0.375)	3/8 (0.375)	4/8 (0.50)	6/8 (0.75)	7/8 (0.875)		0.44
	Strategic Use of Formal Powers	2/8 (0.25)	5/8 (0.625)	3/8 (0.375)	3/8 (0.375)	1/8 (0.125)	3/8 (0.375)	6/8 (0.75)	7/8 (0.875)		0.47
Functional Orientation	Issue Emergence	5/8 (0.625)	5/8 (0.625)	3/8 (0.375)	2/8 (0.25)	1/8 (0.125)	4/8 (0.50)	6/8 (0.75)	7/8 (0.875)		0.52
	Solution Search	5/8 (0.625)	5/8 (0.625)	3/8 (0.375)	1/8 (0.125)	3/8 (0.375)	4/8 (0.50)	1/8 (0.125)	7/8 (0.875)		0.45
	Internal Coordination	5/8 (0.625)	1/8 (0.125)	3/8 (0.375)	1/8 (0.125)	2/8 (0.25)	3/8 (0.375)	1/8 (0.125)	7/8 (0.875)		0.36
	Policy Promotion	5/8 (0.625)	5/8 (0.625)	3/8 (0.375)	2/8 (0.25)	3/8 (0.375)	4/8 (0.50)	6/8 (0.75)	7/8 (0.875)		0.55
	Evaluation	2/8 (0.25)	5/8 (0.625)	0/8 (0.000)	2/8 (0.25)	3/8 (0.375)	3/8 (0.375)	6/8 (0.75)	7/8 (0.875)		0.44

Note: Appendix 2 presents how the different indicators relate to each other. More precisely, for each indicator it shows the share of other indicators exhibiting the very same manifestation. This value is particularly high for 'issue emergence' and 'policy promotion', implying over half of the other indicators always have the exact same manifestation as them. This speaks for the fact that the different indicators do not seem to be completely independent from one another. We do, however, not consider this a problem for our analysis. It is central to the concept of administrative styles that IPAs cluster with regard to the way 'things are done' in organizations. Therefore, the observed interactions between the different indicators simply reflect the patterns of administrative behaviour, which, by definition, constitute administrative styles.

References

Abbott, K. W., Genschel, P., Snidal, D., & Zangl, B. (eds.). (2015). *International organizations as orchestrators*. Cambridge: Cambridge University Press.

Abbott, K. W., Genschel, P., Snidal, D., & Zangl, B. (2018). *The governor's dilemma: competence versus control in indirect governance* (Working Paper No. SP IV 2018–101). WZB Discussion Paper. www.econstor.eu/h andle/10419/177895

Abbott, K. W., Green, J. F., & Keohane, R. O. (2016). Organizational ecology and institutional change in global governance. *International Organization*, 70(2), 247–77.

Abbott, K. W., & Snidal, D. (1998). Why states act through formal international organizations. *Journal of Conflict Resolution*, 42(1), 3–32.

Aberbach, J. D., Putnam, R. D., & Rockman, B. A. (1981). *Politicians and bureaucrats in western democracies*. Cambridge, MA: Harvard University Press.

Acs, A. (2018). Policing the administrative state. *Journal of Politics*, 80(4), 1225–38.

Adam, C., Bauer, M. W., Knill, C., & Studinger, P. (2007). The termination of public organizations: theoretical perspectives to revitalize a promising research area. *Public Organization Review*, 7(3), 221–36.

Adam, C., Steinebach, Y., & Knill, C. (2018). Neglected challenges to evidence-based policy-making: the problem of policy accumulation. *Policy Sciences*, 51(3), 269–90.

Andersen, S. O., Sarma, K. M., & Sinclair, L. (2002). *Protecting the ozone layer: the United Nations history*. London: Earthscan.

Andler, L. (2009). The secretariat of the global environment facility: from network to bureaucracy. In F. Bierman & B. Siebenhüner (eds.), *Managers of global change: the influence of international environmental bureaucracies* (pp. 203–24). Cambridge, MA: MIT Press.

Andonova, L. B. (2017). *Governance entrepreneurs: international organizations and the rise of global public–private partnerships*. Cambridge: Cambridge University Press.

Andrijasevic, R., & Walters, W. (2010). The International Organization for Migration and the international government of borders. *Environment and Planning D: Society and Space*, 28(6), 977–99.

Archer, C. (2015). *International organizations*. New York: Routledge.

Armingeon, K., & Beyeler, M. (2004). *The OECD and European welfare states*. Cheltenham, UK; Northampton, MA: Edward Elgar.

Arrow, K. J. (1984). The economics of the agency. In J. W. Pratt & R. J. Zeckhauser (eds.), *Principals and agents: the structure of business* (pp. 37–51). Boston, MA: Harvard Business School Press.

Ashutosh, I., & Mountz, A. (2011). Migration management for the benefit of whom? Interrogating the work of the International Organization for Migration. *Citizenship Studies*, 15(01), 21–38.

Asongu, S. (2014). How would monetary policy matter in the proposed African monetary unions? Evidence from output and prices. *African Finance Journal*, 16(2), 34–63.

AusAID. (2012a). Australian multilateral assessment March 2012: Food and Agriculture Organization (FAO). Canberra: Australian Government. https://dfat.gov.au/about-us/publications/Documents/fao-assessment.pdf

AusAID. (2012b). Australian multilateral assessment March 2012 International Labour Organization (ILO). Canberra: Australian Government. https://dfat.gov.au/about-us/publications/Documents/ilo-assessment.pdf

Baccaro, L. (2015). Orchestration for the 'social partners' only: internal constraints on the ILO. In K. W. Abbott, P. Genschel, D. Snidal, & B. Zangl (eds.), *International Organizations as orchestrators* (pp. 262–85). Cambridge: Cambridge University Press.

Baccaro, L., & Mele, V. (2012). Pathology of path dependency? The ILO and the challenge of new governance. *Industrial and Labor Relations Review*, 65(2), 195–224. https://doi.org/10.1177/001979391206500201

Balla, S. J., & Gormley, W. T. (2018). *Bureaucracy and democracy: accountability and performance*. Thousand Oaks: SAGE Publications.

Barnett, M. (2001). Humanitarianism with a sovereign face: UNHCR in the global undertow. *International Migration Review*, 35(1), 244–77.

Barnett, M., & Coleman, L. (2005). Designing police: Interpol and the study of change in international organizations. *International Studies Quarterly*, 49(4), 593–620.

Barnett, M., & Finnemore, M. (1999). The politics, power, and pathologies of international organizations. *International Organization*, 53(04), 699–732.

Barnett, M., & Finnemore, M. (2004). *Rules for the world: international organizations in global politics*. Ithaca, NY: Cornell University Press.

Barrett, S. (2007). The smallpox eradication game. *Public Choice*, *130*(1–2), 179–207.

Battilana, J., Leca, B., & Boxenbaum, E. (2009). How actors change institutions: towards a theory of institutional entrepreneurship. *Academy of Management Annals*, *3*(1), 65–107.

Bauer, M. W., & Ege, J. (2013). Commission civil servants and politics: de-politicised bureaucrats in an increasingly political organisation. In C. Neuhold, S. Vanhoonacker, & L. Verhey (eds.), *Civil servants and politics: a delicate balance* (pp. 173–204). Houndmills, UK; New York: Palgrave Macmillan.

Bauer, M. W., & Ege, J. (2016). Bureaucratic autonomy of international organizations' secretariats. *Journal of European Public Policy*, *23*(7), 1019–37.

Bauer, M. W., & Ege, J. (2017). A matter of will and action: the bureaucratic autonomy of international public administrations. In M. W. Bauer, C. Knill, & S. Eckhard (eds.), *International bureaucracy: challenges and lessons for public administration research* (pp. 13–41). London: Palgrave Macmillan.

Bauer, M. W., Knill, C., & Eckhard, S. (eds.). (2017). *International bureaucracy: challenges and lessons for public administration research*. London: Palgrave Macmillan.

Bauer, S. (2007). The ozone secretariat: administering the Vienna convention and the Montreal protocol on substances that deplete the ozone layer (Global Governance Working Paper No. 28). Amsterdam: Global Governance Project, www.die-gdi.de/uploads/media/WP28.pdf.

Bauer, S. (2009). The secretariat of the United Nations Environment Programme: tangled up in blue. In F. Biermann & B. Siebenhüner (eds.), *Managers of global change: the influence of international environmental bureaucracies* (pp. 169–202). Cambridge, MA: MIT Press.

Bauer, S., Andresen, S., & Biermann, F. (2012). International bureaucracies. In F. Biermann & P. H. Pattberg (eds.), *Global environmental governance reconsidered* (pp. 27–44). Cambridge, MA: MIT Press.

Baumgartner, F. R., & Jones, B. D. (2010). *Agendas and instability in American politics* (2nd ed.). Chicago: University of Chicago Press.

Bayerlein, L., & Knill, C. (2019). Administrative styles and policy styles. In William R. Thompson (ed.) *Oxford research encyclopedia of politics*. Oxford: Oxford University Press, https://doi.org/10.1093/acrefore/9780190228637.013.618.

Beach, D. (2004). The unseen hand in treaty reform negotiations: the role and influence of the Council Secretariat. *Journal of European Public Policy*, *11*(3), 408–39.

Beisheim, M., & Liese, A. (2014). *Transnational partnerships: effectively providing for sustainable development?* Basingstoke: Palgrave MacMillan.

Bendor, J., Glazer, A., & Hammond, T. H. (2001). Theories of delegation. *Annual Review of Political Science, 4*, 235–69.

Bennett, O. (2017). The end is nigh for the World Health Organisation. *The Independent*, 5 April. www.independent.co.uk/news/world/politics/obamacare-trump-health-ebola-flu-pandemic-who-reforms-cancer-tb-a7622416.html

Best, J. (2012). Ambiguity and uncertainty in international organizations: a history of debating IMF conditionality. *International Studies Quarterly, 56*(4), 674–88.

Betts, A. (2009). Institutional proliferation and the global refugee regime. *Perspectives on Politics, 7*(1), 53–8.

Betts, A. (ed.). (2011). *Global migration governance.* Oxford: Oxford University Press.

Betts, A. (2012). UNHCR, autonomy, and mandate change. In J. E. Oestreich (ed.), *International organizations as self-directed actors* (pp. 139–61). London: Routledge.

Betts, A. (2013). Regime complexity and international organizations: UNHCR as a challenged institution. *Global Governance: A Review of Multilateralism and International Organizations, 19*(1), 69–81.

Biermann, F. (2007). Reforming global environmental governance, from UNEP towards a world environment organization. In L. Swart & E. Perry (eds.), *Global environmental governance: perspectives on the current debate* (pp. 103–23). New York: Center for UN Reform Education.

Biermann, F., & Pattberg, P. H. (2012). *Global environmental governance reconsidered.* Cambridge, MA: MIT Press.

Biermann, F., & Siebenhüner, B. (2009a). *Managers of global change: the influence of international environmental bureaucracies.* Cambridge, MA: MIT Press.

Biermann, F., & Siebenhüner, B. (2009b). The influence of international bureaucracies in world politics: findings from the MANUS research program. In F. Biermann & B. Siebenhüner (eds.), *Managers of global change: the influence of international environmental bureaucracies* (pp. 319–49). Cambridge, MA: MIT Press.

Biermann, F., & Siebenhüner, B. (eds.). (2009c). *Managers of global change: the influence of international environmental bureaucracies.* Cambridge, MA: MIT Press.

Biermann, F., Siebenhüner, B., Bauer, S., Busch, P.-O., et al. (2009). Studying the influence of international bureaucracies: a conceptual framework. In F. Biermann & B. Siebenhüner (eds.), *Managers of global change: the influence of international environmental bureaucracies* (pp. 37–74). Cambridge, MA: Cambridge: MIT Press.

Biermann, R. (2014). NATO's troubled relations with partner organizations: a resource-dependence explanation. In S. Mayer (ed.), *NATO's post-cold war politics: the changing provision of security* (pp. 215–33). London: Palgrave Macmillan.

Birnholtz, J. P., Cohen, M. D., & Hoch, S. V. (2007). Organizational character: on the regeneration of Camp Poplar Grove. *Organization Science*, *18*(2), 315–32.

Blau, Peter M. (1955). *The dynamics of bureaucracy*. Chicago: University of Chicago Press.

Boschken, H. L. (1988). *Strategic design and organizational change: Pacific coast seaports in transition*. Tuscaloosa: University of Alabama Press.

Boyne, G. A., & Walker, R. M. (2004). Strategy content and public service organizations. *Journal of Public Administration Research and Theory*, *14*(2), 231–52.

Bradley, M. (2017). The International Organization for Migration (IOM): gaining power in the forced migration regime. *Refuge: Canada's Journal on Refugees*, *33*(1), 97–106.

Brechin, S. R., & Ness, G. D. (2013). Looking back at the gap: International Organizations as organizations twenty-five years later. *Journal of International Organizations Studies*, *4*(Special Issue), 14–39.

Broome, A. (2012). The politics of IMF–EU co-operation: institutional change from the Maastricht Treaty to the launch of the euro. *Journal of European Public Policy*, *20*(4), 589–605.

Broome, A., & Seabrooke, L. (2007). Seeing like the IMF: institutional change in small open economies. *Review of International Political Economy*, *14*(4), 576–601.

Broome, A., & Seabrooke, L. (2012). Seeing like an International Organisation. *New Political Economy*, *17*(1), 1–16.

Brown, R. L. (2010). Measuring delegation. *Review of International Organizations*, *5*(2), 141–75.

Burci, G. L., & Vignes, C.-H. (2004). *World Health Organization*. The Hague: Kluwer Law International.

Busch, P.-O. (2009). The OECD environment directorate: the art of persuasion and its limitations. In F. Biermann & B. Siebenhüner (eds.), *Managers of global change: the influence of international environmental bureaucracies* (pp. 75–99). Cambridge, MA: MIT Press.

Busch, P.-O. (2014). Independent influence of international public administrations: contours and future directions of an emerging research strand. In S. Kim, S. Ashley, & W. H. Lambright (eds.), *Public administration in the context of global governance* (pp. 45–62). Cheltenham, UK; Northampton, MA: Edward Elgar.

Busch, P.-O., & Liese, A. (2017). The authority of international public administrations. In M. W. Bauer, C. Knill, & S. Eckhard (eds.), *International bureaucracy* (pp. 97–122). London: Palgrave Macmillan.

Campbell, J. L., Quincy, C., Osserman, J., & Pedersen, O. K. (2013). Coding in-depth semistructured interviews: problems of unitization and intercoder reliability and agreement. *Sociological Methods & Research*, 42(3), 294–320.

Cardesa-Salzmann, A. (2016). Multilateral environmental agreements and illegality. In L. Elliott & W. H. Schaedla (eds.), *Handbook of transnational environmental crime* (pp. 299–321). Cheltenham, UK; Northampton, MA: Edward Elgar.

Carney, T., & Bennett, B. (2014). Framing pandemic management: new governance, science or culture? *Health Sociology Review*, 23(2), 136–47.

CGD. (2013). Time for FAO to shift to a higher gear: a report of the CGD working group on food security. *Center for Global Development*. www .cgdev.org/sites/default/files/FAO-text-Final.pdf.

Chan, L.-H. (2010). WHO: the world's most powerful international organisation? *Journal of Epidemiology and Community Health*, 64(2), 97–8.

Chen, C. (2011). UNEP institutional reform with its impact on developing countries. In K. Ashwani & D. Messner (eds.), *Power shifts and global governance: challenges from South and North* (pp. 301–20). London: Anthem Press.

Chorev, N. (2012). *The World Health Organization between north and south*. Ithaca: Cornell University Press.

Chorev, N. (2013). Restructuring neoliberalism at the World Health Organization. *Review of International Political Economy*, 20(4), 627–66.

Chow, J. C. (2010). Is the WHO becoming irrelevant? Foreign Policy, 8 December, www.foreignpolicy.com/articles/2010/12/08/is_the_who_becoming_irrelevant (accessed 17 February 2020).

Chwieroth, J. (2010). *Capital ideas: the IMF and the rise of financial liberalization*. Princeton: Princeton University Press.

Chwieroth, J. (2011). The crisis in global finance: political economy perspectives on international financial regulatory change. In Centre for International Affairs (ed.), *Beyond national boundaries: building a world without walls* (pp. 1–30). London: Academy of Korean Studies Press. http://eprints.lse.ac.uk/41825/

Chwieroth, J. (2013). 'The silent revolution': how the staff exercise informal governance over IMF lending. *Review of International Organizations*, 8(2), 265–90.

Claude, I. (1984). *Swords into plowshares: the problems and progress of International Organization*. New York: Random House.

Clinton, C., & Sridhar, D. (2017). Who pays for cooperation in global health? A comparative analysis of WHO, the World Bank, the Global Fund to Fight HIV/AIDS, Tuberculosis and Malaria, and Gavi, the Vaccine Alliance. *The Lancet, 390*(10091), 324–32.

Cortell, A. P., & Peterson, S. (2006). Dutiful agents, rogue actors, or both? Staffing, voting rules, and slack in the WHO and WTO. In D. G. Hawkins, D. A. Lake, D. L. Nielson, & M. J. Tierney (eds.), *Delegation and agency in international organizations* (pp. 255–80). Cambridge: Cambridge University Press.

Cox, R. W. (1973). ILO: limited monarchy. In R. W. Cox & H. K. Jacobsen (eds.), *The anatomy of influence: decision making in international organization* (pp. 102–138). New Haven: Yale University Press.

Cox, R. W., & Jacobsen, H. K. (1973). *The anatomy of influence: decision making in international organization*. New Haven: Yale University Press.

Cutler, A. C., Haufler, V., & Porter, T. (1999). *Private authority and international affairs*. Albany: SUNY Press.

Cyert, R. M., & March, J. G. (1963). *A behavioral theory of the firm*. Englewood Cliffs: Prentice-Hall.

Czempiel, E.-O., & Rosenau, J. N. (eds.). (1992). *Governance without government: order and change in world politics*. Cambridge: Cambridge University Press.

Dahan, Y., Lerner, H., & Milman-Sivan, F. (2012). Shared responsibility and the International Labour Organization. *Michigan Journal of International Law, 34*, 675–743.

Das, T. (2010). Basically a house of experts: the production of World Health Organization information. *African Health Sciences, 10*(4), 390–4.

Davies, A. R., Doyle, R., & Pape, J. (2012). Future visioning for sustainable household practices: spaces for sustainability learning? *Area, 44*(1), 54–60.

Davis, J. H., Schoorman, F. D., & Donaldson, L. (1997). Toward a stewardship theory of management. *Academy of Management Review, 22*(1), 20–47.

De Wijk, R. (1997). *NATO on the brink of the new millennium: the battle for consensus*. Dulles: Potomac Books Inc.

del Río, P. (2014). On evaluating success in complex policy mixes: the case of renewable energy support schemes. *Policy Sciences, 47*(3), 267–87.

Dembinski, M. (2012). NATO. In K. Freistein & J. Leininger (eds.), *Handbuch Internationale Organisationen: Theoretische Grundlagen und Akteure*. München: Oldenbourg Wissenschaftsverlag GmbH.

Deni, J. R. (2014). Perfectly flawed? The evolution of NATO's force generation process. in S. Mayer (ed.), *NATO's post-cold war politics: the changing provision of security* (pp. 176–93). London: Palgrave Macmillan.

Desai, R. M., & Vreeland, J. R. (2011). Global governance in a multipolar world: the case for regional monetary funds. *International Studies Review*, *13*(1), 109–21.

DFID. (2011a). *Multilateral aid review: assessment for the Food and Agriculture Organisation of the United Nations (FAO)*. DFID. Retrieved from https://assets.publishing.service.gov.uk/government/uploads/system/uploads/attachment_data/file/224927/FAO.pdf

DFID. (2011b). *Multilateral aid review: assessment of the International Labour Organisation (ILO)*. DFID. Retrieved from https://assets.publishing.service.gov.uk/government/uploads/system/uploads/attachment_data/file/67624/ilo.pdf

DFID. (2011c). *Multilateral aid review: assessment of UNHCR*. Retrieved from https://assets.publishing.service.gov.uk/government/uploads/system/uploads/attachment_data/file/224932/UNHCR.pdf

DFID. (2013a). *Multilateral aid review: the Food and Agriculture Organisation (FAO) – Update 2013*. DFID. Retrieved from https://assets.publishing.service.gov.uk/government/uploads/system/uploads/attachment_data/file/261653/FAO-2013-summary-assessment-update2.pdf

DFID. (2013b). *Multilateral aid review: the International Organization for Migration*. DFID. Retrieved from https://assets.publishing.service.gov.uk/government/uploads/system/uploads/attachment_data/file/260150/IOM-2013-summary-assessment-update.pdf

DFID. (2016). *Raising the standard: the multilateral development review 2016*. DFID. Retrieved from https://assets.publishing.service.gov.uk/government/uploads/system/uploads/attachment_data/file/573884/Multilateral-Development-Review-Dec2016.pdf

Diehl, P. F. (2005). *The politics of global governance: international organizations in an interdependent world*. (3rd ed.). Boulder: Lynne Rienner.

Dijkstra, H. (2008). Council secretariat's role in the common foreign and security policy. *European Foreign Affairs Review*, *13*, 149–66.

Dijkstra, H. (2015). Functionalism, multiple principals and the reform of the NATO secretariat after the Cold War. *Cooperation and Conflict*, *50*(1), 128–45.

DiMaggio, P. J. (1988). Interest and agency in institutional theory. In L. G. Zucker (ed.), *Institutional patterns and organizations: culture and environment* (pp. 3–22). Cambridge, MA: Ballinger.

DiMaggio, P. J., & Powell, W. W. (1983). The iron cage revisited: institutional isomorphism and collective rationality in organizational fields. *American Sociological Review*, 48(2), 147–60.

DiMaggio, P. J., & Powell, W. W. (1991). *The new institutionalism in organizational analysis*. Chicago: University of Chicago Press.

Dingwerth, K., Kerwer, D., & Nölke, A. (eds.). (2009). *Die organisierte Welt*. Baden-Baden: Nomos.

Dionne, G. (2010). Development and organisational practice: ethnography at the food and agriculture organisation of the United Nations (FAO) (PhD Thesis). McGill University.

Douglas, W. A., Ferguson, J.-P., & Klett, E. (2004). An effective confluence of forces in support of workers' rights: ILO standards, US trade laws, unions, and NGOs. *Human Rights Quarterly*, 26(2), 273–99.

Downie, D. L., & Levy, M. A. (2000). The UN environment programme at a turning point: options for change. In P. Chasek (ed.), *The global environment in the twenty-first century: prospects for international cooperation* (pp. 355–77). Tokyo: United Nations University Press.

Downs, A. (1967). *Inside bureaucracy*. Boston: Little, Brown.

Dumiak, M. (2012). Push needed for pandemic planning. *Bulletin of the World Health Organization*, 90(11), 800–1.

Dunleavy, P. (1991). *Democracy, bureaucracy and public choice economic explanations in political science*. New York: Harvester Wheatsheaf.

Durant, R. F. (2009). Theory building, administrative reform movements, and the perdurability of Herbert Hoover. *The American Review of Public Administration*, 39(4), 327–51.

Eccleston-Turner, M., & McArdle, S. (2017). Accountability, international law, and the World Health Organization: a need for reform? *GLOBAL HEALTH*, 11(1), 27–39.

Ecker-Ehrhardt, M. (2018). Self-legitimation in the face of politicization: why international organizations centralized public communication. *The Review of International Organizations*, 13(4), 519–46.

Eckhard, S. (2016). *International assistance to police reform: managing peacebuilding*. Basingstoke: Palgrave Macmillan.

Eckhard, S., & Ege, J. (2016). International bureaucracies and their influence on policy-making: a review of empirical evidence. *Journal of European Public Policy*, 23(7), 960–78.

Eckhard, S., & Kern, C. (2017). A business case for international bureaucrats? Why NATO and the OSCE endure after the Cold War. Presented at the ECPR General Conference, Oslo, 6–9 September.

Eckhard, S., Patz, R., & Schmidt, S. (2016). Coping with the sellout: bureaucratic governance and the UNESCO budget crisis. IPSA 24th World Congress of Political Science, Poznan, 23–28 July.

Eckhard, S., Patz, R., & Schmidt, S. (2019). Reform efforts, synchronization failure, and international bureaucracy: the case of the UNESCO budget crisis. *Journal of European Public Policy*, 26(11), 1639–56.

Ege, J. (2017). Comparing the autonomy of international public administrations: an ideal-type approach. *Public Administration*, 95(3), 555–70.

Ege, J. (2019). Learning from the commission case: the comparative study of management change in international public administrations. *Public Administration*, 97(2), 384–98.

Ege, J., & Bauer, M. W. (2017). How financial resources affect the autonomy of international public administrations. *Global Policy*, 8(S5), 75–84.

Eichengreen, B. (2014). Banking on the BRICS. *Project Syndicate*, 13. www .project-syndicate.org/commentary/barry-eichengreen-is-bullish-on-the-group-s-new-development-bank–but-not-on-its-contingent-reserve-arran gement?barrier=accesspaylog

Elie, J. (2010). The historical roots of cooperation between the UN High Commissioner for Refugees and the International Organization for Migration. *Global Governance*, 16(3), 345–60.

Ellinas, A. A., & Suleiman, E. N. (2011). Supranationalism in a transnational bureaucracy: the case of the European Commission. *JCMS: Journal of Common Market Studies*, 49(5), 923–47.

Elliott, K. A., & Freeman, R. B. (2003). *Can labor standards improve under globalization?* Peterson Institute for International Economics. Retrieved from https://ideas.repec.org/b/iie/ppress/338.html

Ellis, D. C. (2010). The organizational turn in international organization theory. *Journal of International Organizations Studies*, 1(1), 11–28.

Ende, M. (1963). *Jim Button and Luke the engine driver*. London, Bombay: G. G. Harrap.

Enkler, J., Schmidt, S., Eckhard, S., Knill, C., & Grohs, S. (2017). Administrative styles in the OECD: bureaucratic policy-making beyond formal rules. *International Journal of Public Administration*, 40(8), 637–48.

Enticott, G. (2004). Multiple voices of modernization: some methodological implications. *Public Administration*, 82(3), 743–56.

Evans, P., Haggard, S., & Kaufman, R. (1992). The state as problem and solution: predation, embedded autonomy, and structural change. In S. Haggard & R. Kaufman (eds.), *The politics of economic adjustment: international constraints, distributive conflict and the state* (pp. 139–181). Princeton: Princeton University Press.

FAO. (2007). *FAO: the challenge of renewal – report of the independent external evaluation of the Food and Agriculture Organization of the United Nations (FAO)*. Retrieved from www.fao.org/unfao/bodies/IEE-Working-Draft-Report/K0489E.pdf

FAO. (2013). *FAO strategy for partnership with civil society organizations*. FAO. Retrieved from www.fao.org/3/a-i3443e.pdf

FAO. (2017). *Programme evaluation report 2017*. Rome: FAO. Retrieved from www.fao.org/3/a-mt142e.pdf

FAO. (2018). *Evaluation of FAO Strategic Objective 1: contribute to the eradication of hunger, food insecurity and malnutrition*. FAO. Retrieved from www.fao.org/3/I9572EN/i9572en.pdf

Faraj, S., & Xiao, Y. (2006). Coordination in fast-response organizations. *Management Science*, 52(8), 1155–69.

Feldman, M. S. (2003). A performative perspective on stability and change in organizational routines. *Industrial and Corporate Change*, 12(4), 727–52.

Feldman, M. S., & Pentland, B. T. (2003). Reconceptualizing organizational routines as a source of flexibility and change. *Administrative Science Quarterly*, 48(1), 94–118.

Fidler, D. P. (2004). *SARS: governance and the globalization of disease*. Basingstoke; New York: Palgrave Macmillan.

Fidler, D. P. (2009). H1N1 after action review: learning from the unexpected, the success and the fear. *Future Microbiology*, 4(7), 767–69.

Finnemore, M. (1993). International Organizations as teachers of norms: the United Nations Educational, Scientific and Cultural Organization and science policy. *International Organization*, 47(4), 565–97.

Finnemore, M., & Sikkink, K. (1998). International norm dynamics and political change. *International Organization*, 52(4), 887–917.

Flockhart, T. (2014). Post-bipolar challenges: new visions and new activities. In S. Mayer (ed.), *NATO's post-Cold War politics: the changing provision of security* (pp. 71–88). London: Palgrave Macmillan UK.

Fouilleux, È. (2009). À propos de crises mondiales... *Revue Française de Science Politique*, 59(4), 757–82.

Franke, U. (2018). The United Nations and regional security organizations in Africa, Europe and the North-Atlantic region. In Stephen Aris, Aglaya Snetkov, & Andreas Wenger (eds.), *Inter-organizational relations in international security* (pp. 33–49). Abingdon: Routledge.

Freeman, R., & Sturdy, S. (2014). Knowledge, policy and coordinated action: mental health in Europe. In R. Freeman & S. Sturdy (eds.), *Knowledge in policy: embodied, inscribed, enacted* (pp. 61–78). Bristol: Policy Press.

Freitas, R. (2013). The global human mobility architecture. In B. Reinalda (ed.), *Routledge handbook of International Organization* (pp. 473–85). Abingdon: Routledge.

Gasper, D. (2000). Evaluating the 'logical framework approach' towards learning-oriented development evaluation. *Public Administration and Development, 20*(1), 17–28.

Geiger, M., & Pécoud, A. (2010). The politics of international migration management. In M. Geiger & A. Pécoud (eds.), *The politics of international migration management* (pp. 1–20). Basingstoke: Palgrave Macmillan.

Geiger, M., & Pécoud, A. (2013). Migration, development and the 'migration and development nexus'. *Population, Space and Place, 19*(4), 369–74.

Geiger, M., & Pécoud, A. (2014). International organisations and the politics of migration. *Journal of Ethnic and Migration Studies, 40*(6), 865–87.

Georgi, F. (2010). For the benefit of some: the International Organization for Migration and its global migration management. In M. Geiger & A. Pécoud (eds.), *The politics of international migration management* (pp. 45–72). London: Palgrave Macmillan.

Georgi, F., & Schatral, S. (2012). Towards a critical theory of migration control: the case of the International Organization for Migration (IOM). In M. Geiger & A. Pécoud (eds.) *The new politics of international mobility: migration management and its discontents* (pp. 193–222). Osnabrück: Institute for Migration Research and Intercultural Studies (IMIS).

Gerring, J. (2008). Case selection for case-study analysis: qualitative and quantitative techniques. In J. M. Box-Steffensmeier, H. E. Brady, & D. Collier (eds.), *The Oxford handbook of political methodology*. Oxford: Oxford University Press.

Godlee, F. (1998). Change at last at WHO: but will the regions play ball? *BMJ, 317,* 296–300.

Gordenker, L. (1987). *Refugees in international politics*. London: Croom Helm.

Gostin, L. O., Sridhar, D., & Hougendobler, D. (2015). The normative authority of the World Health Organization. *Public Health, 129*(7), 854–63.

Gottwald, M. (2010). *Competing in the humanitarian marketplace: UNHCR's organizational culture and decision-making processes.* UNHCR, Policy Development and Evaluation Service, available at www .unhcr.org/research/working/4cb41ef49/competing-humanitarian-market place-unhcrs-organizational-culture-decision.html.

Gould, E. R. (2006). Delegating IMF conditionality: understanding variations in control and conformity. In D. G. Hawkins, D. A. Lake, D. L. Nielson, & M. J. Tierney (eds.), *Delegation and agency in international organizations* (pp. 281–311). Cambridge: Cambridge University Press.

Grabel, I. (2011). Not your grandfather's IMF: global crisis, 'productive incoherence' and developmental policy space. *Cambridge Journal of Economics*, *35*(5), 805–30.

Graham, E. R. (2014). International organizations as collective agents: fragmentation and the limits of principal control at the World Health Organization. *European Journal of International Relations*, *20*(2), 366–90.

Graham, E. R. (2015). Money and multilateralism: how funding rules constitute IO governance. *International Theory*, *7*(1), 162–94.

Graham, E. R. (2017). Follow the money: how trends in financing are changing governance at International Organizations. *Global Policy*, *8*, 15–25.

Greenwood, R., & Hinings, C. R. (1996). Understanding radical organizational change: bringing together the old and the new institutionalism. *Academy of Management Review*, *21*(4), 1022–54.

Grundmann, R. (2001). Transnational policy networks and the role of advocacy scientists: from ozone layer protection to climate change. In F. Bierman, R. Brohm, & K. Dingwerth (eds.), *Proceedings of the 2001 Berlin Conference on the human dimensions of global environmental change 'global environmental change and the nation-state'* (pp. 405–14). Potsdam: Potsdam Institute for Climate Impact Research.

Haas, E. B. (1964). *Beyond the nation-state: functionalism and International Organization*. Stanford: Stanford University Press.

Haas, P. M. (2008). Climate change governance after Bali. *Global Environmental Politics*, *8*(3), 1–7.

Haas, P. M. (ed.). (2016). *Epistemic communities, constructivism, and international environmental politics*. Abingdon: Routledge.

Haas, P. M., & McCabe, D. (2001). Amplifiers or dampeners: international institutions and social learning in the management of global environmental risks. In *Learning to manage global environmental risks: a comparative history of social responses to climate change, ozone depletion, and acid rain* (Vol. 1, pp. 323–48). Cambridge: MIT Press.

Haftel, Y. Z., & Thompson, A. (2006). The independence of International Organizations – concept and applications. *Journal of Conflict Resolution*, *50*(2), 253–75.

Hall, N. (2013). Moving beyond its mandate? UNHCR and climate change displacement. *Journal of International Organizations Studies*, *4*(1), 91–108.

Hall, N. (2015). Money or mandate? Why International Organizations engage with the climate change regime. *Global Environmental Politics*, 15(2), 79–97.

Hall, N. (2016). *Displacement, development, and climate change: international organizations moving beyond their mandates*. London: Routledge.

Hanrieder, T. (2014). Gradual change in international organisations: agency theory and historical institutionalism. *Politics*, 34(4), 324–33.

Hanrieder, T. (2015). The path-dependent design of international organizations: federalism in the World Health Organization. *European Journal of International Relations*, 21(1), 215–39.

Hanrieder, T., & Kreuder-Sonnen, C. (2014). WHO decides on the exception? Securitization and emergency governance in global health. *Security Dialogue*, 45(4), 331–48.

Harman, S. (2010). *The World Bank and HIV/AIDS: setting a global agenda*. London: Routledge.

Hartlapp, M. (2007). On Enforcement, management and persuasion: different logics of implementation policy in the EU and the ILO. *JCMS: Journal of Common Market Studies*, 45(3), 653–74.

Hawkins, D. G., & Jacoby, W. (2006). How agents matter. In D. G. Hawkins, D. A. Lake, D. L. Nielson, & M. J. Tierney (eds.), *Delegation and agency in international organizations* (pp. 199–228). Cambridge: Cambridge University Press.

Hawkins, D. G., Lake, D. A., Nielson, D. L., & Tierney, M. J. (eds.) (2006). *Delegation and agency in international organizations*. Cambridge: Cambridge University Press.

Heclo, H. (1977). *A Government of strangers: executive politics in Washington*. Washington: The Brookings Institution.

Helfer, L. R. (2006). Understanding change in International Organizations: globalization and innovation in the ILO. *Vanderbilt Law Review*, 59(3), 646–726.

Helfer, L. R. (2008). Monitoring compliance with un-ratified treaties: the ILO experience. *Law and Contemporary Problems*, 71(1), 193–218.

Henderson, D. A. (2016). The development of surveillance systems. *American Journal of Epidemiology*, 183(5), 381–86.

Hendrickson, R. C. (2006). *Diplomacy and war at NATO: the Secretary General and military action after the Cold War*. Columbia, MO: University of Missouri Press.

Hendrickson, R. C. (2014). The changing role of NATO's Secretary General. In S. Mayer (ed.), *NATO's post-Cold War politics: the changing provision of security* (pp. 124–39). London: Palgrave Macmillan.

Hensler, R. (2005). As the UNO celebrates its 60th anniversary, Geneva adopts new mechanisms to serve international community. In D. Dembinski-Gourmard (ed.), *International Geneva yearbook 2005–2006: organization and activities of international institutions in Geneva* (Vol. 19). Geneva: United Nations Publications.

Herz, D., Schattenmann, M., Dortants, S. L., Linke, K., & Steuber, S. (2008). *Professional education for international organizations: preparing students for international public service*. Frankfurt a. M: Peter Lang.

Heymann, D. L., & Rodier, G. (2004). SARS: a global response to an international threat. *The Brown Journal of World Affairs, 10*(2), 185–97.

Hildyard, N. (1991). Editorial: open letter to Eduoard Saouma, Director-General of FAO. *The Ecologist, 21*(2), 43–6.

Hood, C., & Lodge, M. (2006). *The politics of public service bargains: reward, competency, loyalty – and blame*. Oxford: Oxford University Press.

Hooghe, L. (2001). *The European Commission and the integration of Europe: images of governance*. Cambridge: Cambridge University Press.

Hooghe, L., Marks, G., Lenz, T., Bezuijen, J., Ceka, B., & Derderyan, S. (2017). *Measuring international authority: a postfunctionalist theory of governance* (Vol. 3). Oxford University Press.

Hooghe, L., & Marks, G. (2015). Delegation and pooling in International Organizations. *The Review of International Organizations, 10*(3), 305–28.

Howard-Grenville, J. A. (2005). The persistence of flexible organizational routines: the role of agency and organizational context. *Organization Science, 16*(6), 618–36.

Howlett, M. (2003). Administrative styles and the limits of administrative reform: a neo-institutional analysis of administrative culture. *Canadian Public Administration/Administration Publique Du Canada, 46*(4), 471–94.

Howlett, M. (2004). Administrative styles and regulatory reform: institutional arrangements and their effects on administrative behavior. *International Public Management Review, 5*(2), 13–35.

Hughes, S., & Haworth, N. (2011). *The International Labour Organization: coming in from the cold*. Oxford and New York: Routledge.

Hurd, I. (2013). *International Organizations: politics, law, practice*. Cambridge: Cambridge University Press.

Hustedt, T., & Salomonsen, H. H. (2014). Ensuring political responsiveness: politicization mechanisms in ministerial bureaucracies. *International Review of Administrative Sciences, 80*(4), 746–65.

ILO. (2016). *How the ILO works*. Retrieved from www.ilo.org/global/about-the- ilo/how-the-ilo-works/lang–en/index.htm

ILO. (2018). *Programme and budget for the biennium 2018–19*. ILO. Retrieved from www.ilo.org/wcmsp5/groups/public/–ed_mas/–program/documents/genericdocument/wcms_582294.pdf

Imber, M. F. (1994). *Environment, security and UN reform*. London: Palgrave Macmillan.

Inomata, T. (2016). Building institutional and managerial foundations for a new structure for environmental governance with the United Nations system. In T. Kuokkanen, E. Couzens, T. Honkonen, & M. Lewis (eds.), *International environmental law-making and diplomacy: insights and overviews* (pp. 96–110). London: Routledge.

IOM. (2013). *IOM in the EU member states, Norway and Switzerland*. Brussels: IOM. Retrieved from www.iom.int/sites/default/files/country/docs/AUP00550-RO-Brussels-Regional-Strategy.pdf

IOM. (2016). *IOM UK strategic plan 2016–2020*. IOM. Retrieved from https://unitedkingdom.iom.int/blob/AMIfv95pSabRlhQH3ytVDAtcovbBchiNPw6x9EY_jGgMGexJo1Mhm6O8QcO-UUr3u3grY16OCfyxrSOa1XtJXSGZcEn_2JMGH76j1TetsdcNCyNql1Ck6nZy9sFRfBullhWJ4p1es_gMAaatgbX5iydYFnk84aQ_O_4P0TrSOa2jtwQjrtck-6A?type=mime

IOM. (2017a). *Council 108th session: programme and budget for 2018* (No. C/108/6). IOM. Retrieved from https://governingbodies.iom.int/system/files/en/council/108/C-108–6%20-%20Programme%20and%20Budget%20for%202018.pdf

IOM. (2017b). *Constitution and basic texts*. IOM. Retrieved from http://publications.iom.int/system/files/pdf/iom_constitution_en.pdf

Ivanova, M. (2005). Assessing UNEP as anchor institution for the global environment: lessons for the UNEO debate. *Yale Center for Environmental Law & Policy Working Paper Series*, 5(1).

Ivanova, M. (2009). UNEP as anchor organization for the global environment. In F. Biermann, B. Siebenhüner, & A. Schreyögg (eds.), *International Organizations in global environmental governance* (pp. 151–73). Abingdon: Routledge.

Ivanova, M. (2013). The contested legacy of Rio+ 20. *Global Environmental Politics*, 13(4), 1–11.

Jachtenfuchs, M. (2005). The monopoly of legitimate force: denationalization, or business as usual. *European Review*, 13(S1), 37–52.

Jann, W. (2002). Der Wandel verwaltungspolitischer Leitbilder: Von Management zu Governance? In K. König (ed.), *Verwaltung und Verwaltungsforschung: Deutsche Verwaltung an der Wende zum 21. Jahrhundert: Deutsche Verwaltung an der Wende zum 21. Jahrhundert* (pp. 279–303). Speyer: Forschungsinstitut für Öffentliche Verwaltung.

Jinnah, S. (2010). Overlap management in the World Trade Organization: secretariat influence on trade-environment politics. *Global Environmental Politics*, *10*(2), 54–79.

JIU (2012). *Review of management, administration and decentralization in the World Health Organization (WHO). Part I: review of management and administration of WHO*, JIU/REP/2012/6.

Johnson, T. (2016). Cooperation, co-optation, competition, conflict: international bureaucracies and non-governmental organizations in an interdependent world. *Review of International Political Economy*, *23*(5), 737–67.

Johnson, T., & Urpelainen, J. (2014). International bureaucrats and the formation of intergovernmental organizations: institutional design discretion sweetens the pot. *International Organization*, *68*(1), 177–209.

Kamradt-Scott, A. (2016). WHO's to blame? The World Health Organization and the 2014 Ebola outbreak in West Africa. *Third World Quarterly*, *37*(3), 401–18.

Kaplan, L. S. (2004). *NATO divided, NATO united: the evolution of an alliance*. Westport: Praeger.

Kaplan, L. S. (2010). *NATO and the UN: a peculiar relationship*. Columbia, MO: University of Missouri Press.

Karns, M. A., Mingst, K. A., & Stiles, K. W. (2004). *International Organizations: the politics and processes*. Boulder: Lynne Rienner Publishers, Inc.

Kaufman, H. (1960). *The forest ranger: a study in administrative behavior*. Baltimore: Johns Hopkins University Press.

Keck, M. E., & Sikkink, K. (1999). Transnational advocacy networks in international and regional politics. *International social science journal*, *51*(159), 89–101.

Keohane, R. O. (2005). *After hegemony: cooperation and discord in the world political economy*. Princeton: Princeton University Press.

Kingdon, J. W. (1984). *Agendas, alternatives and public policies*. Boston: Little, Brown and Co.

Knill, C. (2001). *The Europeanisation of national administrations: patterns of institutional change and persistence*. Cambridge: Cambridge University Press.

Knill, C., & Bauer, M. W. (2016). Policy-making by international public administrations: concepts, causes and consequences. *Journal of European Public Policy*, *23*(7), 949–59.

Knill, C., Bayerlein, L., Grohs, S., & Enkler, J. (2019). Bureaucratic influence and administrative styles in International Organizations. *Review of International Organizations*, *14*(1), 83–106.

Knill, C., Eckhard, S., & Grohs, S. (2016). Administrative styles in the European Commission and the OSCE-Secretariat: striking similarities despite different organisational settings. *Journal of European Public Policy*, 23(7), 1057–76.

Knill, C., Enkler, J., Schmidt, S., Eckhard, S., & Grohs, S. (2017). Administrative styles of international organizations: can we find them, do they matter? In M. W. Bauer, C. Knill, & S. Eckhard (eds.), *International bureaucracy: challenges and lessons for public administration research* (pp. 43–71). Basingstoke: Palgrave Macmillan.

Knill, C., & Grohs, S. (2015). Administrative styles of EU institutions. In M. W. Bauer & J. Trondal (eds.), *The Palgrave handbook of the European administrative system* (pp. 93–107). Wiesbaden: Springer.

Knill, C., & Lehmkuhl, D. (2002). Private actors and the state: internationalization and changing patterns of governance. *Governance*, 15(1), 41–63.

Knill, C., & Lenschow, A. (2001). 'Seek and ye shall find!': linking different perspectives on institutional change. *Comparative Political Studies*, 34(2), 187–215.

Knill, C., & Lenschow, A. (2005). Compliance, competition and communication: different approaches of European governance and their impact on national institutions. *JCMS: Journal of Common Market Studies*, 43(3), 583–606.

Koch, A. (2014). The politics and discourse of migrant return: the role of UNHCR and IOM in the governance of return. *Journal of Ethnic and Migration Studies*, 40(6), 905–23.

Koremenos, B., Lipson, C., & Snidal, D. (2001). The rational design of international institutions. *International Organization*, 55(04), 761–99.

Koschut, S. (2018). Inter (b)locking institutions: NATO, the EU, the OSCE and inter-organizational European security governance. In Stephen Aris, Aglaya Snetkov, & Andreas Wenger (eds.), *Inter-organizational relations in international security* (pp. 85–103). Abingdon: Routledge.

Koser, K. (2010). Introduction: international migration and global governance. *Global Governance: A Review of Multilateralism and International Organizations*, 16(3), 301–15.

Krasner, S. D. (1999). *Sovereignty: organized hypocrisy*. Princeton: Princeton University Press.

Kydland, F. E., & Prescott, E. C. (1977). Rules rather than discretion: the inconsistency of optimal plans. *Journal of Political Economy*, 85(3), 473–92.

La Hovary, C. (2015). A challenging ménage à trois? *International Organizations Law Review*, 12(1), 204–36.

Laffont, J.-J., & Martimort, D. (2002). *The theory of incentives: the principal–agent model.* Princeton: Princeton University Press.

Lall, R. (2017). Beyond institutional design: explaining the performance of international organizations. *International Organization, 71*(2), 245–80.

Landman, J. C. (2002). The evolution of the OSCE – A perspective from the Netherlands. In Institute for Peace Research and Security Policy at the University of Hamburg /IFSH (ed.), *OSCE Yearbook 2001* (pp. 81–93). Baden-Baden: Nomos.

Lavenex, S. (2016). Multilevelling EU external governance: the role of international organizations in the diffusion of EU migration policies. *Journal of Ethnic and Migration Studies, 42*(4), 554–70.

Lazaric, N., & Denis, B. (2005). Routinization and memorization of tasks in a workshop: the case of the introduction of ISO norms. *Industrial and Corporate Change, 14*(5), 873–96.

Leca, B., & Naccache, P. (2006). A critical realist approach to institutional entrepreneurship. *Organization, 13*(5), 627–51.

Lee, G., Benoit-Bryan, J., & Johnson, T. P. (2012). Survey research in public administration: assessing mainstream journals with a total survey error framework. *Public Administration Review, 72*(1), 87–97.

Lee, K. (2009). *The World Health Organization (WHO).* London: Routledge.

Lenz, T., Bezuijen, J., Hooghe, L., & Marks, G. (2015). Patterns of international organization: task specific vs. general purpose. *Politische Vierteljahresschrift, 49*, 107–32.

Levinson, D. J. (2011). Parchment and politics: the positive puzzle of constitutional commitment. *Harvard Law Review, 124*(3), 659–746.

Liese, A. (2010). Explaining varying degrees of openness in the Food and Agriculture Organization of the United Nations (FAO). In C. Jönsson & J. Tallberg (eds.), *Transnational actors in global governance: patterns, explanations and implications* (pp. 88–108). Basingstoke: Palgrave Macmillan.

Liese, A., & Weinlich, S. (2006). Die Rolle von Verwaltungsstäben internationaler Organisationen. Lücken, Tücken und Konturen eines (neuen) Forschungsgebiets. In J. Bogumil, W. Jann, & F. Nullmeier (eds.), *Politik Und Verwaltung (PVS-Sonderheft 37)* (pp. 491–525). Wiesbaden: Nomos.

Lindley-French, J. (2006). *The North Atlantic Treaty Organization: the enduring alliance.* Abingdon: Routledge.

Lipson, C. (1984). International cooperation in economic and security affairs. *World Politics, 37*(1), 1–23.

Littoz-Monnet, A. (ed.). (2017). *The politics of expertise in International Organizations: how international bureaucracies produce and mobilize knowledge.* Abingdon: Routledge.

Loescher, G. (2001). The UNHCR and World Politics: state interests vs. institutional autonomy. *International Migration Review*, 35(1), 33–56.

Loh, C., Galbraith, V., & Chiu, W. (2004). The media and SARS. In C. Loh (ed.), *At the epicentre: Hong Kong and the SARS outbreak* (pp. 195–214). Hong Kong: Hong Kong University Press.

Lyne, M. M., Nielson, D. L., & Tierney, M. J. (2006). Who delegates? Alternative models of principals in development aid. In D. G. Hawkins, D. A. Lake, D. L. Nielson, & M. J. Tierney (eds.), *Delegation and agency in International Organizations* (pp. 41–76). Cambridge: Cambridge University Press.

Maguire, S., Hardy, C., & Lawrence, T. B. (2004). Institutional entrepreneurship in emerging fields: HIV/AIDS treatment advocacy in Canada. *Academy of Management Journal*, 47(5), 657–79.

Mahon, R., & McBride, S. (2008). *The OECD and global governance.* Vancouver: University of British Columbia Press.

Manulak, M. W. (2017). Leading by design: informal influence and international secretariats. *The Review of International Organizations*, 12(4), 497–522.

March, J. G., & Simon, H. A. (1993). *Organizations.* (2nd ed.). Cambridge, MA: Blackwell.

Marcussen, M., & Trondal, J. (2011). The OECD civil servant: caught between Scylla and Charybdis. *Review of International Political Economy*, 18(5), 592–621.

Margulis, M. E. (2014). Trading out of the global food crisis? The World Trade Organization and the geopolitics of food security. *Geopolitics*, 19(2), 322–50.

Margulis, M. E. (2017). The global governance of food security. In J. A. Koops & R. Biermann (eds.), *Palgrave Handbook of inter-organizational relations in world politics* (pp. 503–25). London: Palgrave Macmillan UK.

Martin, L. (2006). Distribution, information, and delegation to international organizations: the case of IMF conditionality. In D. G. Hawkins, D. A. Lake, D. L. Nielson, & M. J. Tierney (eds.), *Delegation and agency in International Organizations* (pp. 140–64). Cambridge: Cambridge University Press.

Maupain, F. (2013). *The future of the International Labour Organization in the global economy.* Portland: Hart Publishing.

Mayer, P. (2008). Civil society participation at the margins: the case of NATO and OSCE. In J. Steffek & C. Kissling (eds.), *Civil society* participation in European and global governance: a cure for the democratic deficits (pp. 109–15). Basingstoke: Palgrave Macmillan.

Mayer, S. (2014a). Introduction: NATO as an Organization and Bureaucracy. In *NATO's post-Cold War politics: the changing provision of security* (pp. 1–27). Basingstoke: Palgrave Macmillan.

Mayer, S. (ed.). (2014b). *NATO's post-Cold War politics: the changing provision of security*. Basingstoke: Palgrave Macmillan.

Mayer, S., & Theiler, O. (2014). Coping with complexity: informal political forums at nato's headquarters. In S. Mayer (ed.), *NATO's post-Cold war politics: the changing provision of security* (pp. 140–58). Basingstoke: Palgrave Macmillan.

Mayntz, R., & Derlien, H.-U. (1989). Party patronage and politicization of the West German administrative elite 1970–1987 – toward hybridization? *Governance*, 2(4), 384–404.

McCalla, R. B. (1996). NATO's persistence after the cold war. *International Organization*, 50(3), 445–75.

McCubbins, M. D. (1985). The legislative design of regulatory structure. *American Journal of Political Science*, 29(4), 721–48.

McKeon, N. (2009). *The United Nations and civil society: legitimating global governance–whose voice?* London: Zed Books Ltd.

McKittrick, A. (2008). UNHCR as an autonomous organisation: complex operations and the case of Kosovo (No. 50). Working Paper: Oxford, Refugee Studies Centre Oxford University.

McNeil Jr, D. G. (2014). Polio's return after near eradication prompts a global health warning. *The New York Times*. Retrieved from www.nyt imes.com/2014/05/06/health/world-health-organization-polio-health-em ergency.html

Mearsheimer, J. J. (1994). The false promise of international institutions. *International Security*, 19(3), 5–49.

Megens, I. (1998). The role of NATO's bureaucracy in shaping and widening the North Atlantic Treaty Organization. In B. Reinalda & B. Verbeek (eds.), *Autonomous policy making by International Organizations* (pp. 120–33). London: Routledge.

Merton, R. K. (1957). *Social theory and social structure*. Glencoe, IL: Free Press.

Meyer, R. E., Egger-Peitler, I., Höllerer, M. A., & Hammerschmid, G. (2014). Of bureaucrats and passionate public managers: institutional logics, executive identities, and public service motivation. *Public Administration*, 92(4), 861–85.

Michiels, L., & den Boer, R. (2016). *Forging partnerships for the future: IOM and the private sector*. Geneva: IOM. Retrieved from https://publica tions.iom.int/system/files/pdf/ps_photobook.pdf

Miller, G. J. (2005). The political evolution of principal–agent models. *Annual Review of Political Science*, 8(1), 203–25.

Mingst, K. A. (1990). The United States and the World Health Organization. In M. P. Karns & K. A. Mingst (eds.), *The United States and multilateral institutions: patterns of changing instrumentality and influence* (pp. 205–30). London: Routledge.

Mintrom, M., & Norman, P. (2009). Policy entrepreneurship and policy change. *Policy Studies Journal*, 37(4), 649–67.

Moe, T. M. (1990). Political institutions: the neglected side of the story. *Journal of Law, Economics, & Organization*, 6 (Special Issue), 213–53.

Momani, B. (2005). Limits on streamlining Fund conditionality: the International Monetary Fund's organizational culture. *Journal of International Relations and Development*, 8(2), 142–63.

MOPAN (2013). *MOPAN 2013 assessments: World Health Organisation (WHO). Institutional assessment report* (No. 1). MOPAN. Retrieved from www.mopanonline.org/assessments/who2013/MOPAN_2013-_WHO_Vol._I.pdf

MOPAN (2016). *MOPAN 2015–16 assessments: International Labour Organization Institutional assessment report*. MOPAN. Retrieved from www.mopanonline.org/assessments/ilo2015-16/Mopan%20ILO%20[interactive]%20[final].pdf

MOPAN (2017). *MOPAN 2015–16 assessments: United Nations Environment Programme (UNEP) Institutional assessment report*. MOPAN. Retrieved from www.mopanonline.org/assessments/unep2015-16/Mopan%20UNEP%20report%20[interactive]%20[final].pdf

Moravcsik, A. (1999). A new statecraft? Supranational entrepreneurs and international cooperation. *International Organization*, 53(2), 267–306.

Morth, U. (2000). Competing frames in the European Commission: the case of the defence industry and equipment issue. *Journal of European Public Policy*, 7(2), 173–89.

Moschella, M. (2010). *Governing risk: the IMF and global financial crises*. London: Palgrave Macmillan.

Mouritzen, H. (2013). In spite of reform: NATO HQ still in the grips of nations. *Defense & Security Analysis*, 29(4), 342–55.

NATO. (2017a). *Annual report of the Secretary-General*. NATO. Retrieved from www.nato.int/nato_static_fl2014/assets/pdf/pdf_2018_03/20180315_SG_AnnualReport_en.pdf

NATO. (2017b). *The science for peace and security programme*. NATO. Retrieved from www.nato.int/cps/en/natohq/topics_85373.htm?

Nay, O. (2011). What drives reforms in international organizations? External pressure and bureaucratic entrepreneurs in the UN response to AIDS. *Governance, 24*(4), 689–712.

Nay, O. (2012). How do policy ideas spread among international administrations? Policy entrepreneurs and bureaucratic influence in the UN response to AIDS. *Journal of Public Policy, 32*(1), 53–76.

Nelson, R. R., & Winter, S. G. (1982). *An evolutionary theory of economic change*. Cambridge, MA: Harvard University Press.

Nelson, S. C. (2014). Playing favorites: how shared beliefs shape the IMF's lending decisions. *International Organization, 68*(2), 297–328.

Ness, G. D., & Brechin, S. R. (1988). Bridging the gap: international organizations as organizations. *International Organization, 42*(02), 245–73.

Newland, K. (2010). The governance of international migration: mechanisms, processes, and institutions. *Global Governance: A Review of Multilateralism and International Organizations, 16*(3), 331–43.

Nielson, D. L., & Tierney, M. J. (2003). Delegation to international organizations: agency theory and World Bank environmental reform. *International Organization, 57*(02), 241–76.

Niskanen, W. A. (1971). *Bureaucracy and representative government*. Chicago: Aldine.

Noetzel, T., & Schreer, B. (2009). Does a multi-tier NATO matter? The Atlantic alliance and the process of strategic change. *International Affairs, 85*(2), 211–26.

OECD/FAO. (2016). *International regulatory co-operation and international organisations: the case of the Food and Agriculture Organization of the United Nations (FAO)*. OECD/FAO. Retrieved from www.oecd.org/gov/regulatory-policy/FAO_Full-Report.pdf

Oliver, C. (1991). Strategic responses to institutional processes. *Academy of Management Review, 16*(1), 145–79.

Pache, A.-C., & Santos, F. (2010). When worlds collide: the internal dynamics of organizational responses to conflicting institutional demands. *Academy of Management Review, 35*(3), 455–76.

Page, E. C. (1985). *Political authority and bureaucratic power: a comparative analysis*. Brighton: Wheatsheaf.

Page, E. C. (2012). *Policies without politicians: bureaucratic influence in comparative perspective*. Oxford: Oxford University Press.

Palmer, G. W. (1995). *Environment: the international challenge: essays*. Wellington: Victoria University Press.

Palmer, J. R. (2015). How do policy entrepreneurs influence policy change? Framing and boundary work in EU transport biofuels policy. *Environmental Politics*, 24(2), 270–87.

Parmigiani, A., & Howard-Grenville, J. (2011). Routines revisited: exploring the capabilities and practice perspectives. *Academy of Management Annals*, 5(1), 413–53.

Parsanoglou, D. (2015). Organizing an international migration machinery: the intergovermental committee for European migration. In L. Venturas (ed.), *International 'migration management' in the early Cold War. The Intergovernmental Committee for European Migration* (pp. 55–85). Corinth: University of the Peloponnese.

Patz, R., & Goetz, K. H. (2019). *Managing money and discord in the UN: budgeting and bureaucracy*. Oxford: Oxford University Press.

Pécoud, A. (2013). *'Suddenly, migration was everywhere': the conception and future prospects of the Global Migration Group*. Migration Policy Institute. Retrieved from www.migrationpolicy.org/article/suddenly-migration-was-everywhere-conception-and-future-prospects-global-migration-group

Pécoud, A. (2017). What do we know about the International Organization for Migration? *Journal of Ethnic and Migration Studies*, 44(10), 1621–38.

Pentland, B. T., Hærem, T., & Hillison, D. (2010). Comparing organizational routines as recurrent patterns of action. *Organization Studies*, 31(7), 917–40.

Pentland, B. T., Hærem, T., & Hillison, D. (2011). The (n)ever-changing world: stability and change in organizational routines. *Organization Science*, 22(6), 1369–83.

Pernet, C. A., & Ribi Forclaz, A. (2019). Revisiting the Food and Agriculture Organization (FAO): international histories of agriculture, nutrition, and development. *The International History Review*, 41(2), 345–50.

Peters, B. G. (2010). *The politics of bureaucracy* (6th ed.). London: Routledge.

Peters, B. G. (2013). *Strategies for comparative research in political science*. Basingstoke: Palgrave Macmillan.

Peters, B. G., & Hogwood, B. W. (1988). The death of immortality: births, deaths and metamorphoses in the U.S. federal bureaucracy, 1933–1982. *American Review of Public Administration*, 18(2), 119.

Peters, B. G., & Pierre, J. (2004a). Politicization of the civil service: concepts, causes, consequences. In B. G. Peters & J. Pierre (eds.), *The politicization of the civil service in comparative perspective: the quest for control* (pp. 1–13). London: Routledge.

Peters, B. G., & Pierre, J. (2004b). *The politicization of the civil service in comparative perspective: a quest for control*. London: Routledge.

Pierson, P. (2000). Increasing returns, path dependence, and the study of politics. *American Political Science Review, 94*(2), 251–68.

Pollack, M. A. (1997). Delegation, agency, and agenda setting in the European Community. *International Organization, 51*(1), 99–134.

Pollack, M. A. (2003). *The engines of European integration: delegation, agency, and agenda setting in the EU.* Oxford: Oxford University Press.

Pollack, M. A. (2006). Delegation and discretion in the European Union. In D. G. Hawkins, D. A. Lake, D. L. Nielson, & M. J. Tierney (eds.), *Delegation and agency in International Organizations* (pp. 165–96). Cambridge: Cambridge University Press.

Pollitt, C., & Bouckaert, G. (2004). *Public management reform: a comparative analysis.* (2nd ed.). Oxford: Oxford University Press.

Rainey, H. G. (2009). *Understanding and managing public organizations.* San Francisco: Jossey-Bass.

Reinalda, B. (1998). *Autonomous policy making by International Organizations* (Vol. 5). London: Routledge.

Reinalda, B. (2013). *Routledge handbook of International Organization.* London: Routledge.

Reinalda, B., & Verbeek, B. (eds.). (2003). *Autonomous policy making by International Organisations.* London: Routledge.

Rhodes, R., t'Hart, P., & Noordegraaf, M. (eds.). (2007). *Observing government elites: up close and personal.* London: Palgrave Macmillan.

Richardson, J., Gustafsson, G., & Jordan, G. (1982). The concept of policy style. In J. Richardson (ed.), *Policy styles in Western Europe* (pp. 1–16). London: Allen & Unwin.

Risse, T., Ropp, S. C., & Sikkink, K. (eds.). (1999). *The power of human rights: international norms and domestic change.* Cambridge: Cambridge University Press.

Rittberger, V., & Zangl, B. (2006). *International Organization.* Basingstoke: Palgrave Macmillan.

Roberts, N. C., & King, P. J. (1991). Policy entrepreneurs: their activity structure and function in the policy process. *Journal of Public Administration Research and Theory, 1*(2),147–75.

Rochester, J. M. (1986). The rise and fall of international organization as a field of study. *International Organization, 40*(4), 777–813.

Ross, S. (2011). *The World Food Programme in global politics.* Boulder, CO: Lynne Rienner.

Rothgang, H., & Schneider, S. (eds.). (2015). *State transformations in OECD countries: dimensions, driving forces, and trajectories.* Berlin: Springer.

Rourke, F. E. (1969). *Bureaucracy, politics, and public policy.* Boston: Little, Brown.

Sabel, C. F., & Zeitlin, J. (2008). Learning from difference: the new architecture of experimentalist governance in the EU. In C. F. Sabel & J. Zeitlin (eds.), *Experimentalist governance in the European Union: towards a new architecture* (pp. 1–28). Oxford: Oxford University Press.

Salvato, C., & Rerup, C. (2011). Beyond collective entities: multilevel research on organizational routines and capabilities. *Journal of Management, 37*(2), 468–90.

Sandford, R. (1994). International environmental treaty secretariats: stagehands or actors. In H. O. Bergesen & G. Parmann (eds.), *Green globe yearbook of international co-operation on environment and development* (Vol. 17). Oxford: Oxford University Press.

Scharpf, F. W. (1994). Games real actors could play: positive and negative coordination in embedded negotiations. *Journal of Theoretical Politics, 6*(1), 27–53.

Schein, E. H. (1990). Organizational culture. *American Psychologist, 45*(2), 109–19.

Schnapp, K.-U. (2004). *Ministerialbürokratien in westlichen Demokratien: Eine vergleichende Analyse* [Ministerial Bureaucracies in Western Democracies: A Comparative Analysis]. Opladen: Leske & Budrich.

Seabrooke, L., & Nilsson, E. R. (2015). Professional skills in international financial surveillance: assessing change in IMF policy teams. *Governance, 28*(2), 237–54.

Selznick, P. (1949). *TVA and the grass roots: a study of politics and organization.* Berkeley: University of California Press.

Senghaas-Knobloch, E. (2004). Auftrag und Möglichkeiten der Internationalen Arbeitsorganisation (ILO) unter den Bedingungen der Globalisierung. *Arbeit, 13*(3), 236–47.

Sharma, P. (2013). Bureaucratic imperatives and policy outcomes: the origins of World Bank structural adjustment lending. *Review of International Political Economy, 20*(4), 667–86.

Shaw, D. J. (2007). *World food security: a history since 1945.* New York: Palgrave Macmillan.

Shaw, D. J. (2009). *Global food and agricultural institutions.* London: Routledge.

Sikkink, K. (1986). Codes of conduct for transnational corporations: the case of the WHO/UNICEF code. *International Organization, 40*(4), 815–40.

Simmons, B. A., & Danner, A. (2010). Credible commitments and the international criminal court. *International Organization, 64*(2), 225–56.

Simon, H. A. (1997). *Administrative behavior: a study of decision-making processes in administrative organizations.* (4th ed.). New York: Free Press.

Sinclair, D., Isba, R., Kredo, T., Zani, B., Smith, H., & Garner, P. (2013). World Health Organization guideline development: an evaluation. *PLOS ONE, 8*(5), e63715.

Smith, R. (1995). The WHO: change or die. *British Medical Journal, 310* (6979), 543–4.

Snidal, D. (1990). IGOs, regimes, and cooperation: challenges for international relations theory. In M. P. Karns & K. A. Mingst (eds.) *The United States and multilateral institutions: patterns of changing instrumentality and influence* (pp. 221–41). London: Routledge.

Standing, G. (2008). The ILO: an agency for globalization? *Development and Change, 39*(3), 355–84.

Stene, E. O. (1940). An approach to a science of administration. *American Political Science Review, 34*(6), 1124–37.

Stiglitz, J. (2002). *Globalization and its discontents*. New York: W.W. Norton, Inc.

Stone, D. (2008). Global public policy, transnational policy communities, and their networks. *Policy Studies Journal, 36*(1), 19–38.

Stone, R. W. (2011). *Controlling institutions: International Organizations and the global economy*. Cambridge: Cambridge University Press.

Stone, R. W. (2013). Informal governance in international organizations: introduction to the special issue. *The Review of International Organizations, 8*(2), 121–36.

Stone Sweet, A., & Palmer, E. (2017). A Kantian system of constitutional justice: rights, trusteeship, balancing. *Global Constitutionalism, 6*(3), 377–411.

Strang, D., & Chang, P. M. Y. (1993). The International Labor Organization and the welfare state: institutional effects on national welfare spending, 1960–80. *International Organization, 47*(2), 235–62.

Suri, J. (2006). The normative resilience of NATO: a community of shared values amid public discord. In A. Wenger, C. Nuenlist, & A. Locher (eds.), *Transforming NATO in the Cold War: challenges beyond deterrence in the 1960s* (pp. 15–30). Abingdon: Routledge.

Tallberg, J. (2000). The anatomy of autonomy: an institutional account of variation in supranational influence. *JCMS: Journal of Common Market Studies, 38*(5), 843–64.

Tallberg, J., Lundgren, M., Sommerer, T., & Squatrito, T. (2017). *Explaining policy norm adoption by International Organizations* (SSRN Scholarly Paper No. ID 3059442). Rochester, NY: Social Science Research Network. Retrieved from https://papers.ssrn.com/abstract=3059442

Tallberg, J., Sommerer, T., Squatrito, T., & Jönsson, C. (2014). Explaining the transnational design of International Organizations. *International Organization, 68*(4), 741–74.

Tallberg, J., Sommerer, T., Squatrito, T., & Jönsson, C. (2015). *Replication data for: explaining the transnational design of international organizations* [Data set]. https://doi.org/10.7910/DVN/HQ7ZCL

Tallberg, J., Sommerer, T., Squatrito, T., & Lundgren, M. (2016). The performance of International Organizations: a policy output approach. *Journal of European Public Policy, 23*(7), 1077–96.

Tarasofsky, R. (2002). *International environmental governance: strengthening UNEP.* UCN/IAS.

Thomann, L. (2008). The ILO, tripartism, and NGOs: do too many cooks really spoil the broth? In J. Steffek, C. Kissling, & P. Nanz (eds.), *Civil society participation in European and global governance: a cure for the democratic deficit?* (pp. 71–94). London: Palgrave Macmillan UK.

Thouez, C., & Channac, F. (2006). Shaping international migration policy: the role of regional consultative processes. *West European Politics, 29*(2), 370–87.

Tomescu-Hatto, O. (2014). Self-presentation and impression management: NATO's new public diplomacy. In S. Mayer (ed.), *NATO's post-Cold War politics: the changing provision of security* (pp. 89–103). London: Palgrave Macmillan UK.

Tortora, P., & Steensen, S. (2014). Making earmarked funding more effective: Current practices and a way forward. *Better Policies for Better Lives Report*, (1).

Trebilcock, M. J., & Howse, R. (2004). Trade policy & (and) labor standards. *Minnesota Journal of Global Trade, 14*, 261–300.

Trondal, J., Marcussen, M., Larson, T., & Veggeland, F. (2010) *Unpacking International Organisations.* Manchester: Manchester University Press.

Turner, S. F., & Fern, M. J. (2012). Examining the stability and variability of routine performances: the effects of experience and context change. *Journal of Management Studies, 49*(8), 1407–34.

Unger, C. R. (2019). International organizations and rural development: the FAO perspective. *The International History Review, 41*(2), 451–8.

Vabulas, F., & Snidal, D. (2013). Organization without delegation: informal intergovernmental organizations (IIGOs) and the spectrum of intergovernmental arrangements. *The Review of International Organizations, 8*(2),193–220.

Van Daele, J. (2008). The International Labour Organization (ILO) in past and present research. *International Review of Social History, 53*(3), 485–511.

van der Lugt, C., & Dingwerth, K. (2015). Governing where focality is low: UNEP and the principles for responsible investment. In K. W. Abbott, P. Genschel, D. Snidal, & B. Zangl (eds.), *International organizations as orchestrators* (pp. 237–61). Cambridge: Cambridge University Press.

Van Slyke, D. M. (2007). Agents or stewards: using theory to understand the government-nonprofit social service contracting relationship. *Journal of Public Administration Research and Theory, 17*(2), 157–87.

Venturas, L. (ed.). (2015). *International 'migration management' in the early Cold War: the intergovernmental committee for European migration.* Corinth: University of the Peloponnese.

Venzke, I. (2010). International bureaucracies from a political science perspective – agency, authority and international institutional law. In A. Bogdandy, R. Wolfrum, J. Bernstorff, P. Dann, & M. Goldmann (eds.), *The exercise of public authority by international institutions: advancing international institutional law* (pp. 67–98). Berlin; Heidelberg: Springer.

Verbeek, B. (1998). International organizations: the ugly duckling of international relations theory. In B. Reinalda & B. Verbeek (eds.), *Autonomous Policy Making by International Organizations* (pp. 11–26). London: Routledge.

Verhoest, K., Peters, B. G., Bouckaert, G., & Verschuere, B. (2004). The study of organisational autonomy: a conceptual review. *Public Administration and Development, 24*(2), 101–18.

Vermeulen, P., Zietsma, C., Greenwood, R., & Langley, A. (2016). Strategic responses to institutional complexity. *Strategic Organization, 14*(4), 277–86.

Vetterlein, A. (2012). Seeing like the World Bank on poverty. *New Political Economy, 17*(1), 35–58.

Viola, L. A. (2015). The governance shift: from multilateral IGOs to orchestrated networks. In R. Mayntz (ed.), *Negotiated reform: the multilevel governance of financial regulation* (pp. 17–36). Frankfurt: Campus Verlag.

Vogel, D. (1986). *National styles of regulation: environmental policy in Great Britain and the United States.* Ithaca: Cornell University Press.

Vreeland, J. R. (2003). *The IMF and economic development.* New York: Cambridge University Press.

Wallander, C. A. (2000). Institutional assets and adaptability: NATO after the Cold War. *International Organization, 54*(4), 705–35.

Weaver, C. (2008). *Hypocrisy trap: the World Bank and the poverty of reform.* Princeton: Princeton University Press.

Weaver, C. (2010). The politics of performance evaluation: independent evaluation at the International Monetary Fund. *The Review of International Organizations, 5*(3), 365–85.

Weaver, C., & Leiteritz, R. J. (2005). 'Our poverty is a world full of dreams': reforming the World Bank. *Global Governance: A Review of Multilateralism and International Organizations, 11*(3), 369–88.

Webber, M., Sperling, J., & Smith, M. (2012). *NATO's post-Cold War trajectory: decline or regeneration.* Basingstoke: Springer.

Weber, M. (1978). *Economy and society.* Berkeley: University of California Press.

Weible, C. M. (2005). Beliefs and perceived influence in a natural resource conflict: an advocacy coalition approach to policy networks. *Political Research Quarterly, 58*(3), 461–75.

Weinlich, S. (2014). Emerging powers at the UN: ducking for cover? *Third World Quarterly, 35*(10), 1829–44.

Weisband, E. (2000). Discursive multilateralism: global benchmarks, shame, and learning in the ILO labor standards monitoring regime. *International Studies Quarterly, 44*(4), 643–66.

Weiss, T. G. (1982). International Bureaucracy: the myth and reality of the international civil service. *International Affairs, 58*(2), 287–306.

Weiss, T. G., & Pasic, A. (1997). Reinventing UNHCR: enterprising humanitarians in the former Yugoslavia, 1991–1995. *Global Governance, 3*(1), 41–57.

Weller, P., & Yi-Chong, X. (eds.). (2015). *The politics of International Organizations: views from insiders.* Abingdon: Routledge.

WHO. (1980). *The global eradication of smallpox. final report of the global commission for the certification of smallpox eradication* (Vol. 4). Geneva, Switzerland.

Wilson, J. Q. (1989). *Bureaucracy: what government agencies do and why they do it.* New York: Basic Books.

Wilson, W. (1919). The League of Nations. 3 Session 65 Congress. *Senate Document* No. 389: 12–15.

WMO. (2011). *Scientific assessment of ozone depletion: 2010* (Global Ozone Research and Monitoring Project No. 52). World Meteorological Organization. Retrieved from www.wmo.int/pages/pr og/arep/gaw/ozone_2010/documents/Ozone-Assessment-2010-com plete.pdf

Woolf, L. S. (1916). *International government: two reports.* London, Allen & Unwin.

Xu, Y.-C., & Weller, P. (2004). *The governance of World Trade – international civil servants and GATT/WTO.* Cheltenham: Edward Elgar Publishing.

Xu, Y.-C., & Weller, P. (2008). 'To be, but not to be seen': exploring the impact of international civil servants. *Public Administration, 86*(1), 35–51.

Yamey, G. (2002). The WHO in 2002: have the latest reforms reversed WHO's decline? *British Medical Journal, 325*(7372), 1107–12.

Yeager, S. J. (2007). Classic methods in public administration research. In W. B. Hildreth, G. J. Miller, & J. Rabin (eds.), *Handbook of public administration* (pp. 683–794). New York: Marcel Dekker.

Yi-Chong, X., & Weller, P. (2004). *The governance of world trade: international civil servants and the GATT/WTO*. Cheltenham: Edward Elgar Publishing.

Yi-chong, X., & Weller, P. (2018). *The working world of International Organizations: authority, capacity, legitimacy*. Oxford: Oxford University Press.

Young, O. R. (2002). *The institutional dimensions of environmental change: fit, interplay, and scale*. Cambridge, MA: MIT Press.

Zacher, M., & Keefe, T. J. (2008). *The Politics of global health governance: united by contagion*. New York: Palgrave Macmillan.

Zahariadis, Nikolaos (2003). *Ambiguity and choice in public policy: political decision making in modern democracies*. Washington: Georgetown University Press.

Zbaracki, M. J., & Bergen, M. (2010). When truces collapse: a longitudinal study of price-adjustment routines. *Organization Science*, 21(5), 955–72.

Zürn, M., Binder, M., & Ecker-Ehrhardt, M. (2012). International authority and its politicization. *International Theory*, 4(01), 69–106.

Zürn, M., & Checkel, J. T. (2005). Getting socialized to build bridges: constructivism and rationalism, Europe and the nation-state. *International Organization*, 59(04), 1045–79.

Index

Lightning Source UK Ltd.
Milton Keynes UK
UKHW022011270223
417765UK00015B/91